DILEMMAS OF LEADERSHIP

Leadership, as a way of focusing and motivating a group or organization to achieve its aims, is a much discussed but often misunderstood concept. This comprehensive textbook introduces the subject for Masters-level students.

Building on the success of the first edition, this text utilizes an easy-to-follow, map-based approach to take the reader on a journey through the various fundamental dilemmas apparent within leadership studies, dilemmas such as:

- Is a leader born or made?
- How are tensions between ethical dilemmas and economic self-interest resolved?
- How does a leader's desire for control balance with the need to empower members of the organization?

Student-friendly features new to this edition include a wealth of leadership cases, videos, and web-based content regularly updated, so that the book can be studied in the context of the most pressing contemporary leadership issues.

Tudor Rickards is Professor Emeritus at Manchester Business School, University of Manchester, UK. He previously worked at New York Medical College and as a manager within Unilever plc. He has published and lectured extensively on leadership, creativity, and change management, and is a co-editor of *The Routledge Companion to Creativity* (Routledge 2009).

DILEMMAS OF LEADERSHIP

SECOND EDITION

Tudor Rickards

Routledge
Taylor & Francis Group

LONDON AND NEW YORK

First published 2006
by Routledge

Second edition published 2012
by Routledge
2 Park Square, Milton Park, Abingdon, Oxon OX14 4RN

Simultaneously published in the USA and Canada
by Routledge
711 Third Avenue, New York, NY 10017

Routledge is an imprint of the Taylor & Francis Group, an informa business

British Library Cataloguing in Publication Data
A catalogue record for this book is available from the British Library

Library of Congress Cataloging in Publication Data
Rickards, Tudor.
  Dilemmas of leadership/Tudor Rickards. – 2nd ed.
  p. cm.
  Includes bibliographical references and index.
  1. Leadership.   I. Title.
  HD57.7.R522 2012
  658.4′092 – dc23   2011026702

ISBN: 978-0-415-61853-3 (hbk)
ISBN: 978-0-415-61854-0 (pbk)
ISBN: 978-0-203-14425-1 (ebk)

Typeset in Times New Roman and Franklin Gothic
by Florence Production Ltd, Stoodleigh, Devon

Printed and bound in Great Britain by the MPG Books Group

CONTENTS

LIST OF ILLUSTRATIONS

FIGURE

TABLES

BOXES

To Susan, without whose insights and emotional support this book would have been so much poorer.

PREFACE

The first edition of *Dilemmas of Leadership* was written in 2004 as a general handbook or reference text for researchers, students, and practising professionals with leadership responsibilities. In 2010 I needed little persuasion from Routledge to rewrite and update the original material as a graduate textbook. This edition has been designed for use in traditional and blended learning courses on leadership and leadership development.

As its title suggests, the book is based on the premise that leadership development is helped by applying skills for dealing with hard-to-resolve dilemmas. These challenges become critical for effective decision-making. The proposed methodology is described through the metaphors of map-reading, map-making, and map-testing in order to identify dilemmas and challenge personal assumptions about dealing with them.

Some years earlier, I applied paradigm theory to understanding why management education was reluctant to treat creativity seriously while accepting other paradigms, such as strategy, unreservedly. I argued that the teaching of MBA programmes was heavily influenced by assumptions drawing on the Dominant Rational Model map of human behaviours.[1] Furthermore, these beliefs weakened the credibility of ideas coming from different systems of thought.

In conclusion, I noted that:

> Organizational experiences are increasingly revealing gaps in the core topics of business orthodoxy. One of our messages is that actions under conditions of environmental uncertainties can never be completely planned for in advance. That is the paradox of action. Conversely, the orthodoxy known as managerialism has been too readily accepted as a kind of economic predestination within which there is no scope for individual creativity. That is the paradox of inaction.[2]

When the first edition of *Dilemmas of Leadership* was written, Twitter had not been thought of, Facebook was in its infancy[3] and smart phones, iPads and Wikileaks were for the future. China had only recently started to be talked about as an emerging global superpower. The victory of Barack Obama, America's first black president, was attributed in part to a campaign that mobilized a generation able to draw on the power of new media in its communications.

The 'conditions of environmental uncertainties' have persisted into the second decade of the twenty-first century. The financial shocks of 2008–9 were followed by the political upheavals accompanying the so-called Arab Spring of 2011.[4] Social media began to change the way in which knowledge was created and communicated.

Dilemmas of Leadership, like other business texts, faces the challenge of increasingly rapid obsolescence. In our workshops, conventional case studies of leadership were vulnerable to global events that threatened to render their learning messages obsolete. One solution to the dilemma of the increasingly rapid obsolescence of material has been to resort to the updating capabilities of the internet. The wider reference materials now include over 600 posts published electronically as Leaders We Deserve mini-cases. Many were written for use in leadership workshops and have been tested internationally. Also, as far as possible, materials in this new edition have been prepared with an awareness of their intellectual shelf-life.

The book has been applied on teaching assignments in a range of international locations, including the introductory module for all Manchester Business School World Wide MBA programmes. Murray Clark, co-author of the first edition, has also remained active as an inspiring leadership teacher internationally, from his base at Sheffield Hallam University. Murray's scholarship continues to shine through these pages.

Another constant is the principle that, as stated in the first edition, 'the most important leader you will be studying is yourself'. As was observed:

> In one of his poems, W.H. Auden tells the story of a reader confronting a rider undertaking a mysterious journey. The reader is passive and not inclined to take the risks of the rider. Do you suppose, the reader asks the rider, that 'diligent looking' will 'discover the lacking'? In other words, why become so involved, when you can never be sure that searching will help you discover what you are looking for? Auden is comparing the passive kind of knowledge of the reader, with the inevitably risky knowledge of the rider, or the person who becomes involved in a personal search.

> We want our readers to become riders, who set off on their own journeys of exploration, engaging in 'diligent looking', even though the looking may not completely 'discover the lacking'. We welcome readers to start by asking what are the contemporary ideas about leadership, and to continue by relating the information to their own leadership experiences and aspirations. The personal search is how the reader becomes both a rider and a leader. Borrowing a style influenced by Auden's poem, we offer the following lines to capture our 'take' on the dilemma.

> 'O where are you going?' says reader to leader

> 'And who is in charge of the compass and maps?'

'The charts are unfinished' said leader to reader,

'You must journey alone to fill in the gaps'

The invitation to each reader/leader is to go on, to search for what is lacking.
The design is intended to offer powerful support for the processes of personal
reflection, critique of knowledge, and leadership development.[5]

The second edition has been built around contributions from many colleagues. Dr Murray
Clark was co-author of the first edition, and this text still owes much to his deep
knowledge of leadership as well as his experiences in teaching the subject. Susan Moger,
my long-term collaborator and much more, developed many ideas of creative leadership for
our *Handbook for Creative Team Leaders*.[6]

Other colleagues who researched this subject with us included Professors Abdullah Al
Bereidi, Ming-Huei Chen, Fernando Gimenez, Faisal Khokhar, and Zain Mohamed.
Practical and scholarly advice came from the tutors of leadership programmes within the
Manchester Business School World Wide (MBSW) operations: Professors Jeff Ramsbottom
and Pikay Richardson were among the international tutors who helped to develop for
international audiences the Manchester courses initiated with Susan Moger and Murray
Clark. Other substantial contributions came from Dr Kamel Mnisri, Dr David Allen,
Dr Dina Williams, Leigh Wharton, and Stephen Parry. Alex Hough helped enormously
through his 'content capture' work on programmes, and through his formidable knowledge
of and skills in information technology and social media. His experience as an unobtrusive
observer and video-maker generated many vivid examples of creative leadership, filmed
from what became known as the creativity corner at Manchester Business School.

At Routledge, Terry Clague has been an encouraging commissioning editor, working
closely with Alexander Krause in the critical period as deadlines approached.

At the University of Manchester there has been an array of colleagues providing
invaluable support. Professor Elaine Ferneley, Dr Alistair Benson, and Nigel Banister
were powerful influences in establishing leadership as a core element in MBSW
programmes. At the risk of omitting names, I can at least acknowledge advice from
Professors Michael Bresnen, Margaret Bruce, Fang Lee Cooke, Gary Davies, John Hassard,
Peter Kawalek, Katharine Perera, and from Dr Lazlo Czaban, Dr Damian O'Doherty,
Dr Ismael Erturk, and Dr Eunice Maytorena. An emerging team of researchers into action
learning and leadership development includes Professor Paul Jackson, Dr Mark Batey,
Dr Mandy Chivers, and Dr Richard Common.

The wider community of researchers and leaders gave freely of their experience and
knowledge. These included Professors Paul Adler, Nancy Adler, Teresa Amabile, Barry
Bozeman, Jan Buijs, Gian Casimir, Raewyn Connell, Christian de Cock, Sandra Dingli,
Kurt Dirks, Alice Flaherty, Horst Geschka, Charles and Elizabeth Handy, Cynthia Hardy,
Margaret Heffernan, Helga Hohn, Olaf Fisscher, Cameron Ford, Todd Lubart, Mathew
Manimala, Paddy McNutt, Michael Mumford, Laurie Mullins, Mike Pedler, Gerard Puccio,
Mark Runco, Todd Reeser, Richard Thorpe, Kevin Scholes, Frido Smulders, Sandra
Sucher, Charles Wankel, Ingo Winkler, Petra de Weerd-Nederhof, and Fangqi Xu.

Many distinguished leaders have also contributed to the ideas found in this book. I would particularly like to acknowledge John Adair, Admiral Lord Boyce, Mike Brearley, Lord Terry Burns, Jim Cassells, Mandy Chivers, Fran Cotton, Dawn Gibbins, Will Hutton, Grigor McClelland, Kelly Marks, Tom Mullarkey, John Peters, Monty Roberts, and Cheng-Hock Toh.

The text has been enhanced by suggestions from these varied sources, which include the authors of most of the major texts cited in the book. It is also more than an author's ritual on my part to acknowledge how so many students and colleagues have acted as 'co-creators' of the final product. Nor do I feel this to be inconsistent with the author's convention of admitting responsibility for residual errors of style, omission, and commission.

NOTES

1   Rickards, T. (1999) *Creativity and the management of change*, Oxford: Blackwell.
2   Ibid., p. 189.
3   Geier, T. et al. 'The 100 greatest movies, TV shows, albums, books, characters, scenes, episodes, songs, dresses, music videos, and trends that entertained us over the 10 years', *Entertainment Weekly*, New York (1079/1080), pp. 74–84.
4   See, for example, Froud, J., Johal, S., Leaver, A., & Williams, K. (2006) *Financialization and strategy*, Oxford and New York: Routledge.
5   Rickards, T., & Clark, M. (2005) *Dilemmas of leadership*, Oxford: Routledge, p. 10.
6   Rickards, T., & Moger, S.M. (1999) *Handbook for creative team leaders*, Aldershot, Hants: Gower Press.

DILEMMAS OF LEADERSHIP

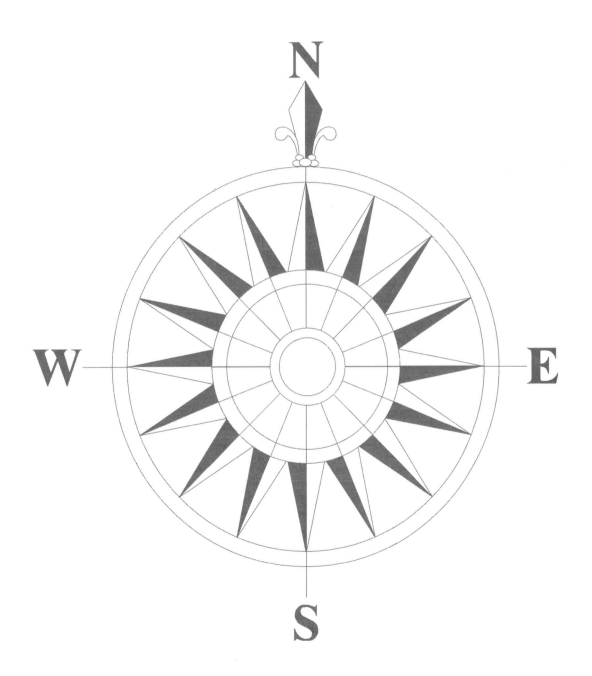

CHAPTER LEARNING OBJECTIVES

Learning focus

Key issues

Dilemmas

Platforms of understanding
- POU N.1
- POU N.2

Contextual materials
- CM N.1
- CM N.2
- CM N.3
- CM N.4

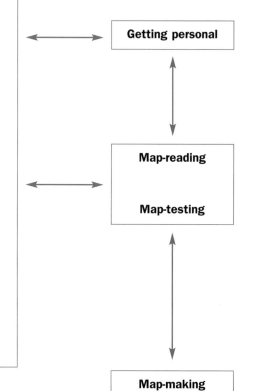

Getting personal

Map-reading

Map-testing

Map-making

INTRODUCTION

Dilemmas are what your boss talks about when he says, 'You're in charge, Fosdick, but make sure Susannah is on board.'[1]

As a leader, maps can help you a lot, but you need something even more important than maps . . . You need to know yourself and have the capacity to enter an unknown terrain that has not been mapped, where you draw the map as you walk the terrain.[2]

To benefit from business orthodoxy we have to be skilled at challenging its wisdom.[3]

I am a big fan of leadership research . . . but the study of others cannot supplant the study of self.[4]

Dilemmas of Leadership, as its title suggests, concerns itself with leadership challenges that are difficult to resolve. Its approach is one that helps the reader in the processes of dealing with difficult practical and theoretical issues. The methodology involves the use of a metaphor of knowledge representation as a map. Map-reading, map-making, and map-testing are proposed as leadership skills enabling leadership development and more effective action possibilities in dealing with complex and uncertain situations.

Each of the chapters in *Dilemmas of Leadership* has a common format that can itself be seen as a map of the chapter. Their common structure can be seen in 'Chapter learning objectives' on the facing page of this Introduction.

This is the first map of the book. It is a slightly simplified version of a similar map found at the start of all 11 chapters. You will be advised to study each introductory map sufficiently for you to feel that you have an indication of the more detailed materials you will encounter in the chapter. You will see from the map that you will be expected to carry out map-reading, map-testing, and map-making.

1 *Learning Focus* First there will be an indication of the broad learning focus. The focus of these introductory pages is to provide a sense of the overall structure and contents of the chapters of the book.
2 *Key Issues* As you carry out the three mapping processes you will encounter several key issues. These may introduce background information and suggest themes that assist the mapping processes.
3 *Dilemmas* The map-testing process will suggest leadership dilemmas. Suggestions for these are made although you will be encouraged to test even these dilemmas and look for additional ones. In particular, active efforts at seeking dilemmas are proposed as ways of revealing assumptions and beliefs so that more effective decision-making processes may occur.
4 *Platforms of Understanding (POUs)* These are not presented in the introduction. POUs may be regarded as maps constructed to deal with the general aspects of a situation or a text topic being studied. They attempt to pull together shared beliefs. POUs are good starting points for map-reading and map-testing. They may be regarded as maps constructed to deal with the general aspects of a situation or a text topic being studied. In each chapter you will find two POUs, providing a map of wide scope and often drawing on a thorough study of many other maps.
5 *Contextual Materials (CMs)* These, too, are not presented here in the introduction. CMs are more specific summaries of topics than are POUs and are often briefer, each dealing with a more specific issue. Each chapter has four or five CMs which, when studied, are useful for comparing issues and findings in different specific contexts such as organizational cultures, professional disciplines, and international institutional arrangements.

In map-testing, the active practice of seeking dilemmas is encouraged. In this way, assumptions and beliefs of personal maps are easier to reveal, which permits more effective analysis and leadership decision-making.

The metaphor of mapping is well known within the social sciences. It may be seen as a less formal way of dealing with what are sometimes referred to as paradigms, a term popularized half a century ago by Thomas Kuhn.[5] The terminology of mapping has been preferred because it is easier to relate to everyday and personal experiences. In contrast, 'paradigm' tends to be a term mostly reserved for widely shared belief systems. Thinking processes within a paradigm or map can be too unreflective. The active search for contradictions within a map and across maps often reveals dilemmas of leadership and in this way can help in rethinking personal beliefs.

Each of the chapters in *Dilemmas of Leadership* has a common format which itself can be seen as a map of the chapter. The reader is encouraged to develop skills in identifying dilemmas and considering how the process may support personal insights into leadership development. In most chapters the dominance of the Dominant Rational Model (DRM) becomes clear. So, for example, in Chapter 2 it becomes clear why the search to identify and measure the characteristics of natural, born leaders was influenced by the DRM. By considering the implications of humanistic psychology (among others) it becomes easier to see why leadership may be more than a fixed set of abilities or traits.

Chapter 1 is somewhat different from the other chapters because it is more focused on the various aspects of map-reading, map-testing, and map-making that are applied throughout the rest of the book. For this reason, the learning materials in this chapter are somewhat atypical. The first POU deals the methodology of the mapping approach for developing personal leadership maps. The second POU provides a brief historical review of leadership maps, as a demonstration of how the approach can be applied to a very complex set of maps to extract dilemmas and insights for leadership development purposes.

The chapter also proposes an important way of understanding definitions. A distinction may be made between theoretical and personal or working definitions. A theoretical definition indicates grounds for examining its claims. In contrast, a working definition is self-justifying and may be taken as a starting-point for sharing POUs.

Chapter 2 concentrates on the well-known leadership issue sometimes stated as the 'born or made dilemma'. The POUs of Chapter 2 indicate how the 'leaders are born' position fits understandings drawing on the DRM. Alternative possibilities draw on maps which propose that 'leaders can be developed' through learned experiences and the acquisition of appropriate skills.

Chapter 3 deals primarily with project management, one of the most successful practical systems of implementing organizational goals. The approach draws primarily on the DRM. Among its perceived strengths is its capacity for the efficient control and coordination of project teams.

Closer inspection reveals dilemmas associated with the coordination and control of work groups. Why is project leadership so little discussed in comparison to project management? How might individuals in highly coordinated and controlled project groups at the same time be expected to be motivated, entrepreneurial, and empowered?

One important element of project maps has been characterized as a focus on identifiable and measurable functions. An approach based on functionalism turns out to be well equipped for achieving well-specified goals in relatively surprise-free contexts. This appears to result in dilemmas in more complex and turbulent conditions.

Chapter 4 examines the ancient concept of charisma. It might be expected that the DRM would have wiped out all traces of such pre-modern thinking. Yet charisma, far from being overcome, was partially reinvented (or tamed) by the New Leadership thinking of the 1980s. Transformational leadership, with its uneasy relationship with its pre-modern features, is shown to be a modern version of charismatic leadership that is more accommodating of the rationality of action implied in the DRM.

Chapter 5 introduces the theme of symbolic leadership. Here we have a radical challenge to maps drawing on the DRM. A ferment of ideas has been introduced into organizational theory, drawing on a range of disciplines and favoured among social scientists. Symbolic leadership ideas are found under various labels such as post-structuralism, symbolic interactionism, social constructivism, sense-making, critical theory and postmodernism. These maps are collectively opposed to the dominance and limitations of the DRM.

Chapter 6 examines trust. Although this is considered an important concept within social science research,[6] it receives only a superficial treatment in executive education textbooks. The disinterest is in part because the DRM has little need of constructs to explain the emotional relationships between leaders and followers. More attention is needed if sense is to be made of what President Obama referred to as America's 'deficit of trust'.[7]

A concern for trust brings with it leadership dilemmas. The charismatic leader, for example, induces trust by means that go beyond rationality and that risk criticism as being manipulation of others. The challenges of trust-based processes have become a focus of attention for the emerging interest in authentic leadership.

Chapter 7 examines maps of strategy. These remain central to the business school curriculum, where the traditional treatment of the subject has been clearly influenced by rational means for formulating and implementing strategy. The approaches (as those found in Chapter 3 on project management) are oriented to functionalist treatments. Contemporary strategy texts continue to give priority to the traditional rational analysis of planned strategy. Leadership is implied, and reveals itself as an emergent strategy within implementation processes.

Chapter 8 provides students of leadership with a guide for dealing with power relationships, discrimination, and diversity. Discussions of power can be found within organizational leadership texts, although often in rather fragmented form. Any opposition to leadership power is implicitly assumed to be disruptive and contrary to the interests of the organization. Some of the most powerful alternative maps to the DRM have arisen through attempts to challenge this basic assumption. The approaches, particularly those based on critical theory, enquire who has legitimate rights to exercise power in and beyond organizations. The approaches differ fundamentally in their belief that 'reality' is socially constructed, and cannot be addressed by the reality-testing methods inherent in the dominant rational model.

Chapter 9 considers the ethical dilemmas facing leaders. As in Chapter 8, it reveals the difficulties of retaining a thoroughly rationalist treatment of leadership dilemmas. The central dilemma is presented as the conflicts often encountered between organizational pragmatism and moral belief. Although these are among the most intractable of dilemmas, their study offers alternatives to leadership decision-making's ignoring of ethical considerations.

Chapter 10 examines leadership in the context of creativity, innovation, and change. It suggests a perspective for dealing with leadership dilemmas that is summed up as treating creativity as a leader's secret weapon. This chapter explains how creativity is a powerful means of generating imaginative and effective leadership responses to professional dilemmas. It also provides a well-grounded explanation of intrinsic motivation as important for both leadership and creativity theory and practice.

Chapter 11 provides further opportunities for the reader to reflect on the journeys of exploration and the ways in which they have assisted personal learning. It attempts to identify the emerging themes that are occupying leaders and leadership researchers at present, and into the future.

The design of the book invites readers to study each chapter by starting and finishing with exercises to reflect on personal maps. Even those not engaged in a formal course of study are encouraged to tackle the exercises. They will be found to be relatively painless and will help in understanding and reinforcing the key learning points offered in the book.

Box I.1 assumes the existence of widely held and largely taken-for-granted belief systems or paradigms that structure socially shared belief systems and individual actions. Paradigms are assumed to change only marginally over time, until some substantial paradigm 'switch' occurs as a result of identification of contradictions and dilemmas. The diagram also suggests that personal beliefs and actions may be changed through a process of paradigm study (map-reading, testing, and making).

Box I.1: Paradigms and Maps

Debates over the nature of paradigms and paradigm change have been waged for many years. Kuhn proposed that the most fundamental belief systems (for example, that regarding the nature of scientific truth) become established as the dominant way of seeing things. So much so, that change is limited to rare and radical rupture of a paradigm (scientific revolution) or to frequent incremental changes at the margins of the paradigm.

One of the broadest of sociological paradigms of modern times is that of scientific rationalism. For example, education has widely accepted the principle of developing individual capacity to reason logically. Skills involving the categorization of objective components and processes are valued. Even terms such as 'objective' and 'subjective' are applied in ways that indicate the dominance of the rational over less dominant (and, by implication, inferior) ways of thinking, seeing, and acting.

The concept of a paradigm has been applied to various professional fields to explain mental rigidities or mind-sets. Cultural breakthroughs have been described in terms of paradigm shifts, perhaps accompanying a radical personal insight or creative breakthrough. Conversely, strategic 'blindness' is associated with psychological processes of functional fixedness, of not being able to see beyond existing maps.

These varied ideas suggest that personal learning requires efforts to overcome habits of thought. Social scientists have argued that the dominance of a paradigm reduces the ease with which alternative ideas become accepted.[8]

For over two centuries, the dominant paradigm of the industrial era has provided the basis of scientific reasoning. It has strongly influenced education and practices within the professions, including that of business management. We will refer to it as the Dominant Rational Model (or DRM). The DRM has a considerable historical pedigree from earlier eras. It became further associated with progress and innovation in the modern industrial age, reinforcing it as the basis of formal education and enlightened social behaviours.

So much so, that its emphasis on logic, reason, and rationality is largely taken for granted and applied, often unreflectively, beyond the professional and technical fields of its most successful applications.

Students of finance, engineering management, and information systems, as well as those with education in the natural and applied sciences are particularly familiar with the DRM.

There are alternative broad maps of the nature of knowledge and these will become evident in the chapters that follow.

Leadership scholars are among those social scientists examining the limitations of the DRM under labels such as critical theory and postmodernism. Among the issues that are brought into focus are those of discrimination, ethics, social responsibility, and the legitimacy of power.

The recommended processes of map-testing and map-making will be shown to go some way to overcoming personal preferences and beliefs over-influenced by taken-for-granted maps.

NOTES

1   Stewart, T.A. 'The nine dilemmas leaders face', http://faculty.css.edu/dswenson/web/lead9.html, downloaded 18 April 2011.
2   www.avivshahar.com/developing-leaders/, downloaded 18 April 2011.
3   Rickards, T. (1999) *Creativity and the management of change*, Oxford: Blackwell, p. xiv.
4   Thomas, R.J. (2008) *Crucibles of leadership*, Boston: Harvard Business Press, p. xii.
5   Burrell, G., & Morgan, G. (1979) *Sociological paradigms and organisational analysis: Elements of the sociology of corporate life*, London: Heinemann.
6   Kramer, R.M. (2011) 'Trust and distrust in the leadership process: A review and assessment of theory and evidence', in Bryman, A., Collinson, D., Grint, K., Jackson, B., & Uhl-Bien, M. (eds) (2011) *The Sage handbook of leadership*, London: Sage, pp. 136–150.
7   In his first State of the Union address to Congress, cited in ibid., p. 137.
8   Masterman, M. (1970) 'The nature of a paradigm', in Lakatos, I., & Musgrave, A. (eds) *Criticism and the growth of knowledge*, Cambridge: Cambridge University Press, pp. 59–89.

CHAPTER LEARNING OBJECTIVES

Learning focus
- How to apply a mapping approach to study and reflect on leadership experiences and knowledge

Key issues
- Map-reading, map-testing, map-making
- Platforms of understanding
- The nature of dilemmas
- Leadership maps, past and present

Dilemmas
- The credibility of authority
- Definitional dilemmas

Platforms of understanding
- POU 1.1 Map-reading, Map-testing, and Map-making
- POU 1.2 A Short History of Leadership Thought

Contextual materials
- CM 1.1 On Defining Definitions
- CM 1.2 The Map Is Not the Territory
- CM 1.3 Examining Dilemmas as a Means of Critical Thinking in Map-Testing
- CM 1.4 Why All Leaders Face Dilemmas: Effective and not so Effective Ways of Dealing with Them

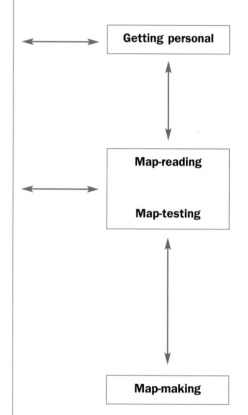

Getting personal

Map-reading

Map-testing

Map-making

1 LEADERSHIP JOURNEYS, DILEMMAS, AND MAPS

As soon as we try to define leadership we immediately discover that leadership has many different meanings.[1]

We do not distinguish between leaders and managers because the terms are often used interchangeably in the literature.[2]

Nobody has proposed that managing and leading are equivalent. But the degree of overlap is a point of sharp distinction.[3]

ORIENTATION

This chapter starts our leadership journey by introducing the approach to leadership development based on the metaphors of map-reading, map-testing, and map-making.

You will become familiar with the ways maps are constructed when they are based on the Dominant Rational Model (DRM) of knowledge management. Its influence has been pervasive for so long in educational and professional fields that it is largely taken for granted. You will learn how the DRM gained ascendancy over earlier beliefs about the workings of the natural world, thus paving the way for the methods of scientific reasoning and rational actions in modern civilizations around the world.

For all its successes, the DRM has posed dilemmas for social scientists who have studied the nature of individual and group behaviours. You will be introduced to ways of reviewing their assumptions and beliefs about leadership and testing their credibility. By examining the dilemmas that are uncovered, promising new approaches are revealed.

The chapter also addresses the difficulties of dealing with definitions. You will learn of ways to distinguish between working definitions and theoretical ones. You will become familiar with technical terms important for dealing with maps and map-making. You will learn how map-testing is a powerful way of evaluating the strengths and weaknesses of any text you study, including a way of understanding books, reports, films, even situations as forms of text.[4] In these ways you will be able to think more deeply about the fundamental question: 'What is leadership?'

By way of introduction you are invited to carry out a reflective exercise as a benchmark of your current leadership maps (Exercise 1.1).

Each chapter in the book will have its own overview map with a similar structure. The orientation section is followed by a section divided into a small number (usually two) of important general readings. These are described as platforms of understanding (POUs). A POU is information that captures a set of shared beliefs about a theme or concept.

One of the ways to think about communication is as a means of establishing a shared POU. The sharing may be widespread, or more localized into professional groupings, organizations, or even smaller social groups such as families. Even the most respected POU is open to further testing.

The POUs of the chapter are followed by a slightly larger number of contextual materials (CMs) selected as being briefer and more focused on a specific context. Each CM may be regarded as a POU of more limited scope.

If you study any text to understand its content you are mainly engaged in map-reading. Even that is a very important and useful skill. When you study to test the POU, comparing it with other knowledge you have, you are map-testing. Such active efforts at map-testing will produce an awareness of dilemmas. You will find plenty of examples for practice throughout the book, starting with the POUs and CMs in this chapter.

Exercise 1.1: Your Now and Future Leadership Maps

This exercise is for personal preparation and reflection. First impressions are worth recording. You will be able to complete the exercise in 10 to 20 minutes of undisturbed work. For a classroom activity, it is suited to students working in pairs, each sharing and refining individual maps.

Produce a personal reference document outlining your current ideas and beliefs about leadership, and your future plans (however unclear they may be). Do not search for any information at this stage. Keep your notes for reference because they will provide a benchmark to refer to during later stages of your leadership studies.

Exercise 1.1 Discussion Questions

1 Describe briefly, in everyday language, what you understand by the term 'leadership'. This is your working definition.
2 What questions about leadership do you have, about which you hope to learn more from this book?
3 What do you know about leadership from direct or indirect experience that has already influenced your thinking and/or actions?
4 What do you think are your personal leadership strengths and weaknesses?
5 Is there a particular leader who has influenced your leadership behaviours? Who? Why?
6 Do you have any leadership goal that you have promised yourself you will try to achieve?

The first POU of all introduces the core method advocated to support your leadership development: learning through the application of map-reading, map-testing, and map-making.

PLATFORMS OF UNDERSTANDING

POU 1.1: Map-reading, Map-testing, and Map-making

Our first POU introduces the key aspects of the processes of map-reading, map-testing, and map-making. It also explains more about the importance of the active examination of information within any book or other text in order for you to become more aware of aspects of your own mental maps and how you may be able to revise them. The POU also touches on the nature of experiential learning and critical thinking.

The metaphor of map-reading has already been used, and will recur in all future chapters. It is probably a familiar one, representing life as a journey or quest, in which we use aids such as maps, guides, and compasses to help us on our way.

Many students (even experienced managers) struggle with assessing the quality of leadership information that they come across. The data may or may not be accurate. Case histories are even harder to evaluate than the more technical reports with which they are familiar. In this book, we offer an approach that is a simplification of the scholarly approach taught as research methodology.[5] We have described it in terms of map-reading, map-making, and map-testing.

Maps and map-making have played an invaluable part in the advancement of human knowledge and discovery processes. Early maps have been dated as having been made over nine thousand years ago in Anatolia. Other maps dated at over 2,000 years old have survived in China and Mesopotamia. Maps supported trade, exploration, and military ventures, becoming increasingly diverse and accurate, drawing on (and creating) technological advantages. The creation of a map inevitably draws on knowledge of previous maps of which the map-maker will be aware. It is likely that the modifications have been made because of dissatisfactions with the older map, based on study or experience.

As a first exercise in map-reading, making and testing, you are invited to carry out a thought experiment, putting yourself in the place of a business graduate shortly after joining an international organization. Exercise 1.2 is suitable for private study or for tutorial or classroom discussion.

Perhaps you were surprised at what sense you were able to make about a book you had not read. Because you did not have an opportunity to read the entire book you had to rely on attempts to reconstruct what a map of the book would look like. You were trying to reproduce the POU of the book's author, by information collecting and sorting.

The process usually overlaps with evaluating the information and, in this example, the book. This is map-testing. You are examining a map for the sense it makes to you.

At some stage you may revise your understanding of the book, but you may also make a new map. Map-making involves a revision of your own previous assumptions, and beliefs could change in any way. This might be about the book or about the process through which you test books for their reliability. Map-making, then, is part of the process of critical and reflective thinking. If the process reveals dilemmas, so much the more promising. Finding a previously hidden dilemma is a move towards finding new ways of dealing with it.

These processes require the development of new habits for the active study of any book or text. It is not possible to suggest a simple formula for how long to spend on the stages of map-reading, making, and testing. In practice, the stages merge with one another, and you will find yourself returning to a stage with which you are dissatisfied.

Map-reading is familiar in principle to many students. The processes of map-testing and map-making are likely to be found more difficult and unfamiliar.

Exercise 1.2: The Departure Lounge Dilemma

The Departure Lounge Dilemma challenges you to deal with a dilemma using the principles of map-reading, map-testing, and map-making. You have to evaluate a business book quickly. You have never seen it before. The book is called *Leadership is for Winners not Whingers*. It is what is sometimes referred to as an inspirational self-development book. It is easy to read, and appears to have many aspects in common with other books for sale in the business section of bookshops, promising a solution to the problems that leaders face.

You have never heard of the publishers, Victor Ludorum Press of Woodford, Cheshire in England. The author, Tex Writter, is a former high-school football coach who has also coached the Moldovan national team. The front cover tells you that this book will change your life and improve your skills in influencing your colleagues and employees.

You are a recently graduated MBA who has just been appointed to work as a personal aide to the director of strategy of an international organization. Your employers were looking for someone able to contribute to the organization's strategic plans. A broad knowledge of international business and change programmes, and an ability to analyse complex situations were also considered important.

Our story begins as you are waiting for a plane in the departure lounge of an international airport. A few minutes ago your manager handed you a copy of a new book on leadership. He had discovered the book a few weeks earlier, and you are accompanying him to a strategy review meeting where he will announce his intention to use its approach as a cornerstone for developing future strategy.

You are to draft this part of his speech, and you have the length of the eight-hour flight to decide what to put in it. From the flyleaf of the book, you learn that the author claims to have found a new method of identifying winners and losers in business, based on his experiences as a football coach. He argues that business follows the same patterns of behaviour as football. Following his method, the business leader can identify winners and deal with losers. This involves identifying people who have the winning gene and those who do not. Those who do not may be tried out in jobs as followers of the winners, as a proportion of these non-winners are needed to carry out the leader's goals.

Note down your first reactions to the book as a guide to the future of leadership.

Exercise 1.2 Discussion Questions

1 What information did you take into account that helped you to reach your conclusions about the credibility of the book?
2 Can you identify any map-testing that you carried out in your attempts to evaluate the book?
3 If so, can you see how map-testing might lead you to develop a more general approach for evaluating business information provided in books, articles, or other forms of professional activity?

Throughout *Dilemmas of Leadership*, you will find leadership stories and opportunities to relate your maps to personal experiences, beliefs, and goals. This treatment may be thought of as a means for you to study well-established maps so that you can test them and then construct from them maps for your personal leadership journeys. A recent review has suggested the term 'critical thinking' as capturing the essential features of the process.[6]

Critical thinking allows us to examine and explain (to ourselves and to others) why we have arrived at the conclusions we have reached. It is a universal component of our mental hardware. It helps in the understanding of the most important (i.e. critical) issues within an area of enquiry. The focus of attention could be a written text such as a business case, or a book, or a business presentation. Critical thinking relies on prior knowledge ('knowing that') and on higher-level knowledge ('knowing how'). Reasoning of a logical kind comes into the process, but is far from the only mental characteristic. Reflection and judgement (sometimes described as intuition) are also important.

David Kolb and colleagues at Case Western in the 1980s suggested that personal learning occurs through repeated processes[7] within which experience connects with reflection, abstract concept formation, and active experimentation. The process also can be seen as associated with more recent theories of knowledge-acquisition cycles from 'tacit to explicit' forms.[8] Kolb describes the connecting process as one of reflective observation. Another scholar has described it as like having a conversation with the situation.[9] Through reflection, the learner is able to make new sense of experience in terms of codified knowledge, and also to make new sense of codified knowledge in terms of reflection. We become better leaders through reflecting on experience (our own and that of others), and through linking theory and practice.

In our courses for business students and executives, we encourage reflection, which we see as going hand in hand with critique.

POU 1.2: A Short History of Leadership Thought

POU 1.2 provides a historical overview of leadership. It has been assembled from several widely accepted maps. One of its purposes is to introduce the reader to the ways in which map-makers have identified dilemmas and proposed alternatives to the most widely accepted maps of their times. The texts that have been major influences in the construction of POU 1.2 are shown in Box 1.1.

This 'map of maps' shows how even the most widely accepted leadership maps become challenged and changed through a process involving their testing and the identification of dilemmas. In particular, the dilemmas leading to challenges of assumptions based on the DRM have been highlighted.

It would appear, from archaeological evidence, that all early societies had some form of leadership. Indeed, it has been argued that '"the beginning" for leadership scholars is the beginning of recorded history, not the beginning of Homo Sapiens'.[10]

Box 1.1: Construction of a 'Map of Maps' of Leadership

Map-making always draws on knowledge of earlier maps. The 'Map of Maps' studied in POU 1.2 drew on a large number of such maps. The following texts (maps) were particularly important in its construction as major sources of information for map-reading and map-testing.

Leadership in Organizations, by Gary Yukl[11]

Leadership: Theory and Practice, by Peter Northouse[12]

Changing Theories of Leadership and Leadership Development, by John Story[13]

Leadership in Organizations, by Alan Bryman[14]

The Ancestor's Tale, by Richard Dawkins[15]

Beliefs about the patterns of the seasons and human existence were based on assumptions about spiritual phenomena that existed in animals and inanimate objects. Much has been learned from the earliest paintings and other artefacts when they are studied as leadership maps.

These ancient beliefs were challenged by the powerful concept that humans were able to overcome predestined fate through the application of reason. This probably happened over a long period of time. Eventually, however, the application of reasoned argument became accepted as a powerful means of testing beliefs. Influential scholars from Europe and the Middle East spread the new idea around the world. Rationality became accepted as the way forward for understanding and influencing the natural world. The Rational Model became accepted to such an extent that it began to dominate earlier beliefs. One of its strengths was its power of testing and challenging prior knowledge.

The Dominant Rational Model heavily influences more specific personal and cultural maps. Its methods of enquiring into knowledge are forms of map-reading, testing, and making. However, it is worth noting that the arrival of a dominant map does not eliminate all traces of the knowledge associated with earlier maps. As we shall see, a significant aspect of the records of pre-modern societies was the representation of leadership through study of the natural world and, in particular, of the animals they encountered. Not all ancient knowledge should be dismissed.

For example, recent work on complexity theory examines the ways in which leadership 'emerges' within flocks of birds and shoals of fish.[16] Evolutionary biologists[17] argue that species find ways of surviving, and that leadership has survival advantages for the species. The DRM provides understanding of leadership in humans by its scientific study in animals (Table 1.1).

Table 1.1 Leadership as a Biological Phenomenon

Insects	Role specialization and biologically distinct 'leaders' of a swarm or colony (bees, termites, etc.).
	Foraging involves information leaders that report back and are able to lead others to a source of food they have discovered.
Fish	'Shoaling' fish have no obvious leader(s). The movements of the shoal can be modelled as instinctive patterns influenced by signals of fluid turbulence.
Reptiles	Fight–flight survival instincts favour winners/leaders in territorial and sexual competition.
Birds	Pecking-order principle is evidence of dominance, hierarchy, and leadership.
	Flocking appears to reveal pathfinder leader/followers.
	Display activities to attract mates favour development of non-functional attributes (the peacock's tail phenomenon).
Predators	Hunting packs show strong social systems of dominance and hierarchy (alpha and beta animals of both sexes).
	Learning through play.
Herd creatures (horses, elephants)	Herds show social systems of dominance, hierarchy, and matriarchal 'schooling'.
Primates (mandrills, monkeys, chimpanzees)	Colonies show a wide range of social interactions (grooming, communications patterns) while retaining hierarchical patterns of dominance.
	Intelligence becomes an observable factor among leaders in species that are close 'relatives' to human beings (chimpanzees).

The ancient beliefs about the natural world were gradually clarified by the methods of science. Some instinctive behaviours, such as aggression and territorialism, are widely shared across species. In contrast, attributing aspects of morality to other species is to risk the error known as anthropomorphism, which is attributing human emotions and motives to animals. We must think carefully of what sense we are making of a term such as 'leader' applied to a flock of wild geese, or a line of ants being 'led' to a source of food.

It is worth noting that maps in the modern era have not eliminated the older metaphors of leadership that draw on observed animal behaviours. For example, the vocabulary of alpha males and pack leaders is often found in contemporary professional leadership texts.[18]

The DRM has provided guidance for knowledge-seeking and testing for at least two millennia. It has a built-in capacity to help us reinvent our understanding of our world. It took on particular importance over the last two centuries, in the era marked by the so-called Industrial Revolution. Its dominance roughly corresponds with the political and conceptual upheavals of the Enlightenment in Western thought in the eighteenth century.

An important map historically came from the work of the great sociologist Max Weber. He studied contemporary and historical sources of authority. He thought that pre-modern society had leaders accepted through long-established traditions and beliefs. There was a pre-modern form of leader who changed such beliefs, and for whom Weber reintroduced the term 'charismatic'.

Weber considered that both these leadership types were less suited to the conditions found in a modern industrialized society and its institutions.[19] His widely accepted portrait of a modern leader is that of someone operating within a rational framework of legally accepted rules and regulations.

Weber appears to have confined traditional and charismatic leadership forms to the dustbin of discarded historical theories. As we will see in Chapter 4, charismatic leadership has not been completely removed from contemporary leadership maps.

Psychologists also applied modern scientific methods to develop maps of leadership. For over a century, the focus of these approaches was the application of scientific rigour to discovering the traits or stable personality characteristics of successful leaders. The so-called trait era of leadership is generally considered to have been severely weakened by the work of the American psychologist Ralph Stogdill. His encyclopaedic handbook amassed evidence that the search for traits was proving fruitless.[20]

The dominance of trait mappings declined towards the middle of the twentieth century, and became replaced with maps examining leadership behaviours and skills. An important implication is that skills are considered to be less inherent, and more trainable. That is to say, the possibility opened up that leaders could be developed. The change of emphasis also resulted in greater attention being paid to leaders at lower levels in organizational hierarchies, a shift permitting easier access to a far larger population of leaders.

The shifts in leadership beliefs and mappings were still failing to establish clear links between observed behaviours and leadership performance. The focus began to move from studies of leaders to studies of leadership processes. By the 1970s, the field of leadership studies had recognized the dilemmas in trait theories and the incompleteness of the attempted replacements.

The story took a new turn in the 1980s, under the label of New Leadership. The change is widely told as having received its impetus from an earlier study of great political leaders by historian James MacGregor Burns. His most influential book was simply entitled *Leadership*.[21] It contrasted contemporary maps that Burns viewed as being based on economic (and rational) transactions with a new map of transformational leadership.

His work suggested that the behaviours of exceptional transformational leaders could also be found in many less famous leaders, in less spectacular contexts. In the process, he unintentionally updated a much older concept of charismatic leadership, which turned into a dilemma within the story of (new) transformational leadership.

New Leadership put considerable emphasis on the management of meaning. The 1980s had also seen the rise of popular business books placing emphasis on processes of transformation and change. The most popular books were enthusiastic about the older idea of charismatic leadership because of its capability of motivating people through powerful, emotionally engaging visions. Transformational leadership addressed the dilemma through studies that drew on the methods of modern psychological investigations. As we will see, this was to produce considerable debate about whether transformational leadership was charismatic leadership in a modern guise.

In summary, the 'Map of Maps' illustrates how the dominance of an older map is challenged as dilemmas are revealed. Pre-modern maps and their dilemmas in explaining the natural world gave way to the DRM, whose methods of truth-seeking were far more successful. These persisted into modern time. In leadership studies, Burns considered that these maps still presented a dilemma concerning the transformative powers of leaders. This was resolved when transformational leadership was incorporated into New Leadership approaches. The old idea of charisma had been 'tamed' into modern form.

CONTEXTUAL MATERIALS

Contextual materials (CMs) have been selected as being briefer and more focused on a specific context than a POU. Each CM may be regarded as a POU of more limited scope. Their study reveals different perspectives and permits more opportunities for map-testing, for example, by examining assertions made within the POUs against information found within any of the CMs.

CM 1.1: On Defining Definitions

This book departs from a common practice of offering authoritative definitions of important terms being considered. Instead, it suggests that definitions are open to testing within a mapping approach. It places emphasis on the provisional nature of definitions within our personally constructed maps or belief systems. These are referred to as working definitions.

Definitions play an important part in attempts to learn and to deal with unfamiliar ideas and situations. The question of definition is particularly important for understanding leadership, which has perhaps suffered from an excess of definitions.

Communication relies on assumptions about the meanings of words and other symbols used. In everyday discussions we rarely define terms. What appears to be happening is that conversation is itself a means of testing for shared POUs situated within a social context. Just as we use the concepts of map-making and map-testing to side-step more complex theories of knowledge, we use the notion of working definitions to side-step problems of theoretical generalization. Working definitions offer a starting-point for sharing beliefs and POUs. In practical terms, this means that a working definition has the powerful property of being self-referential. That is to say, it provides its own justification. A working definition stops short of offering proof to a wider group. So for leadership, you may start a discussion by saying what you mean by leadership. You might say '. . . when I use the term leadership I mean . . .' before completing your statement.

When we are challenged even further to explain what we mean, we are expected to clarify by offering more formal explanations. A theoretical definition of leadership is presented in a way that makes it possible to test its claims to be trusted. This explanation is taking us towards the point that engaging in discussions involving definitions is a form of map-testing and seeking a shared POU from which to work.

CM 1.2: The Map Is Not the Territory

A well-known saying in management courses is that the map is not the territory. The point being made is that a conceptual map is a representation or a way of seeing. The idea has been popularized by the distinguished organizational theorist Karl Weick in several of his books and lectures. His accounts can be traced to a poem by Miroslav Holub[22] about a Hungarian reconnaissance unit lost in the Alps. In the poem, the soldiers faced an icy death, until their leader found a map which he used to lead the platoon to safety. On their return, however, it was found that the map was not of the Alps, but of the Pyrenees:

> . . . we considered ourselves
>
> lost and waited for the end. And then one of us
>
> found a map in his pocket. That calmed us down.
>
> We pitched camp, lasted out the snowstorm and then with the map
>
> we discovered our bearings.
>
> And here we are.
>
> The lieutenant borrowed this remarkable map
>
> and had a good look at it. It was not a map of the Alps
>
> but of the Pyrenees.[23]

The story can itself be interpreted in various ways. It can be seen as indicating how a map does not have to be accurate to be a means of finding your bearings. But the effort is an active one, and map-reading also requires experiential learning through what has been described, in a grand-sounding term, as a 'situationally enacted capability'.[24]

The map-making metaphor can also be found in the behavioural theory of neurolinguistic programming (NLP). This clinical discipline is based on the belief that individuals have cognitive structures or maps whose fundamental features have been widely tested. The mental maps provide individuals with differing perceptions of their psychological worlds.[25] Understanding the maps from observed behaviours permits better communication and POUs. The process may be seen as 'reading' an individual through their behaviours.

We use the term 'map' as a metaphor for a representation of a conceptual territory. In later chapters the maps cover territories such as charismatic leadership, project management, strategy, symbolism, and ethics.

CM 1.3: Examining Dilemmas as a Means of Critical Thinking in Map-Testing

Becoming skilled at identifying dilemmas is a powerful approach for developing new understandings of leadership when you are faced with difficult situations. Before considering the dilemmas of modern business leaders, let us briefly look at dilemmas whose resolution may have life-and-death consequences. The extreme examples are all too familiar. Hostage-takers face their negotiators with dilemmas through their demands for military concessions. To the outsider, the dilemma presents itself as a struggle between two utterly different ('incommensurate') sets of values, each violated by the two obvious sets of actions. To concede to the hostage-takers' demands is ethically dubious, perhaps politically or socially unacceptable. To reject the demands is likely to place in mortal danger the lives of hostages caught up in events. Little wonder that the processes of negotiating are increasingly acknowledged as requiring the most skilful of mediators (who are examples of a special kind of leader).[26]

The Judaeo-Christian tradition teaches the dilemmas of leadership through stories and parables. The future King David is said to have been engaged in a fierce battle during which three of his chosen captains dared to break through enemy lines to secure him a pitcher of water. His dilemma: to drink while his warriors went thirsty, and while such great risks had been taken on his behalf to obtain it.

David carried out a symbolic act of pouring the water onto the sands of the desert, saying it was too precious to drink. We may think of this as a symbolic act of leadership self-denial. The story is backed up by many similar ones in military history. The leader has to find a powerful way of shifting the perspective of the followers, so as to avoid the most obvious and most undesired actions (to accept a gift or to refuse it).

In another story, a child was brought to King Solomon, with two women each claiming, tearfully, to be the real mother. King Solomon dealt with the dilemma of the child, by drawing his sword and announcing that he would kill the child so that each of the women could have one half of it. The anguished cries of one of the women revealed the real mother and resolved the dilemma.

The ancient stories have the power to captivate, bewilder, and disturb, both emotionally and intellectually. In one sense, this is how leaders are 'supposed to' deal with tough situations, and as we relive in our imaginations these dramatic stories, we may contrast them with our own indecisiveness.

If the actions were decisive, they were also unexpected and unpredictable. As in the account of any heroic story, we may speculate on what 'really' happened at the time, but we can have no doubt that the leader is described as acting in an exceptional and unexpected way. In present-day language we might refer to their actions as being consequential for leaps of lateral thinking,[27] which change the perceptions of those around them.

Organizational leaders repeatedly face dilemmas. The issues are generally less dramatic than those that require the wisdom of Solomon, yet they will still have those aspects of a dilemma described by one executive as 'what keeps leaders awake at night'.[28]

These maps show how dilemmas may be seen as hard-to-solve problems. Some systems researchers have considered them in this fashion.[29] It should be noted that, technically, a dilemma presents an either–or decision that has no acceptable answer. Logic puzzles couched as dilemmas have amused philosophers since the time of Socrates. Even so, many people seem to assume, in everyday conversation, that every problem has a right answer (and presumably quite a few wrong ones).

Leaders resolve dilemmas through action. Their actions often are seen, in hindsight, as escaping from a mind-set that is blocking off effective action. In so doing, the leader demonstrates creativity. There are many examples throughout the book, particularly in Chapter 10, where leadership is seen as inherently a creative practice.

CM 1.4: Why All Leaders Face Dilemmas: Effective and not so Effective Ways of Dealing with Them

The term 'dilemma' originally referred to a philosophical position that defeats logical attempts to resolve it. One of two outcomes has to be accepted, yet each contradicts previously held beliefs and their logical consequences. The early philosophers talked of being on the horns of a dilemma – where the choice is to be impaled by one or the other horn of an angry bull. Other powerful metaphors also illustrate what dilemma is like: 'It's being between a rock and a hard place'; 'It's a choice between the devil and the deep blue sea'; or 'Sailing too close to the rocks or the whirlpool' (Scylla and Charybdis were the terms used in mythology).

The essence of a dilemma is that there is no satisfactory choice that suggests itself on the basis of the evidence available. Each action seems to carry with it undesired consequences. This even applies to the action of doing nothing and waiting to see what happens. The explanation lies in the uncertainties surrounding leadership decisions, and strategic decisions in particular. There is incomplete information about the consequences of the decisions. Even the sophisticated methods of probability and risk analysis are unable to provide more than indications of what might happen. As all leaders operate with less than complete information, it may be argued that all leaders face dilemmas in reaching decisions.

A common but ineffective way of dealing with a dilemma is to deny its existence. Denial of the ambiguities of a situation can be found in leaders who act decisively, but upon wrong decisions, ignoring 'uncomfortable' information that might warn of the dangers of the proposed strategic action.

At least, the strategy of coping through denial is consistent with the image of the leader as bold and decisive. The leader who is unable to act does not even have that consolation. Inevitably, the blame falls on the hapless leader. Military schools are particularly sensitive to the battles that have been lost through indecision. So much so, that their own leadership training puts at a premium the need to act as swiftly as necessary, accepting the risks involved. The actions, however, follow the best appraisal that can be made under the circumstances, with the best intelligence that can be obtained. But military training has not succeeded in eliminating, under battle conditions, either the over-hasty and impulsive action (denial of the complexities of the situation) or indecision and hesitancy under pressure (being overwhelmed by the uncertainties). The case is also true in commercial life. Then the accusations appear of a 'rudderless' company, one that is unable to steer a path through its turbulent sea of troubles.

There is no 'magic bullet' or technique that guarantees leaders ways of overcoming their most pressing dilemmas. Almost by definition, dilemmas are not susceptible to formulaic treatments. However, there is an approach that has proved itself repeatedly in developing skills so that dilemmas are stripped of their potential for producing over-hasty actions, on the one hand, or action paralysis, on the other.

The process, basically, is one in which you are trying to become more skilled at finding beliefs and assumptions at work or in social environments. You may help others, or find it helpful to see yourself having your own 'conversation with the situation'. The following questions suggest possible starting-points for such conversations, whether alone or amongst others.

1   *Examining a Single Map*

■   What's familiar about this map?
■   What's new and unexpected?
■   Does the new and unexpected present a dilemma (between what was expected and what was found)?

2   *Integrating the Information from Several Maps*

■   In comparing more than one map, are there contradictions and confusions?
■   Do these suggest dilemmas?
■   Might the dilemmas arise because of different maps or POUs that appear to explain the map?

INTEGRATION

Chapter 1 deals in the knowledge and skill-sets that will support improved study and leadership actions. It shows the benefits derived from examining knowledge in terms of map-reading, making, and testing. The identification of dilemmas offers insights into ways of dealing with hard-to-resolve issues.

The brief history of leadership would be difficult to appreciate without examining its dilemmas. These show how the authority of a dominant map is challenged by a subsequent authority. The ancient ideas of a fatalistic world persisted through early civilizations. These maps were challenged by the authority of the DRM. Its ideas of rationality and logic as a means of establishing truth have been refined, but its map has retained its authority.

This brings us to the important dilemma of the credibility of authority. Some ancient ideas resist the implications of the new orthodoxy. Charisma, for example, persists, and may even survive attempts to transform it through applying the methods of modern psychological investigations.

A second important dilemma, partly related to the first, is that which deals with multiple definitions. Clearly, if there were one absolute authority, there would likely be one non-contested definition of leadership. This is far from the case.

Box 1.2: Changing Eras, Changing Definitions

Differing views of leadership (maps) produce differing definitions. One definition has been accepted, since it was proposed by Stogdill in his *Handbook*, which has continued to be regarded as almost uncontested in authority:

> Leadership may be considered as the process (act) of influencing the activities of a group in its efforts towards goal setting and goal achievement.[30]

Bryman later noted that the definition is not adequate for distinguishing between leadership and management. This lack of differentiation contributes to difficulties in distinguishing leadership and management processes. He also suggests a 'New Leadership' definition dealing with the management of meaning:

> The leader gives a sense of direction and purpose through the articulation of a compelling world view [the defining characteristic of which is] the active promotion of values which provide shared meanings about the nature of organization.

An understanding of maps as representations of reality helps to explain how the most accepted definitions change. Different eras have different maps (Box 1.2). Stogdill's authority helped to establish his map of leadership and his definition. Several decades later, Bryman challenged Stogdill's map on the grounds that it failed to distinguish between leaders and managers. His own proposal was to result in increased attention to New Leadership. New eras, new authorities, new definitions.

GETTING PERSONAL

A great deal of this chapter offers insights of personal value. Much confusion exists about the nature of concepts such as leadership. Without some ideas of map-making, many people assume that an answer is to be found by looking up a definition in a dictionary or in its modern substitute, via an internet search by way of Google or Wikipedia. These are excellent starting-points for collecting information. This chapter has shown why any knowledge acquired in these ways has to be tested. Any definition needs to be set against your working definitions. In that way you will find opportunities for learning when its dilemmas are discovered.

SUMMARY

The metaphors of map-reading, map-testing, and map-making presented in Chapter 1 are retained throughout the book. Consistent with the metaphor, the book is a support for leadership development journeys. The maps of various other map-makers offer guides for the journey. Ultimately, however, the reader takes responsibility for preparing for his or her personal leadership journeys in the future.

The processes require knowledge of various terms. A set of working definitions is shown in Box 1.3.

Box 1.3: Working Definitions of Key Terms

The following working definitions will provide a starting-point for your studies of Dilemmas of Leadership. You will be able to deepen your understanding and find more formal definitions during your journeys of exploration.

Critical thinking A form of consciously controlled thinking directed towards understanding what to believe and what to do. It involves reflective thought, drawing on experience as well as on perception and memory.[31]

Critique The processes whereby information is studied and judged, applying analytical techniques so as to reveal its implications for specified purposes.

Definition An attempt to express the meaning of a term.

Dilemmas Hard-to-resolve but important issues in theory and practice. Logical dilemmas arise when formal analysis (including critique) reveals more than one (usually two) possibility, each of which contradicts a starting contention or proposition. Action dilemmas arise when someone (such as a leader) has identified more than one (most often two) course of action, none of which is acceptable in practice. Ethical dilemmas may be between two sets of ethical values, or between one ethical set and other practical, 'real-world' considerations.

Dominant Rational Model (DRM) The term used to indicate the universally accepted approach, based on logic, to assessing the claims made about any form of knowledge. The DRM is also associated with beliefs in the rationality of human action.

Leadership journey An expedition into a leadership territory, for purposes of discovery or experience. Journeys are supported by appropriate maps, which may involve personal map-making.

Leadership map A representation of the territory likely to be covered by a proposed leadership journey.

Map Unless specified otherwise, the term is used to indicate a representation of a conceptual 'territory' in which 'journeys of exploration' take place.

Metaphoric models Metaphors are ways of expressing concepts so that a less familiar concept is connected to a more familiar one. We have resorted to metaphors of maps and territory to help us deal with concepts associated with experiential learning, personal development, and critical analysis.

Modernism The culture of the modern industrial era, which places emphasis on technological advances. The term is often used to draw attention to the dehumanizing effects of such maps.

Paradigm A widely held world-view or belief system.

Personal map-making The creation of personalized maps, based on individual goals and experience, and with specific journeys in mind. Personal maps tend to rely on examination of previously well-established, but general, maps.

Platform of understanding (POU) A conceptual map of a body of knowledge. The course materials capture POUs that are then reinterpreted by readers. The 'map' is deeply influenced by assumptions about the 'territory', the arbiters of which are authorities or experts. Communication may be seen as attempts to achieve a shared POU.

Working definition An indication of the sense made of a term. Working definitions are particularly useful in communicating personal POUs. They have their own form of self-justification, although testing the definition may result in refinements, a form of map-testing and map-making.

The leadership materials studied are based on shared belief systems, which are described as POUs. A map is a simplified representation of a territory. It conceals uncertainties. Map-testing involves testing the maps for those concealed uncertainties. The recommended comparative approach is to look for unexplained differences between maps. This approach reveals the differences as dilemmas, which are hard-to-resolve but important issues. Dilemmas, by definition, have no 'right answer'. Instead, leaders have to make decisions based on personal examination of the dilemmas for specific leadership challenges, drawing on personal mapping processes.

The DRM is shown to apply to many aspects of professional life, including that of leadership. However, at its core is a method of challenging and even falsifying assumptions and beliefs. This is one of its strengths: the DRM has a built-in way of testing its own assumptions, a powerful form of map-testing and map-making.

Such map-testing has contributed to scientific and technological advances. However, as has been shown, it can also lead to the denial of the value of alternative paradigmatic maps. The following chapters will draw attention to the dilemmas which the DRM has been found inadequate for resolving. They address issues found to be relevant in contemporary organizations, such as power relationships, inequalities, ethics, conflicts and conflict resolution, and change management.

We will be encountering definitional variety in several chapters throughout the book. The starting-point for map-testing, unless stated otherwise is a working definition of leadership as a process of influence. It borrows from a much-quoted definition by Stogdill: 'Leadership may be considered as the process (act) of influencing the activities of a group in its efforts towards goal setting and goal achievement.'

Readers interested in a final effort at map-testing might be able to identify how Stogdill's definition may be interpreted as drawing on the values and methods of the DRM.

NOTES

1   Northouse, P.G. (2004) *Leadership theory and practice*, 3rd edn, Thousand Oaks, CA: Sage, p. 2.
2   Dirks, K.T., & Ferrin, D.L. (2002) 'Trust in leadership: Meta-analytic findings and implications for research and practice', *Journal of Applied Psychology*, 87, 4, 611–628, who cite Yukl, G., & Van Fleet, D.D. (1992) 'Theory and research on leadership in organizations', in Dunnette, M.D., & Hough, L.M. (eds) *Handbook of industrial and organizational psychology*, Vol. 3, pp. 147–197. The Dirks and Ferrin meta-analysis of trust is studied in Chapter 6 of this edition of *Dilemmas of Leadership*.
3   Yukl, G.A. (2002) *Leadership in organizations*, 3rd edn, Englewood Cliffs, NJ: Prentice Hall, p. 5.
4   Since the publication of the first edition of *Dilemmas of Leadership*, a version of the airport lounge exercise has been applied in leadership workshops around the world. Participants are invited to share their favourite leadership book, article, or film. Subsequent discussion considers how to develop skills in evaluating such materials (in other words, skills needed by the MBA graduate to perform well in the airport lounge example). The map-making, map-testing, and map-reading approach is contrasted with the possible dilemma of the unconditional acceptance or rejection of a book or other text. The dilemma is examined further in http://leaderswedeserve. wordpress.com/2010/07/06/peter-drucker-baseball-and-a-manga-heroine/.

5   DePoy, E., & Gitlin, L.N. (1998) *Introduction to research: Understanding and applying multiple strategies*, St Louis: Mosby.

6   Smith, G.F. (2003) 'Beyond critical thinking and decision-making: Teaching business students how to think', *Journal of Management Education*, 27, 1, 24–51.

7   Kolb, D.A. (1985) *Experiential learning*, Englewood Cliffs, NJ: Prentice Hall; Kolb, D.A., Rubin, I.M., & McIntyre, J.M. (eds) (1990) *Organizational psychology: A book of readings*, 5th edn, Englewood Cliffs, NJ: Prentice Hall.

8   Nonaka, I., & Takeuchi, H. (1995) *The knowledge creating company: How Japanese companies create the dynamics of innovation*, Oxford: OUP.

9   Schon, D.A. (1983) *The reflective practitioner*, New York: Basic Books.

10 Grint, K. (2011) 'A history of leadership', in Bryman, A., Collinson, D., Grint, K., Jackson, B., & Uhl-Bien, M. (eds) (2011) *The Sage handbook of leadership*, London: Sage Publications Ltd, pp. 3–14.

11 Yukl, G.A. (2002) *Leadership in organizations*, 3rd edn, Englewood Cliffs, NJ: Prentice Hall.

12 Northouse, P.G. (2004, 2011) *Leadership: Theory and practice*, 3rd edn, 5th edn, Newbury Park, CA: Sage.

13 Story, J. (2004) 'Changing theories of leadership and leadership development', in Story, J. (ed.) *Leadership in organizations: Current issues and key trends*, London: Routledge, pp. 11–37.

13 Bryman, A. (1996) 'Leadership in organizations', in Clegg, S.R., Hardy, C., & Nord, W.R. (eds) *Handbook of organization studies*, London: Sage, pp. 276–292.

15 Dawkins, R. (2005) *The ancestor's tale*, London: Orion.

16 http://66.102.1.104/scholar?hl=en&lr=&newwindow=1&q=cache:WjX_Q2CwVZ4J:www.emergence.org/Emergence/Archive/Issue1_1/Issue1_1_3.pdf+author:%22Goldstein%22+intitle:%22Emergence+as+a+Construct:+History+and+Issues%22+.

17 Dawkins, R. (1989) *The selfish gene*, 2nd edn, Oxford: OUP; (2005) *The ancestor's tale*, London: Orion.

18 An illustrative example can be found in http://briandoddonleadership.com/2010/09/10/65-characteristics-of-alpha-male-leadership/, downloaded 1 May 2011.

19 Weber, M. (1947) *The theory of social and economic organization*, Henderson, A.M., & Parsons, T. (trans.), Parsons, T. (ed.) New York: Free Press (original work, 1924).

20 Another influence was Mann, R.D. (1959) 'A review of the relationships between personality and performance in small groups', *Psychological Bulletin*, 56, 241–270.

21 Burns, J.M. (1978) *Leadership*, New York: Harper & Row.

22 Holub, M. (1977) 'Brief thoughts on maps', *Times Literary Supplement*, 4 February, p. 118.

23 Basbøll, T., & Graham, H. (2006) 'Substitutes for strategy research: Notes on the source of Karl Weick's anecdote of the young lieutenant and the map of the Pyrenees', *Ephemera*, 6, 2, 194–204.

24 Orlikowski, W.J. (2002) 'Knowing in practice: Enacting a collective capability in distributed organizing', *Organization Science: A Journal of the Institute of Management Sciences*, 13, 3, 249.

25 Ibid.

26 See Kohlrieser, G. (2007) 'Hostage at the table', Jossey-Bass, www.hostageatthetable.com/, downloaded 2 May 2011.

27 De Bono, E. (1992) *Serious creativity: Using the power of lateral thinking to create new ideas*, London: Harper Collins.

28 http://cgblog.org/2008/09/15/what-keeps-senior-leaders-awake-at-night/.

29 Armson, R. (2011) *Growing wings on the way: Systems thinking for messy situations*, Axminster, Devon: Triarchy.

30 Stogdill, R.M. (1950) 'Leadership, membership, and organization', *Psychological Bulletin*, 47, 1–14, at p. 3; Bryman, A. (1996) 'Leadership in organizations', in Clegg, S.R., Hardy, C., & Nord, W.R. (eds) *Handbook of organization studies*, London: Sage, pp. 276–292, at p. 276.

31 Smith, G.F. (2003) 'Beyond critical thinking and decision-making: Teaching business students how to think'. *Journal of Management Education*, 27, 1, 24–5.

CHAPTER LEARNING OBJECTIVES

Learning focus
- Applying mapping techniques to appreciate the 'born or made' dilemma

Key issues
- Inherited leadership maps
- Developmental maps

Dilemmas
- Are leaders born or made?
- The fatalistic nature of inherited leadership
- The unpredictability of developmental leadership

Platforms of understanding
- POU 2.1 Bryman's Leadership Eras
- POU 2.2 Day's Personal Development Approaches

Contextual materials
- CM 2.1 History and Destiny
- CM 2.2 The Family Firm
- CM 2.3 Impact Studies (CCL)
- CM 2.4 John Adair and Action Centred Leadership
- CM 2.5 Intentional Change Theory

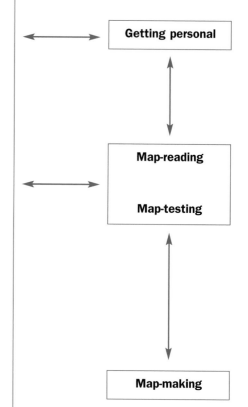

Getting personal

Map-reading

Map-testing

Map-making

2 BORN OR MADE?
DILEMMAS OF DESTINY AND DEVELOPMENT

Plato was one of the first to write about the importance of leaders and leadership [suggesting] that 'some natures which are fitted for the task . . . and others who are not born to be [leaders] and are meant to be followers'.[1]

Executives who believe that leaders are born, give less attention both to their own personal development as well as the development of those they lead. They are focused on selecting leaders with the 'right stuff,' and expect that those leaders' natural abilities will mean organizational success. But nothing could be further from the truth.[2]

It is a fact that some men possess an inbred superiority, which gives them a dominating influence over their contemporaries, and marks them out unmistakeably for leadership . . .[3]

The majority of researchers today believe that the origins of leadership go beyond genes and family to other sources . . . current research suggests that experiences on the job play an important catalytic role in unlocking leader behavior.[4]

ORIENTATION

The leadership dilemmas examined in this chapter are those which arise from the familiar question 'Are leaders born or made?' After studying the chapter you will see how different perspectives on the question offer different answers, drawing on differing beliefs or maps about the nature of leadership. One map draws on assumptions about the characteristics of the natural or predestined leader. The other assumes that leadership skills can be instilled and nurtured, the so-called developmental position. We will see that these ideas relate to the broader issues of nature versus nurture in human behaviours.

Before going further into the chapter, you are invited to make a quick self-assessment of your current beliefs regarding the 'born or made' question by attempting Exercise 2.1, which is suited to personal study or tutorial discussion.

The much-debated question of whether leaders are born or whether they can be developed has become a dilemma because of the existence of two widely shared sets of beliefs. One assumes that effective leaders have fixed traits, the other that leader effectiveness can be developed. The issue is a special case of the wider, unresolved matter of the influence of 'nature' and 'nurture' on human behaviours and life chances.[5]

The first of the two POUs studied in this chapter is already partly familiar, as it was touched upon in Chapter 1. In this chapter, in POU 2.1, Alan Bryman suggests that, regardless of the apparent variety of definitions, there is a widely shared platform of understanding of leadership as some form of *influencing* process. This provides a working definition that is found or implied in many books on leadership.

The earliest human beliefs presumed that leaders were born. In POU 2.1, Bryman concentrates on maps made in more modern times that, for the most part, reveal a common platform of understanding based on the DRM.

Bryman argues that, since the nineteenth century, leadership studies were attempts to improve accepted understanding of leadership as essentially a transactional exchange

Exercise 2.1: The 'Born or Made' Question

1 Based on your experiences and studies of leaders and leadership, do you agree that leaders are generally appointed by virtue of special characteristics of breeding and/or background? Say why you agree or disagree.

2 Do you think that most people could develop enough skills to become an effective leader regardless of breeding or background?

3 Can you see why some people might believe leaders are born, and some people might believe that leaders are more the products of training and development?

between leaders and followers. He proposed the label of 'New Leadership' for the emerging ideas of the 1980s. The most powerful new idea within the New Leadership map was that of a transformational leader capable of initiating and supporting visionary change in organizations and organizational employees. The New Leadership maps recognized the need for maps dealing with processes of leadership development.

Day (POU 2.2) studies the New Leadership map of leadership development. The work was conducted at the start of the twenty-first century, within the period of interest in New Leadership ideas. Widespread enthusiasm in organizations was reported for programmes intended to develop leaders. There was considerable self-reported evidence of acceptance of the programmes. However, Day pointed out an evaluation dilemma. It was not easy to disentangle the contributions of the various change initiatives carried out using performance measures acceptable within a DRM of map-testing.

The 'pre-ordained fate' view of leaders is shown in POU 2.1 to be most closely associated with traditional, trait-dominated views. POU 2.2 outlines work concerning the view that leaders can and perhaps must be developed. Note, however, that even 'pre-ordained' leaders can be prepared for their destined roles through various development processes (see Box 2.1 for two examples).

Box 2.1: How Dynastic Leaders Are Developed

The Indian province of Gujarat was ruled for many years by maharajahs. The rajah reigned from a magnificent palace in the centre of the bustling town of Baroda (Varodora). From birth, the dynastic successor, the eldest son of the maharajah, was prepared to rule. For this to occur, the would-be maharajah was brought up as ruler in the little palace – a sort of maharajah finishing school a few miles from the main palace – where he became accustomed to being the unquestioned leader, to giving unchallenged orders, while being surrounded by servants and wise advisors in a luxurious environment not too dissimilar to what he would find in his future palatial home. The practice reveals how, even in the most traditional of dynasties, succession went hand in hand with 'leadership schooling'.

A young Kenyan manager on an MBA programme reflected on the 'born or made' dilemma. He pointed out that a 'born leader' is sometimes forced to choose from many children, recalling King Mawati of the Southern State of Africa, who had 14 wives, and his father, King Mawati Senior, who had 56 wives, and who both had numerous children. He recalled, from his own family, how his uncle had 13 children, of whom 6 were boys. Most of the children stayed with their father in Nairobi. The three youngest stayed in the rural farm with their grandparents. The youngest of all was given the role of attending to his weakening grandfather. But, as a consequence, he learned all the decision-making and dispute-settling from the old man as elder of the village. This has 'made' the young man develop into a wise leader who is now increasingly consulted by his elder brothers and whose acquired wisdom is needed by them.

The contextual materials (CM 2.1–CM 2.5) provide a range of maps contributing to the debate on natural born leaders and the possibility of leadership development.

PLATFORMS OF UNDERSTANDING

POU 2.1: Bryman's Leadership Eras

Alan Bryman is one of the most cited of leadership researchers. POU 2.1 concentrates on his review chapter written in the 1990s and updated in 2006.[6] Bryman takes a historian's approach, and suggests distinct eras in leadership theory and research. His time span begins when studies had already accepted the DRM of scholarly enquiry.

The Trait Era (1880s–1940s) In trait theories emphasis is placed on the essential characteristics of leaders, which were presumed to originate in what today would be called genetically determined factors. The rise of trait theories followed the first attempts to conduct a scientific survey of genius, many years earlier, by Francis Galton.

The Style Era (1940s–1960s) refocused on what leaders did (rather than on their inherent traits). The most influential organizational studies, such as the Ohio State investigations, set a trend for investigating the reports of followers (a trend followed in the subsequent contingency era). Researchers attempted to reduce styles to a few overarching variables, often producing a two-dimensional model of *people orientation* and *task orientation*. This conceptual parsimony provided elegance, at the expense of excluding other factors that were introduced in the subsequent contingency era.

The Contingency Era (late 1960s–early 1980s) Contingency theories may be seen as more complex style theories, incorporating situational variables. A contingent variable is one whose significance in a theory is contingent on circumstances. A people-oriented leadership style may be more or less effective according to the level of training and education of followers.

The New Leadership Era (1980s–1990s) The distinguishing features of the New Leadership Era are due to beliefs which reject an objective essence of leadership, replacing them with interpretive beliefs. That is to say, leadership is concerned with the perceptions of meanings that are attributed to leaders. This is also referred to as a social constructionist approach.

The Post-Charismatic and Post-Transformational Era (2000s) Ideas which were gaining in influence in maps of leadership at the start of the twenty-first century.

The final era, Post-Charismatic and Post-Transformational leadership, suggests that New Leadership had not proved sufficient to address the various dilemmas of the previous eras. Leadership knowledge has become more accepting of diverse maps, including those of distributed leadership, and a wide range of non-cognitive considerations which depart further from the constraints of the DRM.

In our examination of the emergence of leadership development, the historical eras become the context in which New Leadership ideas emerged. Yet the DRM retained its influence, particularly in the methods used to test the validity of maps.

An important observation was made by Bryman and his co-worker, Parry, in the revised version of the original chapter some years later:

> Like its predecessors, much if not most New Leadership writing is wedded to a rational model of organizational behaviour.[7]

The radical shift was, perhaps, not as radical as was implied in its labelling. Nevertheless it gave momentum to a departure from unreflective acceptance of 'a rational model of organizational behaviour', and the era intruded into many of the newer maps considered in subsequent chapters of *Dilemmas of Leadership*.

POU 2.2: Day's Personal Development Approaches

American business scholar David Day carried out a thorough examination of leadership development from three interrelated perspectives: theory, practice, and research.[8] One of the broad findings of his meta-analysis was that the practice of leadership development offered many recipes for conducting programmes for achieving desired organizational goals. He also identified an unexpected difficulty in demonstrating the relative effectiveness of the development approaches in contributing to the achievement of corporate goals.[9] You can see more about how a meta-analysis is carried out by studying Box 2.2.

Box 2.2: How a Meta-analysis Is Carried Out

A meta-analysis involves a thorough examination (generally requiring statistical manipulations) by which data from different studies of a subject of shared interest are studied. Specifically, such an analysis often seeks to explain why factors appear to be positive in some circumstances, and negative in others. This is often the case with concepts of a high level of generality, particularly when applied in a range of different contexts.

The power of a meta-analysis lies in its potential for revealing major factors and their interrelationships in a topic of interest. A weakness lies in the need to redefine the original data sets in order to produce a common standard for statistical manipulation.

In this chapter we see the results of a meta-study on leadership development by Day (POU 2.2). Other meta-studies, on trust (Chapter 6) and on the differences between genders in studies of leadership styles (Chapter 8), are reported later in the book.

Day gives a clear illustration of one of the ways in which leadership research is particularly complex to study and execute. Leadership development embraces the individual focus, rather than replacing it.[10] He examines six of the most influential techniques for leadership development:

1 *360 Degree Feedback* involves assessment processes within which executives (leaders) give feedback to, and receive feedback from, 'significant others', if possible at higher, lower, and equivalent levels in the organization. The 360 degrees nomenclature implies something that works in all directions. It collects and examines views of 'lower downs' and peers, as well as 'higher ups'. The technique gained widespread corporate attention in the 1990s, when a majority of Fortune 500 companies were reporting as using it or claimed to be planning to use it. Even for this, the least embedded of the approaches (to use Day's terminology), it has proved difficult to provide strong claims for benefits in leadership development. Advocates assert that it offers competitive advantage, while others see yet another management fad. It remains a popular assessment and development methodology.

2 *Coaching* The next two approaches, coaching and mentoring, are two overlapping means of developing leadership competences. Both stretch back to ancient civilizations as educational approaches. Both approaches fit well into the idea of passing on experience through direct encounter between a less (almost always younger) experienced person and a more experienced one.
   Coaching is a term generally associated with the provision of specific sets of behavioural skills (negotiation, communication, and presentation skills would be typical leadership examples). The processes tend to assume that codified knowledge is transferred from coach to learner. The term has a particularly wide set of connotations, from developing skills for sporting leaders to relevant support systems for students of all ages facing examinations and other competitive-entry educational requirements.[11]

3 *Mentoring* is the classical term for the relationship between a personal guide with deep and relevant knowledge and experience and a less experienced recipient (see Box 2.3 for a brief history). Unlike in coaching, the knowledge transfer is less concerned with specific skills and the acquired knowledge is more likely to be diffuse.

4 *Networking* Formal programmes have been implemented to encourage business leaders to develop their personal networks, in the interests of their organizations. Motorola has focused, at the level of vice-presidents, on a programme seeking to identify and capitalize on entrepreneurial activities. The programme also seeks to transfer knowledge about the company's heritage and culture (achievements also associated with mentoring).[12]
   Networking theories are concerned with the development of social relationships through information management. Such processes are increasingly mediated electronically.[13]

5 *Job Assignments* have played a part in management development programmes for many years. The simple assumption (not necessarily therefore wrong!) is that individuals learn by being exposed to varied challenges of relevance to current or future jobs. The argument has been widely applied to justify business exchanges,

---

Box 2.3: Mentoring as an Ancient Form of Leadership Development

In traditional dynastic societies there was recognition that future rulers could be educated into their destined role by wise counsel. Odysseus, before leaving for the Trojan War, placed his trusted friend, Mentor, in charge of his son, Telemachus, and of his palace.[14] Since that time, mentors have been found within social structures which accepted the hereditary right of rulers. Mentors speeded up the emergence of the identified successor.

In more recent times, mentoring has come to mean a process of supporting personal development through the interventions of a person skilled in mentoring. Bozeman and Feeney carried out a rich conceptual review and provided a descriptive definition:

> Mentoring is a process for the informal transmission of knowledge, social capital, and the psychosocial support perceived by the recipient as relevant to work, career, or professional development; mentoring entails informal communication, usually face-to-face and during a sustained period of time, between a person who is perceived to have greater relevant knowledge, wisdom, or experience (the mentor) and a person who is perceived to have less (the protégé).[15]

---

foreign delegations, even overseas school trips. It will be noted that a job assignment programme will inevitably entail change in the networking activities of those involved, so that the evaluation of the one technique against the other is a complex matter.

6   *Action Learning* is a term applied to a wide range of experiential learning processes. The processes tend to involve projects such as the vehicle for learning, often directed to important business problems.

The term is sometimes used interchangeably with the term 'action research', associated initially with Kurt Lewin and the Group Relations school in the United States, and subsequently with the Tavistock Institute in the United Kingdom. Action research introduced a revolutionary thought into the conduct of organizational research – the notion of deliberate involvement (rather than deliberate detachment) of researchers. Discovery processes occur 'from the inside'.

Another application of action learning comes from the work of the British social science innovator Reg Revans. His book *Action Learning* summarizes his influential approach.[16] Revans developed a learning methodology involving managers (leaders) from different industries in applying their collective know-how in turn to problems within an action learning group or set. Leadership is assisted by a facilitator experienced in action learning, although the broad principle is that the group members make decisions as to the content of the meetings.

CONTEXTUAL MATERIALS

CM 2.1: History and Destiny

Shakespeare wrote with brilliant insight into leadership, many centuries ago. Today, his historical dramas are studied in leadership courses. It was Shakespeare who pointed out how some leaders are born great, while others acquire greatness.

His plays had powerful messages about issues that were of utmost importance to his audiences, and the exercise of power was a frequent theme. It was a time when the institution of the monarchy in England was under threat. There was no serious question that there was a right to rule and an obligation for others to obey the ruler. As in other cultures of earlier times, it was just widely accepted, and was a necessary component of a stable social system. That is not to say that conflicts were absent. Shakespeare told vividly of the struggles following claims to rule. They were often to produce great social upheavals and wars. They were disputes that were fought out and justified around questions of birth, and thus around the legitimacy of rulers and would-be rulers.[17] Shakespeare suggests various ways in which a king may be made – he may 'make it', by achieving greatness; he may be 'made King', as the chroniclers put it. In some cases the king may accept the burdens of leadership by having the role 'thrust on him'.

One consequence of a belief in the rightful leader by reason of birth is acceptance that the next leader will come from the same bloodline. Leadership through bloodline is a principle that is likely to produce a stable succession, sometimes labelled a dynasty.

The terms 'dynasty' and 'dynastic' have a Greek root implying power. The head of a dynasty (a dynast) has extensive powers, which are exercised to maintain authority and preserve the dynasty. Historians have regarded dynastic rule as one of the most common features of the earliest human societies (Box 2.4). However, this has not prevented opposition, and revolt against the primacy of an unpopular dynastic ruler.

Succession by virtue of bloodline results in the installation of a dynasty. Weber identified dynastic succession as part of an important social structure found in traditional societies, which he anticipated would be replaced by more rational forms of succession, particularly in economic organizations. Yet, at the start of the twenty-first century, the ancient processes of succession to top leadership positions often reveal versions of appointment in dynastic fashion.

Heads of state continue to have an affinity for the old idea of dynastic succession. The Kennedy 'clan' in the United States was widely regarded as a form of dynasty whose claim to the presidency came almost by birthright. In the 1990s, President Lee Kuan Yew of Singapore was widely believed to be grooming his son for ultimate accession to his rightful position as his heir. It is at least plausible to assume that George W. Bush may have gained some advantage from being the son of a former president. Dynastic succession and birthright still matter in the early twenty-first century, as much in economic institutions as in political leadership around the world.

Box 2.4: The Widespread Occurrence of Dynasties

Weber theorized that dynastic rule was a universal cultural response to the challenges of authority and control. The widespread occurrence of dynastic rule supports his proposition.

Three Sovereigns and Five Emperors [Ancient Chinese] Dynasties (ca. 2850 BC–2205 BC) The stories of the earliest Chinese dynasties have been retold as cultural stories of mythological heroes and rulers.

The Eighteenth [Egyptian] Dynasty (1550 BC–1292 BC) Akhenaten with his wife, Nefertiti, instituted what many identify as the earliest recorded monotheistic state religion. Now famed for the archaeological discoveries, including those from the tomb of Tutankhamun.

Eastern Zhou Dynasty (770 BC–256 BC) A dynastic period in which Emperor Qin Shihuang (also called the First Emperor) was the founder of the first unified empire in the history of China. He established an autocratic state with centralized power over a feudal society and built the line of defence now known as the Great Wall.

The Japanese Dynasty (660 BC–present day) The Emperor (天皇) symbolizes the state and unity of the Japanese people. He is the head of the Japanese imperial family, the oldest continuing hereditary monarchy in the world. He is also the highest authority of the Shinto religion.

The Nanda Dynasty (424 BC–321 BC) The Nandas are sometimes described as the first imperialists (empire builders) in the recorded history of India. According to historical reports, Dhana Nanda was deposed, thus ending the dynasty, because he was hated and despised by his subjects for his venality.

The Duguwa Dynasty (700 BC–1081) is the line of kings (*mai*) of the Kanem empire prior to the rise of the Islamic Seyfawa dynasty in 1081.

The Inca Empire (ca. 1400–1572) was the largest empire in pre-Columbian America. Inca leadership encouraged the worship of Inti, the sun god, and identified the king as 'child of the sun'.

The Māori Kīngitanga dynasty (1858–) In New Zealand, each Māori king is appointed on the day of the previous monarch's funeral by the leaders of the tribes involved in the Kīngitanga movement. However, all Māori monarchs have been direct descendants of Pōtatau Te Wherowhero, the first Māori king.

Struggles for leadership and control were recorded in the oral and written accounts of ancient civilizations. Some have been retained and studied for their relevance to modern-day leaders. In them we find insights into the leadership of sages and spiritual father figures such as Laozi (老子) and military leaders such as Julius Caesar and the Greek military general Xenophon.[18] Since the fifteenth century, *The Prince*, a book written by Niccolò Machiavelli, has been an important and controversial historical document in Western discussions on the ethics of leadership.[19]

CM 2.2: The Family Firm

Dynastic succession is not confined to the political estate. It can be found around the world in organizations, and nowhere more obviously than in the ways of family firms (Box 2.5).

The success of dynasties in Chinese and other Eastern cultures is widely recognized, although made more complicated as founding entrepreneurs became engaged in the construction of the mighty state conglomerates (*zaibatsu* in Japan; *chaebôl* in South Korea). Dynasties such as the Yi family (Samsung) in South Korea, and Mitsui and Sumitomo in Japan would be significant examples.

Rupert Murdoch appeared to have dynastic aspirations in the 1990s, with both son and daughter being encouraged to find high office in his own and other organizations.

Even in the United States, proud of its contributions to defining the democratic 'way of life', family firms continue to have dynastic features.

Box 2.5: Modern Business Dynasties

Weber proposed that the dynasties that were integral to the rule of traditional societies would be less appropriate for modern institutional forms relying on legal-rational principles. The evidence runs contrary to Weber's postulate.

Joe Kennedy created a business dynasty even before his heirs went on to build a political one, which reached its highest influence in the presidency of J.F. Kennedy.

Three generations of Fords have headed the dynasty founded by Henry Ford.

An Wang was creating a dynasty through his electronic calculators and other innovations before control passed from his son as a result of restructuring of the firm.

In popular American culture, the cult TV series *Dynasty* offered a distorted but recognizable view of a world outside the box long before the romanticized view of criminal dynasties fictionalized in sagas such as *The Godfather* and *The Sopranos*.

In the UK, the business empires of William Lever (Unilever), Richard Cadbury (Cadbury Schweppes), Joseph Rowntree and Thomas Cook all flourished down generations of family governance.

Meyer Amschel Rothschild founded a banking dynasty which, likewise, prospered for over two centuries under family control.

An early TV example of the fictional English dynastic family was Galsworthy's *Forsyte Saga*.

Jamsetji Tata founded the Tata dynastic conglomerate, based on his original cotton mills.

Culture theorist Fons Trompenaars suggests that family-style corporate cultures are characterized by a special kind of power, involving obligations on high-status leaders (usually 'father') of businesses towards lower-status 'family' members, and loyalty towards the leader from the employees/followers. The power, as in social family groups, is seen as pervasive, perhaps strict, but essentially benign. He suggests that many examples of family-style cultures can be found in nations that were late to industrialize. He cites Greece, Italy, Japan, Singapore, South Korea, and Spain. Trompenaars also describes the privileges of family over non-family, citing an example of a Brazilian owner arranging for his young and inexperienced nephew to have major responsibility in an international joint venture. The Brazilians saw it as a signal of commitment from the family, while their Dutch partners were puzzled by what must have seemed to be a lightweight choice of leader.[20]

CM 2.3: Impact Studies (CCL)

The Center for Creative Leadership (CCL) is regarded as among the leading and most experienced leadership development organizations in the world. CCL was founded as a non-profit educational institute in 1970. From its original headquarters in Greensboro, North Carolina, it has developed into a global institution with sites in North America, Europe, and Asia. Its commitment over the years to research and training has resulted in a community of researchers that has produced over a hundred books on leadership development. An estimated 400,000 professionals participated in its programmes in its first 30 years of operation. As its name implies, the Center for Creative Leadership has pioneered interest in the link between creativity and leadership. Many leading researchers from around the world have been attracted as visitors and collaborators.[21]

Impact studies

Impact studies of its leadership development programmes have been assessed on:

- increasing self-awareness
- improving leadership capabilities
- increasing ability to learn from experience
- valuing differences
- building and maintaining relationships
- giving and receiving developmental feedback
- setting and achieving goals
- communicating effectively
- developing others
- building effective teams
- developing strategies for life balance.

One empirical study cited as representative of CCL's wider experience lists the learning gains most frequently reported by participants:

- self-awareness (75%)
- understanding and valuing others (24%–19%)
- self-improvement (40%)
- work climate (29%)
- direct deliverables (product and process outcomes, 14%).[22]

CM 2.4: John Adair and Action Centred Leadership

It is hard to overestimate the contributions of John Adair to leadership education in the United Kingdom and beyond. Adair's contributions to leadership courses at the prestigious military college at Sandhurst in the 1960s gave him unrivalled access to the military commanders and heroes of the Second World War. His unusual career (adjutant to a Bedouin regiment in the Arab Legion; deckhand on an Arctic trawler; military historian) gave his writings a combination of insight from wide experience and great scholarship. Numbers of participants in subsequent programmes around the world based on his Action Centred Leadership (ACL) approach have been estimated at approximately one million. To understand the intentions of his approach, we have to examine the deeper ethical and conceptual grounding which he tried to retain within his development programmes.

John Adair's action-centred approach is among the most widely diffused approaches to leadership development. Originally provided for British military officers at Sandhurst, it has subsequently been applied internationally across industry sectors. His writings are grounded in the view that leadership can be developed, a perspective that he believes can be traced back to the time of Socrates. He cites the military general Xenophon, a student of Socrates:

> As Xenophon implied, some degree of leadership potential has to be there in the first place. Many people possess it without being aware of the fact. Given the need or opportunity to lead, some encouragement, and perhaps a leadership course or programme, most people can develop this potential. Those with [more natural potential] can become greater [within their particular circumstances] providing that they are willing to work hard at becoming leaders.[23]

As a historian, Adair regards leadership as drawing on three sources, which have become particularly integrated within the European culture of leadership. A *tribal tradition* treats a leader as 'first among equals', anticipating a more egalitarian and democratic society. An *Eastern tradition* has provided us with the view of the leader as the cultural transmitter of moral values. According to this tradition, the leader has to avoid the (all too human) trait of arrogance. The links with ethical leadership (see Chapter 9) are clear. The approach also reduces the dilemma of the tyrannical leader ('the Hitler problem'). The *Western tradition* derives from the teachings and philosophy stretching back at least two and a half millennia to Socrates and his group in Athens. The key concept is that authority flows from knowledge, the origins of the DRM of human thinking and behaviour. This tradition has become associated with democratic beliefs – that knowledge is not an inherited gift, but rather something that may be cultivated through education. Through this long tradition, the notions of parliamentary democracy and freedom, and the forms of leadership required in their development, were worked out.

At Sandhurst, Adair worked on an approach to military leadership development which he saw as drawing on the motivational theories of Maslow and Hertzberg, and on classical managerial theories, particularly those of Henri Fayol.[24] He describes his work as a functional model. That is to say, he focuses on what can be most closely observed in a system, namely its functional elements of planning, initiating, controlling, and so on. These were retained as he extended his work beyond its original military setting.

Adair represented his leadership model as three overlapping circles. His map of task, team, and individual became synonymous with the principles and teaching of ACL.

Adair considered the three overlapping circles a powerful learning and communications device, although he regretted a tendency for it to lose much of its conceptual grounding when replicated later in leadership books and courses.[25]

ACL shows how different situations require different leadership styles. In the Bryman classification (POU 2.1) it is a contingency theory map.[26] A leader assesses the involvement of the team in any task according to the situation. For immature groups, the leader may have no better option than to 'tell or sell'; for more mature and development groups, the leader is able to involve and delegate. Adair argued that involvement and participation were prerequisites for team motivation.

This presents a possible dilemma of being ineffectively predictable or changing style and risking being seen as unpredictable. Contingency theory and situational leadership reveal this dilemma. Adair notes a group's need for consistency in a leader, while recognizing that situational needs may result in a leader's enacting various decision styles over a short space of time.

CM 2.5: Intentional Change Theory

A group of influential researchers into experiential learning emerged in the 1980s. Within it, an active advocate of the merits of leadership development was Richard Boyatzis. He collaborated with David Kolb, whose experiential learning cycle remains one of the most-cited. Their work connected with David Goleman's exploration of emotional intelligence (EI). Boyatzis and Kolb headed a formal leadership development programme within the Weatherhead School of Management at Case Western Research University.[27]

Competencies are the capabilities of individuals for effective action. According to Boyatzis, there are three clusters of competencies germane to leadership: cognitive abilities, self-management skills, and social skills. Management programmes (and particularly MBA programmes) are mostly concerned with the first cluster, cognitive abilities (use of concepts; quantitative analysis; written communications, and so on). The other two clusters are more closely associated with EI, which has gained considerable research interest (and controversy) following claims in the 1990s that EI is a stronger indicator of leadership effectiveness than are cognitive skills as measured by classical IQ measures.[28]

Boyatzis bases his work on careful measures of the performance of executives undertaking executive education programmes. He offers evidence that performance on the EI factors increases because the programme is geared more towards social skills and self-management.

Intentional Change Theory proposes that leader development programmes support personal change through offering ways in which intentional change strategies are organized. The principles behind this model are shared by the ideas of other personal development practitioners.[29]

The model focuses on perceptions of *actual* and *ideal* self-images as an individual moves towards achieving individual leadership goals. The focus is enhanced through experimentation in a climate of trust that is augmented by coaching (one of the six developmental systems noted above in Day's meta-study).

For Boyatzis, coaching is a means of helping others in their intentional change efforts. Under such conditions, the individual seeks (and is more likely to find) understanding of gaps between the actual and ideal self (image), and also acknowledgement of strengths (when ideal and actual perceptions are similar).

The theory further suggests that positive emotional experiences are more promising for developmental change than are negative ones. Thus, the attention should be more on finding future possibilities and building on strengths, rather than on attempting 'gap-filling' strategies to reduce the effects of perceived individual weaknesses.

As self-directed and intentional change develops, the individual is better able to cope with unexpected changes and shocks. Such experiences become less threatening, less disorienting, and less likely to be assessed as potentially catastrophic. Positive psychology has become a focus for debate, and has attracted both supporters and detractors.[30] The concepts and applications have widespread application within personal development programmes.

INTEGRATION

The eras of leadership map reveals changing maps of leadership. For the longest period of time, leaders were assumed to be born. The assumption is central to traditional, bloodline succession, such as in tribal and monarchical systems.

The trait era holds to two assumptions: first, that the 'best leader' is dictated by bloodline, so there are no questions of identifying and selecting from a wide range of pretenders. The second assumption is that the young leader benefits from development. These assumptions carried over from succession in traditional cultures to the governance of family firms, where it is still often taken for granted that there is a succession 'right' for the eldest son to leadership of the firm.

For Bryman, the various eras up to the 1980s were variations on one map, albeit one which could be divided into trait, style, and contingency/situational eras. The New Leadership map differs in radical ways. It opened the way to maps which departed further from explanations of leadership based on the DRM. These maps come into focus in the chapters that follow.

Day explores the map of leadership development in order to determine under what circumstances leadership development is most effective. His observation of the dilemma of embedded actions is particularly important.

To study and gain convincing information about programmes' influence on leadership, you need simple programmes, with one or two defining operational characteristics. The 360 Degree programmes would be a good example. According to Day, development programmes are often relatively simple and disconnected from other factors required for change to take place. Conversely, researchers deploying complex designs such as Action Learning will find evidence of change, but will have far more difficulty in showing a direct causal link between the programme and the changes or outputs from the programme. The embeddedness of programmes presents leaders with a dilemma in attempting to isolate the impact of a programme of developmental learning.

Overall, the materials reveal the influence of the DRM. Era followed era, but changes considered as improvements to older ideas made little impact. In the 1980s the introduction of more transformational ideas was hailed as revolutionary, but even its advocates later conceded that the DRM retained a considerable hold. By the twenty-first century, a range of 'post-charismatic' ideas were beginning to challenge that dominance.

GETTING PERSONAL

Do I have the 'Right Stuff' of Leadership?

Few people have unswerving belief in their own leadership potential, so such doubts need not disqualify you as a 'wannabe' leader. Perhaps you may now be reflecting on the question, taking the above information into account. How have your views been influenced? Have you been sustained by an encouraging mentor, or a family member? Or have you been more influenced in environments closer to the one that Alan experienced (Box 2.6)?

Many leaders spent their early days with their leadership potential unnoticed. One of many examples is the young Thomas Edison, a giant of technological discovery, and ultimately the founder of a great industry (electric power) and a mighty organization. We have seen

---

Box 2.6: 'I Know I'm not a Born Leader'

Alan had left his employment as a professional in a financial institution and was studying for his Masters in Business Studies when he related the following self-history:

> I just wanted out of banking. I hoped maybe I could learn more about being a leader, although I know for sure I'm not a natural leader.

How had he arrived at that conclusion? Mainly from his work experiences, he replied. In groups at work, he had felt most comfortable as a loyal follower, finding a niche through supporting the ideas and proposals of more dominant group members. He recalled what happened at his leaving party. His boss read out the conclusions of some personal inventory through which Alan had been assessed.

'He probably meant it as a joke', Alan reflected. 'It more or less said I was not cut out for being a leader. I have had other psychological tests, and they all seem to be saying pretty much the same thing. My preferred style at work is to be a team player. I suppose my boss was telling me that I shouldn't bother going to business school. I don't have what it takes to become a leader.'

Alan went on to describe how the decision to go back to 'school' had turned out to be a good one for him. He found that he was accepted by his new colleagues from various parts of the world, who sought him out as a team colleague. Although some were more obvious leaders than he was, in their various group activities he developed a newly found confidence that at times he could take the lead.

Alan says that he knows 'for sure' that he is not a natural leader. But his action in studying leadership within a formal course of business studies suggests that he believes (or maybe wants to believe) that he can become some kind of leader. Furthermore, other course members respected him as demonstrating leadership qualities in tasks that he had carried out during the course.

---

that leadership is, in any case, no longer assumed to be a special set of attributes that you are born with. With the more systematic examination of leader characteristics (fixed traits), the bloodline assumption became increasingly open to question, particularly in firms, where the assumption was not backed up by recourse to a divine right to rule. In the absence of identifiable sets of traits, the leadership dilemma of selection or development emerged.

For those in search of intentional personal change, it now becomes more appropriate to ask the developmental questions suggested by Boyatzis. One of the Intentional Change Theory elements outlined in CM 2.5 is the benefits accruing from a positive orientation to work and life. Can you think of strengths that will help you to achieve your leadership goals?

Box 2.7: Positivity and Pollyanna: A Leadership Challenge

There are various arguments in favour of a leader's optimistic orientation. We have touched on one theoretical justification in the Intentional Change Theory of Richard Boyatzis. Another, related view can be found in many writings on stimulating creativity in individuals and teams.[31] Yet another justification has been made, that positivity arouses positive emotions and supports willingness to accept change.

If we test this map we may recall that we encountered executives who are too positive. They appear to display naive, impulsive, and unconditional positivity towards all ideas and suggestions. This is sometimes referred to as a Pollyanna outlook.[32] This raises the question: 'Does positivity in a leader risk blindness to real dangers and difficulties?'

This is a reasonable opposing view. It might be countered with the question: 'Might the risks of taking a positive perspective outweigh the dangers of becoming less sensitive to opportunities for effective change and decision-making?'

Look back at people who had a deep and long-term constructive influence on you. These are ways in which role-modelling works, so that you draw from what you have heard, and are thus able to retain enthusiasm and motivation in times of leadership crisis. The leadership challenge of Box 2.7 may help in an examination of these questions.

SUMMARY

This chapter has confined itself to two main maps of leadership. Over the major portion of the period under discussion, researchers attempted to identify the fundamental elements of leadership as relatively stable behavioural traits. It took approximately a century for acceptance that this approach was not successful in revealing the universal traits of successful leaders. When that acceptance came in the 1960s, either the DRM model could have been abandoned, or the search for universal traits could have been discarded. It was the latter that happened, assisted by acceptance of the influence of Bass and his co-workers and their advocacy of the reorientation of efforts towards leadership styles rather than traits.

As Bryman indicated, this move left the DRM still influential in a methodology which mirrors that of the natural sciences and was now being directed towards behavioural styles. The shift was from what leaders are to what leaders do. It might have opened the door to work on how to develop leaders. While there were some moves in that direction, the DRM influence meant that most researchers were still following established paths. In the 1980s, that rupture was hailed as coming from a New Leadership map. The forces that assisted this change came from growing recognition of a kind of leader who demonstrates skills of a transformational kind. This aligned well with enthusiasm in organizations for a leadership that supported creativity, innovation, and change. Somewhat ironically, the shift was partly a retreat to older concepts that were current long before the rational mode. This applied to the New Leadership interest in aspects of charismatic influence. It also advocates accepting the premise of leadership development that leaders can be 'made' through appropriate interventions of an educational kind.

Some leadership researchers have pointed out this tendency for swings back to older leadership ideas as part of a move away from more modern ones. The reinvigoration of a modified trait theory (Box 2.8) is one example of this 'retreat into newness'.

We also have plenty of evidence of the continued existence of leaders by dynastic bloodline in modern organizations (see Box 2.5), which is somewhat contrary to the widely accepted maps of organization theory.

We have started a journey that takes us closer to the dilemma of whether leaders are born or made. It is a journey that reveals no clear-cut answer. However, it has indicated how a dominant set of beliefs (the DRM) has encouraged researchers to look for other explanations for leadership behaviour. On the other hand, the journey shows how the search has remained rather closely anchored in the methods of knowledge exploration of the DRM, and to some degree in its core beliefs in rational human actions in professional life.

Future chapters will introduce maps that offer various challenges to the rational model. Methodologies such as critical theory and sense-making break with the methodology of the DRM. Beyond New Leadership, as Parry and Bryant noted, we will find maps of Post-Charismatic and Post-Transformational leadership forms.

Box 2.8: How Trait Theories Were Reappraised after the Rise of New Leadership Maps

Traits are considered by psychologists as fixed, psychometrically measurable characteristics that differentiate leaders from non-leaders. By the 1990s, Stogdill's colleague Bass was wondering whether the accumulated evidence had sounded the death knell for trait theories.[33]

But even as the New Leadership maps were emerging, fresh empirical evidence revealed that leaders could be differentiated from non-leaders by trait-like factors.[34] These factors included intelligence, adjustment, extraversion, conscientiousness,[35] openness to experience,[36] and general self-efficacy (self-belief in capabilities).[37]

The evidence was complicated by claims for other leadership characteristics which became referred to as traits or trait-like.[38] The search for universalistic traits defining leadership has disappeared. Interest in exploring the contribution of traits in a more modest role remains.

Exercise 2.2: A Map-Testing Challenge Applied to Trait Research

Traits are relatively stable personality characteristics. They have increasingly become regarded as having a strong genetic component. It follows that traits are not characteristics that can be changed. Kouzes and Posner[39] reported research which identified five leadership traits, as follows:

■ honest   ■ forward-looking   ■ competent   ■ inspiring   ■ intelligent.

Exercise 2.2 Discussion Questions

1 Do you believe that each of these characteristics is a 'strongly genetically determined' trait?
2 Do you believe that any or all of these characteristics could be determined to some degree by the impression a leader makes on others?
3 Do you believe that any or all of these characteristics might be (or be perceived as) different in different situations?
4 How has thinking about these questions contributed to your own map of trait theories of leadership?

NOTES

1 Antonakis, J. (2011) 'Predictors of leadership: The usual suspects and the suspect traits', in Bryman, A., Collinson, D., Grint, K., Jackson, B., & Uhl-Bien, M. (eds) *The Sage handbook of leadership*, London: Sage, pp. 269–285, at p. 269.
2 Riggio, R.E. (2010) 'Are leaders born or made? Why the question itself is dangerous', www.psychologytoday.com/blog/cutting-edge-leadership/201012/are-leaders-born-or-made-why-the-question-itself-is-dangerous, downloaded 7 May 2011.
3 Dr Hensley, Bishop of Durham, quoted in Adair, J. (1989) *Great leaders*, Guildford, UK: Talbot Adair, p. 13.
4 Maltby, D.E. 'Leaders: born or made? The state of leadership theory and training today', www.biola.edu/academics/professional-studies/leadership/resources/leadership/bornormade/, downloaded 6 April 2011.
5 Ridley, M. (2003) *Nature via nurture: Genes, experience, and what makes us human*, New York: Harper Collins; Ceci, S.J., & Williams, W.M. (eds) (1999) *The nature–nurture debate: the essential readings*, Oxford: Blackwell.
6 Bryman, A. (1996) 'Leadership in organizations', in Clegg, S.R., Hardy, C., & Nord, W.R. (eds) *Handbook of organization studies*, London: Sage, pp. 276–292; Parry, K.W., & Bryman, A. (2006) 'Leadership in organizations', in Clegg, S.R., Hardy, C., Lawrence, T.B., & Nord, W.R. (eds) *Handbook of organizational studies*, 2nd edn, London: Sage, pp. 447–468.
7 Parry, K.W., & Bryman, A. (2006:453) 'Leadership in organizations', in Clegg, S.R., Hardy, C., Lawrence, T.B., & Nord, W.R. (eds) *Handbook of organization studies*, 2nd edn, London: Sage.

8 Day, D.V. (2001) 'Leadership development: A review in context', *Leadership Quarterly*, 11, 4, 581–613.

9 Day's meta-analysis of leadership development in the 1980s discussed the problem identified earlier by Fiedler as the difficulty in assessing effectiveness of leadership programmes. Fiedler attempted to resolve the problem by proposing an intermediate range of situations outside of which leadership would be unlikely to make a difference.

10 He also differentiates between leader development and leadership development. The former focuses on the individual leader, and historically was the more important of the two treatments ('This is what leaders are and do; this is what you need to do to be more like them'). The latter explores the wider picture of the overall dynamics of organizations within which leaders and others engage in their work.

11 Polanyi, M. (1967) *The tacit dimension*, New York: Anchor. More recent models of knowledge management have continued to see the conversion of tacit knowledge into explicit knowledge which can be codified and contribute to personal development. See Nonaka, I., & Takeuchi, H. (1995) *The knowledge creating company: How Japanese companies create the dynamics of innovation*, Oxford: OUP.

12 Day, D.V. (2001) 'Leadership development: A review in context', *Leadership Quarterly*, 11, 4, 581–613, p. 596. See also Kilduff, M., & Balkundi, P. (2011) 'A network approach to leader cognition and effectiveness', in Bryman, A., Collinson, D., Grint, K., Jackson, B., & Uhl-Bien, M. (2011) *The Sage handbook of leadership*, London: Sage, pp. 118–135.

13 Von Krogh, G., Roos, J., & Kleine, D. (eds) (1998) *Knowing in firms: Understanding, managing and measuring knowledge*, London: Sage.

14 See Roberts, A. (1999) 'The origins of the term mentor', *History of Education Society Bulletin*, 64, 313–329.

15 Bozeman, B., & Feeney, M.K. (2007) 'Toward a useful theory of mentoring: A conceptual analysis and critique', *Administration and Society*, 39, 6, 719–739. See also Kram, K.E. (1983) 'Phases of the mentor relationship', *Academy of Management Journal*, 26, 4, 608–625; Kram, K.E. (1985) *Mentoring at work: Developmental relationships in organizational life*, Glenview, IL: Scott Foresman.

16 Revons, R. (1980) *Action learning*, London: Blond & Briggs.

17 A challenger to the leadership of the state is known as a pretender. The wedding-night activities of a king and his queen were attended by observers, to minimise the risks of any false heir being declared in the future.

18 Adair, J. (1989) *Great leaders*, Guildford, UK: Talbot Adair, p. 13.

19 For an accessible account of the importance of Machiavelli's work today see Sucher, S.J. (2008) *The moral leader: Challenges, insights and tools*, Oxford: Routledge.

20 Trompenaars, F. (1993) *Riding the waves of culture: Understanding cultural diversity in business*, London: Economist Books, pp. 141–145.

21 McCauley, C., Moxley, D.M., & VanVelsor, E. (eds) (2003) *The CCL handbook of leadership development*, San Francisco: Jossey-Bass.

22 Proportions increased to 53 per cent, 58 per cent, and 45 per cent respectively after four months.

23 Adair, J. (1989) *Great leaders*, Guildford, UK: Talbot Adair, p. 37.

24 Adair, J. (1979) *Action centred leadership*, Epping, Essex: Gower.

25 Adair, J. (1990) *Understanding motivation*, Guildford, UK: Talbot Adair.

26 Adair acknowledged a situational component in his work, drawing on Tannenbaum, R., & Schmidt, W.H. (1973) 'How to choose a leadership pattern', *Harvard Business Review*, 51, May–June, 162–175, 178–180 (reprinted from *Harvard Business Review*, 36 (1958), 95–101).

27 Boyatzis, R.E. (1982) *The competent manager: A model for effective performance*, New York: Wiley; Boyatzis, R.E., Stubbs, E., & Taylor, S.N. (2002) 'Learning cognitive and emotional intelligence competences through graduate management education', *Academy of Management Learning and Education*, 1, 2, 150–162.

28 Goleman, D. (1995) *Emotional intelligence*, New York: Free Press.

29 Pedler, M., Burgoyne, J., & Boydell, T. (2001) *A manager's guide to self-development*, 4th edn, London: McGraw Hill.

30 Seligman, M.E.P., & Csikszentmihalyi, M. (2000) 'Positive psychology: An introduction', *American Psychologist*, 55, 1, 5–14. Martin Seligman has become acknowledged as the pioneering influence in the Positive Psychology movement. See www.huffingtonpost.com/amy-tardio/is-the-world-ready-for-a_b_233741.html. Tardio, A. (2009) 'Is the world ready for a positive psychology?', *Huffington Post*, 19 July.

31 Parnes, S.J. (ed.) (1992) *Sourcebook for creative problem-solving*, Buffalo, NY: Creative Education Foundation.

32 Pollyanna was a little girl, noted for her optimistic nature, in a novel by Eleanor Porter (1868–1920).

33 See Bryman, A., Collinson, D., Grint, K., Jackson, B., & Uhl-Bien, M. (2011) *The Sage handbook of leadership*, London: Sage, p. 277.

34 Kenny, D.A., & Zaccaro, S.J. (1983) 'An estimate of variance due to traits in leadership', *Journal of Applied Psychology*, 68, 678–685.

35 Arvey, R.D., Rotundo, M., Johnson, W., Zhang, Z., & McGue, M. (2006) 'The determinants of leadership role occupancy: Genetic and personality factors', *Leadership Quarterly*, 17, 1–20; Judge, T.A., Bono, J.E., Ilies, R., & Gerhardt, M.W. (2002) 'Personality and leadership: A qualitative and quantitative review', *Journal of Applied Psychology*, 87, 765–780; Tagger, S., Hackett, R., Saha, S. (1999) 'Leadership emergence in autonomous work teams: Antecedents and outcomes', *Personnel Psychology*, 52, 899–926.

36 Judge, T.A., Bono, J.E., Ilies, R., & Gerhardt, M.W. (2002) 'Personality and leadership: A qualitative and quantitative review', *Journal of Applied Psychology*, 87, 765–780.

37 Smith, J.A., & Foti, R.J. (1998), 'A pattern approach to the study of leader emergence', *Leadership Quarterly*, 9, 147–160; Foti, R.J., & Hauenstein, N. (2007) 'Pattern and variable approaches in leadership emergence and effectiveness', *Journal of Applied Psychology*, 92, 347–355.

38 Zaccaro, S.J. (2007) 'Trait-based perspectives of leadership', *American Psychologist*, 62, 6–16.

39 Kouzes, J.M., & Posner, B.Z. (1974) *The leadership challenge*, San Francisco, CA: Jossey-Bass; Kouzes, J.M., & Posner, B.Z. (1995) *The leadership challenge: How to keep getting extraordinary things done in organizations*, San Francisco, CA: Jossey-Bass.

CHAPTER LEARNING OBJECTIVES

Learning focus
- The functional nature of project management and how project leadership meets the challenges of a functional approach

Key issues
- Team work and team leadership
- Distributed leadership
- Team development processes

Dilemmas
- The limitations of a functional approach to team work
- Coordination and control dilemmas of project work

Platforms of understanding
- POU 3.1 Action Teams: A Meta-analysis
- POU 3.2 Innovation Teams

Contextual materials
- CM 3.1 Self-Managing Work Teams
- CM 3.2 Tuckman's Stage Model of Team Development
- CM 3.3 Sporting Teams and Their Development
- CM 3.4 Team Pathologies

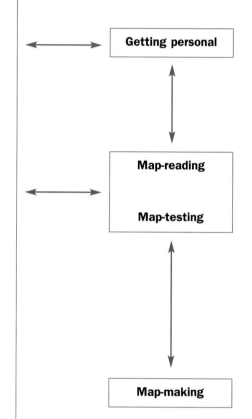

Getting personal

Map-reading

Map-testing

Map-making

3 PROJECT TEAMS AND THE DILEMMAS OF FUNCTIONAL LEADERSHIP

A project is a non-routine set of activities carried out to achieve a specified outcome such as a new product, service, or resolution of a problem.[1]

There are many definitions of what constitutes a project.[2]

In January 2010, Toyota shares plummeted, as the company prepared to recall eight million vehicles globally . . . Toyota's UK spokesman denied that the firm had delayed recalls, stating it was a quality rather than a safety issue.[3]

Shudder if you enter a ward advertising 'team nursing'. In my experience this is a euphemism for no-one in charge and everyone doing their own thing as and when they choose to do so.[4]

ORIENTATION

This chapter deals with work activities organized into projects. Although the importance of *project leaders* and *project leadership* have become recognized, the majority of textbooks and articles on the subject prefer to use the terms *project managers* and *project management*. Before reading any further, you are invited to consider your current understanding of project management and project leadership by studying Exercise 3.1

As can be seen in the definitions above, projects have been described as largely rationally planned activities. Project management training concentrates on acquiring the skills of applying project procedures as established by professional institutions.

The procedures provide the structures believed to be necessary for the coordination and control of project activities and for effective team functioning. However, dilemmas arise because the coordination and control mechanisms imposed on individuals are contrary to conditions favouring individual motivation and initiative-taking.[5]

In this chapter we will examine maps of business processes that give less priority to leadership than to the structures and processes that permit the effective functioning of organizational activities. The approach is known as functionalism. In project management, the functional orientation results in dilemmas for leaders, which are exacerbated when the unexpected and the unplanned occur.[6] Risk-management processes in project-based operations can, in hindsight, be seen to have collapsed.[7]

Exercise 3.1: Project Management and Project Leadership

Project management has become a widely accepted professional discipline. The processes of project management are taught on courses and captured in standard (and comprehensive) 'how to do it' manuals. Project managers are in demand in a wide range of industrial and commercial sectors, as is evidenced in the job vacancy pages of professional periodicals. There may be mention that project managers need to show leadership skills, but this is a benefit rather than a primary consideration.

Exercise 3.1 Discussion Questions

1 What can be concluded from the description of projects as being 'managed' rather than led?
2 If teams are the most common form of project structure, why are the manuals not described as 'project leadership' documents?

[Exercise for individual reflection or classroom or tutorial discussion.]

In this chapter we will use the term 'project team' to cover action teams, innovation teams, and self-managing work groups.

Project management has become an essential component of management education courses. The subject is widely taught as a component of technological and operational programmes.

Project management remains strongly influenced by the DRM as a means of understanding and influencing purposive human actions. Its features reveal the influences of Max Weber, for his analysis of organizational structures, and of F.W. Taylor, for pioneering ideas of scientific management.[8] Taylor's ideas also provided an explanation of the effectiveness of mass-production systems, typified by those introduced into automobile manufacture by Henry Ford. So much so, that the term 'Fordism' is still used interchangeably with 'Taylorism'.[9] Both sets of ideas were compatible with those of Adam Smith from a century earlier, and in particular with the concept of the efficient division of labour.[10]

Each project is characterized by 'unique one-time efforts with a distinct beginning and an end'.[11] In the 1970s, the established orthodoxy of management theories was being challenged. Its critics were dissatisfied with the theorizing of an organization as a 'top-down pyramid' of activities to be carried out by individuals acting as rational agents. Alternatives to Taylorism and Weberian structures were proposed.[12] These are introduced in subsequent chapters as critical theory[13] and 'post-structuralism'.[14]

Project management orthodoxy thoroughly based on the DRM still fits the belief systems of technical professionals engaged in projects. There are sectors, such as construction and consultancy, in which the entire organization is dominated by project activities.[15]

The project team has become the structure most closely associated with work in which the task requires some innovative outcome.[16] It has also become the cornerstone for implementing the processes involved in the worldwide quality movement.[17] Consistent with the principles of scientific management, the emphasis has been more on processes involving the structuring and activities of the project than on its leadership. These issues are explored in the platforms of understanding (POU 3.1–3.2) and the contextual materials (CM 3.1–3.4).

PLATFORMS OF UNDERSTANDING

POU 3.1 reveals how project teams (described as action teams) have achieved results within an approach focused on observable functions or activities (functionalism). The complexities of team projects result in the allocation of differing roles and responsibilities within the team. This gives rise to a dilemma of coordination and control for the team leader.

POU 3.2 focuses on innovation projects. Again, the functionalist approach is considered to produce similar dilemmas, with additional issues requiring coordination (boundary-spanning) leadership work.

POU 3.1: Action Teams: A Meta-analysis

Stephen Zaccaro and Andrea Rittman of George Mason University, and co-worker Michelle Marks of Florida International University, conducted a survey of team leadership.[18] They imply its defining characteristics to be the observable and plannable activities of teams in action, referring to this as a functionalist or action approach.

They offer a definition of an action team which reveals its functionalist nature:

> a distinguishable set of two or more people who interact, dynamically, interdependently, and adaptively toward a common and valued goal/objective/mission who have been assigned specific roles or functions to perform and who have a limited lifespan of membership.[19]

The researchers identify 'action teams' as a covering term for functional teams, including performing and production teams. They see this as a sub-set of all possible teams, citing also project teams, service teams, and parallel teams. Thus, their work spans from the complexities of leading a team with members working around the world (Boeing and Airbus projects) to the challenges of a local community trying to fund-raise for facilities for a local community centre, to the team assembled to create an advertising campaign.

Zaccaro and colleagues regard the activities of an action team as being directed towards a process of *social problem-solving*. This distinction acknowledges that the processes are essentially social. As implied in the definition, the model places emphasis on the *interdependencies* of individuals. The researchers suggest that in a great deal of the extensive literature on teams the emphasis has been on the *differentiation* of roles, rather than on the way in which the activities (functions) of differing roles require *integration* or *coordination*.

A three-stage sequence of activities in social problem-solving is presented as:

1 Solution finding (generation)
2 Solution selection
3 Solution implementation.

Four main dimensions, each with two components, are associated with the stages: two are informational dimensions, and two are resource dimensions:

Informational dimensions

- Search for information
- Structuring of information.

Resource dimensions

- Personnel
- Material resources.

Individuals will have different functional responsibilities within the allocated team roles. This results in dilemmas of coordinating the roles while retaining control over the effective functioning of the team.

Associated with the division of roles is the leadership issue of coordination within a team across role boundaries. (The boundary-spanning coordination between a team and its organizational and market environments is considered in POU 3.2.[20])

Three management features are identified as relevant to internal leadership coordination processes:

- Shared mental models
- Collective information processing
- Team metacognition.

The development of shared mental models may be seen as efforts directed towards a more coherent set of beliefs, such as a POU around a common task. Collective information-processing often occurs with well-codified activity structures such as brainstorming, stage-gate sequencing, and decision matrices.

Metacognition is a term generally referring to 'knowing about knowing' processes, such as personal or group discovery processes. Structures and actions associated with such discovery learning, creativity, self-insight, and development all help in enhancing a team's metacognitive processes, learned skills, and performance outcomes.[21]

The development of the metacognitive skills helps leaders to promote learning and deal with behavioural issues within action teams (see Box 3.1 for an example).

However, for many project team leaders in industrial organizations, the functional approach is conducted within a culture of acceptance of actions consistent with a rational model of behaviour. From such a perspective, emotional reactions are regarded as irrational disturbances to effective group work, and unhelpful for team effectiveness.

Box 3.1: How Team Leaders Promote Learning in Interdisciplinary Action Teams

To explore what leaders of action teams do to promote speaking up and other proactive coordination behaviours, I analysed data from 16 operating room teams learning to use a new technology for cardiac surgery. Team leader coaching, ease of speaking up, and boundary spanning were associated with successful technology implementation. The most effective leaders helped teams learn by communicating a motivating rationale for change and by minimizing concerns about power and status differences to promote speaking up in the service of learning.[22]

POU 3.2: Innovation Teams

Innovation is widely referenced as occurring in project teams.[23] Professor Jürgen Hauschildt was a pioneering influence in innovation studies in Europe. With colleagues Karl Brockhoff and Anil Chakrabarti, he reviewed work in the field.[24]

Hauschildt traced the influence of the economist Josef Schumpeter, who had proposed the innovation leader as a style re-emerging within the emerging industrial organizations, and particularly within technological departments of the modern era.

In the 1960s, Donald Schon had introduced the term 'product champion' for this type of leader.[25] NASA further popularized the term in the 1970s, identifying it as a key success indicator in innovation projects. Across a wide range of projects, the overwhelming proportion of successful ones had product champions, while the converse was true for unsuccessful projects.[26]

In Germany, the concepts of entrepreneurial leader and project champion were subsequently reinterpreted as three leadership roles, providing different contributions to the group's innovative performance:

■ The *power promoter* (Machtpromotor) contributes resources and hierarchical potential, and is generally in a high-status position within the organization.
■ The *technology promoter* (Fachpromotor) contributes specific technical knowledge to the innovation process, and influences through know-how, rather than high status.
■ The *process promoter* catalyses or supports the processes of change, and may be seen as a form of team facilitator whose role is to enable, rather than to direct change.

Hauschildt considers the process promoter as the more behavioural role, helping to overcome the dilemmas of leadership in innovation teams. He considers also the importance of leadership and the boundary-spanning role.[27] However, he notes that the model remains a rational approach to leadership. When emotional issues arise, the prescriptions for their resolution tend to be cognitive and rational. The structures within innovation teams place emphasis on formal organizational tools such as matrix management, Gantt charts, and stage-gate procedures. In contrast, behavioural issues have tended to be down-played. Hence the significance of the process promoter as a leadership role.

CONTEXTUAL MATERIAL

CM 3.1: Self-Managing Work Teams

Manz and Sims contributed to the popularization of the concept of self-managed work teams.[28] Their work contains the powerful idea that many of the responsibilities assumed by traditional leaders have become shared, empowering the wider team. The Superleader (the title of one of their books) is effectively the *collective* leadership contributions of an entire team. Leadership may be thought of as *distributed* among the team members. The leader is not so much a hero as a maker of heroes. For this reason it is unfortunate that the term 'Superleader' has echoes of a far older concept of the Great Man theory of leadership.[29]

Manz and Sims contrast their Superleader to three earlier leadership types:

- The strong man
- The transactor
- The visionary leader.

The strong man style is portrayed as the bullying and uncaring leader. They suggest that the style is commoner than is generally admitted, even in successful and highly regarded organizations. They cite a president of the Kellogg organization who had been ousted for reasons to do with his ultra-abrasive style. They list other examples, such as PepsiCo's culture, which *Fortune* described as being like a boot camp, rewarding the survivors and making it easy for those not comfortable with the arrangements to drop out. Those who are comfortable and effective in this culture receive the spoils. Those who are not comfortable tend to leave early in their career.

Transactors are similar to the task-oriented leaders modelled in Chapter 2. Their influence style is based on the exercise of direct transactional rewards and punishments to subordinates. The style is particularly inappropriate for situations calling for radical or transformational change.

Visionary leaders, while recognized as often engaged in radical change processes, are described as being vulnerable to ignoring succession dilemmas, and failing to develop others. As a consequence, visionary leaders may succeed only in developing dependency. You will find overlap of this basic concept with the maps of charismatic leadership processes in Chapter 4.

All three forms of leadership are considered to have weaknesses that can be overcome through a more distributed leadership way of operating, leading to a 'superteam' (rather than a team with one Superleader, as found in the traditional maps).[30]

The work of Manz and Sims challenged American work practices in the 1980s, which were criticized for poor quality of production, absenteeism, high labour turnover, and disruptive behaviours. They argued that such weaknesses were associated with the prevailing leadership styles that they had identified. The premise is that such styles alienate the workforce through failing to provide a genuine sense of involvement in, and commitment to, corporate goals. The basic challenge is seen as being to find ways of 'power sharing' in the interests of productivity gains. The proposed approach is through participation and involvement.

Examples were emerging around the world of self-managed work teams. In Europe and America the initiators of the projects were sometimes outside the top-echelon team at corporate headquarters. In the USA, managers, often at plant level, had been conducting unofficial practices which, they believed from experience, could achieve substantial improvements by introducing more participative structures. These procedural innovations tended to be in plants physically remote from the scrutiny of a head office.

Manz and Sims reported in detail an illustration of such an approach. The team system was found in a small-parts manufacturing plant. The site had been set up some years earlier as an experiment in innovative work practices, and was located in the southern United States. At the time of the research, the evidence collected suggested that the plant was running at a 20 per cent gain in productivity over what might be expected from traditional work design systems. The local workforce was non-unionized and approximately 320 employees worked at the plant. The ultimate owner was described as a large corporation.

The degree of autonomy of the teams in this particular example was actually found at a rather modest level. The increased ownership of the self-managed teams over their roles was confined to discretion over in-group methods of work. It did not provide for discretion over work targets as such. It included the right to allocate differential payment levels to group members, yet not discretion over the overall size of the group-salary budget. The more strategic levels of decision-making remained the province of others at a different (higher) level in the organization, which still had distinct layers of management, if not a traditional pyramid of control.

The upper level was the classical executive level, dealing with the overall planning and client-interface responsibilities. The middle layer included the people who were regarded as the external coordinators of the self-managed teams. It is at this level that we find the innovation in project leadership. The role of *team coordinator* had emerged as the plant developed its self-managing team approach. It was a role that had considerable ambiguities – for example, was it a leadership role? If so, it had different kinds of leadership responsibilities from any experienced before. Manz and Sims took the coordinator to be a new form of external leader, and examined the characteristics and context of the role.

Teams were trained in ways that enhanced their skills, for example in problem-solving, and in communicating in supportive as well as task-specific areas of their work. The teams would sometimes invite their coordinators to join them for specific problem-solving meetings, while retaining the team culture, which sought to avoid deference towards status or expertise. The coordinators were themselves trained in a facilitative rather than a directive style. This style avoids reinforcing the dilemma of leadership dependency. The researchers concluded that the leadership functions of the coordinator and team-selected internal leader were significantly different from leader roles to be found according to prevailing 'top-down' leadership theory.

In subsequent work, Manz and Sims collected and described numerous examples of such leadership roles and practices, both from their own experience and from other sources. They suggest that the original idea has become aligned with a wider range of innovative approaches concerned with achieving high performance through high-commitment teams. The concept of self-managed teams remains a promising means of dealing with the dilemmas of coordination of interests and of dependency. It is finding particular application in not-for-profit operations.

CM 3.2: Tuckman's Stage Model of Team Development

Much of the work on project teams and team leadership makes the assumption that the team, once assembled, is immediately able to execute its required team goal or objective. This is another assumption within a DRM mind-set. However, projects are often assembled from individuals who have not worked closely together in the past. Leaders face a dilemma of dealing with development needs that have not been adequately accommodated in the project mission and plans.

One approach to team development has become widely accepted as a template for understanding the process. In the 1960s an American educationalist, Bruce Tuckman, proposed a synthesis of existing research of groups and group development. He suggested that teams pass through the stages of:

1 Forming
2 Storming
3 Norming, and
4 Performing.[31]

With the subsequent addition of a closure stage,[32] the Tuckman model became a widely accepted map of team-development processes. It has the considerable merit of making sense to people, who are able to recognize and discriminate each stage from personal experience.

In practice, attempts to research the stages thoroughly suggest a more complex story.[33] Questions were raised relating to the storming and outperforming processes, such as:

'What happens when a team fails to pass the storm stage?'

'What happens when a team outperforms expectations?'

One suggestion is that the model conceals two different kinds of barrier.[34] Some teams, even with adequate resources for the task, seem to spend far too long in a storming mode. Furthermore, a minority of teams exceed expectations. These two refinements to Tuckman's map have been linked to the possibility that a facilitative or creative leadership style may be particularly suited to achieving progress. A facilitative style encourages openness among team members, thus reducing the barrier often found at the storming stage. The style is also effective in encouraging teams to challenge their own mental maps and thus discover unexpected and innovative possibilities for change.[35]

CM 3.3: Sporting Teams and Their Development

The effectiveness of sports teams has been a matter of direct interest for sporting managers, specifically, the special roles of front-line manager or performance coach and on-field captain. Both kinds of team leader have become popular additions to the executive lecture circuit, outlining their ideas. Their relevance to more general leadership issues is a beguiling possibility, although specific contextual features (as so often) must not be ignored.

For example, in team sports like football the coach remains isolated from the team when it is in operation, acting as non-playing leader. There is an on-field captain, who may be able to provide direct leadership instructions during periods of 'time out' (rugby, football of various kinds, etc.). The coach may have a similar opportunity during a half-time break. In less professional circumstances, coaches are often former players with no specific technical training. Prior reputation may help to establish their credentials as coach, and many leadership principles with which we have become familiar come into play – charismatic coaches are common.

In sport, various such systems of distributed leadership are commonplace. They present the first sporting dilemma: 'Who is in charge?' From time to time, the on-field captain and non-playing coach disagree. In one infamous incident, the captain of a World Cup football team attacked the lack of training facilities and the general leadership failures of the coach in a dressing-room confrontation. The matter could not be resolved to everyone's satisfaction and the captain was sent home and was not selected again, even though he was rated the best player in the team. The remaining members of the team rose to the challenge they were facing and performed as well as might be expected. However, the coach did not survive the captain in his post for much longer than the competition lasted.

In the World Cup competition of 2001–2, a distributed leadership approach to football team leadership was introduced into the England football team by Sven-Göran Eriksson. The team had, arguably, under-performed for many years when coached by former players. Reluctantly, the Football Association of England opted for Eriksson, the first-ever non-English manager of the team. The team qualified, against the odds, and lost a close game to the eventual winners, Brazil. Eriksson's overall approach was in contrast to that of his predecessors, who had a more experience-based style. He brought with him a developed theory of on-field leadership, in association with Swedish psychologist Willi Railo, that draws on visualization, positive thinking, and cognitive reframing.[36]

According to this theory, a successful football team of 11 requires about three leaders – one of whom is designated as captain. These form a core demonstrating the required leadership behaviours that work to promote the necessary behaviours from others. The performance in the team is then sustained by the behaviours and influence of the core leaders, which are effective in countering reactions from less positive players that could spread rapidly and negatively, particularly after set-backs in play. The outcome is a culture in which *performance anxiety* is reduced. This adds to more familiar team characteristics (visionary thinking, mutual respect and support of all team members, ambitious goals, concern for quality).

CM 3.4: Team Pathologies

There is a large body of work referring to the weaknesses of teams at the level of the team. We will take a look at the theories of team dysfunction here, leaving the issue of the dysfunctional leader to the next chapter.

An approach drawing on various psychodynamic influences was developed by workers associated with the Tavistock Institute in Europe.[37] One pioneer, Wilfred Bion, is widely acknowledged for his work on the displacement of the planned and rational activities of social groups by largely unconscious influences.

One of Bion's distinctions extends the intra-personal concepts of Freudian psychology to intra-group concepts. Bion considered that some groups retain a strong grounding in the reality of the present. Other groups were more influenced by unconscious and emotionally charged forces. He described the former as task groups and the latter as basic assumption groups.

Specifically, he identified three forms of basic assumption:

■ dependency
■ fight–flight
■ pairing.

He suggested that the basic assumption provided the group with its reality, a world *as if* the hate object is an enemy to be defeated; or *as if* the leader is the all-providing and all-knowing saviour, who may also become another hate object. The conceptual grounding of basic assumption theory remains a matter of the deepest debate within the psychoanalytical community.

Social groups offer protection from anxiety, although the means may be through a distortion or denial of the direct evidence of their working experiences. In extreme cases (maybe not even extreme cases) the work of the group becomes filled with fantasies of what might be happening and what might happen in the future.

Understanding the principles and applications of group psychodynamics requires many years of study and learning from involvement in practical work. For our purposes we may simplify the discipline as involving the exploration of patterns of group behaviour through which groups avoid becoming prey to deep emotional beliefs. The exploration is conducted in ways that help the group members to develop towards more fully functioning collaborative relationships.

The Group Relations movement has conceptual and experiential similarities with the various laboratory methods developed in the United States which became well known as T-Group methodologies.[38] The origins of this can be traced to the National Training Laboratories Institute, which was founded in Bethel, Maine in 1947. The movement acknowledged its debt to Kurt Lewin (who died in the year of its inception), who had also been associated with the Tavistock studies.[39]

Learners in Group Relations approaches are encouraged to explore group processes and gain insights into behaviours and explanations for themselves and other participants. The movement has burgeoned into a wider community of researcher/practitioners. It has its own scholarly publication, the *Journal of Applied Behavioral Science*. The broad movement has survived considerable controversy on the dangers of its methods to participants.[40]

INTEGRATION

The maps of the project management terrain in the POUs and contextual materials (CM 3.1–3.4) have been rich in detail and depth. However, there are a few recurring themes, as shown in Box 3.2.

Box 3.2: Recurring Themes in Project Management and Leadership

POU 3.1 Zaccaro et al.: Functionalism, need for coordination of functions

Teams require social skills to develop shared mental models, assisted by a participative style that encourages empowerment through dealing with both rational and behavioural (personal, emotional) needs. More leadership efforts are needed to deal with coordination and interdependencies. Functionalism of dominant map stronger on control than on dealing with behavioural issues to achieve coordination.

POU 3.2 Hauschildt: Innovation

Teams requiring innovative outcomes require a combination of leadership roles to deal with power and status, and information. The roles include that of a facilitative or process leader. Leadership at the boundaries ('boundary-spanning') of the project is also important.

CM 3.1 Manz and Sims: Self-managed teams

Leadership styles of contemporary teams; considered weak or inadequate for motivating (empowering) members. Visionary (charismatic) leadership can be bullying or uncaring and fail to develop others. Task-orientation (transactional leadership) is inappropriate if situations require nurturing and transformational change. Shared or distributed leadership addresses needs to coordinate individual interests. Collectively, the combined leadership actions of members of a self-managed team may be seen as that of a 'superleader'.

CM 3.2 Tuckman's team-development model

Teams do not perform their required functions from the start of a project. Before they reach operational maturity a development process is involved that overcomes personal needs and conflicts. A facilitative leadership style may help to achieve innovative results that go beyond expectations and standard operating procedures (creativity). The majority of teams follow functional requirements.

CM 3.3 Eriksson's approach to sports team leadership

Sport often involves an 'off-field' coach or manager. Traditional coaches may be charismatic or rely on former success (reputation status). The Eriksson approach seeks to achieve distributed leadership, which involves delegation and power-sharing.[41]

CM 3.4 Dysfunctional teams

POU 3.1 and 3.2 and CM 3.1 to CM 3.3 have assumed as a given that project teams follow the traditionally accepted scientific and rational approach to project management. Deviations from that norm can be remedied as a team incorporates coordination mechanisms (POU 3.1) and gives more attention to social factors and leadership roles and to team maturity or development (CM 3.2). In CM 3.4 the assumption is that there are deeper-rooted dysfunctions within teams, which need to be addressed skilfully by a facilitative leader so as to overcome unhelpful basic assumptions about reality and the possibilities of change.

POU 3.1, provided by Zaccaro and colleagues, makes clear that the dominant map of project management retains the rational management approach that it had inherited from earlier maps of scientific management.[42] The authors argue that project management is widely regarded as primarily concerned with the roles involved, and particularly with what functions are required in various roles. They consider this to give project teams their functionalist nature. Such an emphasis pays less attention to the interdependencies required for groups working on complex projects. The corpus of knowledge on project teams has tended to ignore the processes through which individual efforts are channelled into a group purpose. This introduces the theme that recurs throughout the materials here, the dilemma of coordination and control. The focus on control in functionalist treatments of project management has tended to reduce the degree of attention paid to requirements for the coordination and reconciliation of personal needs.

Zaccaro's proposition is that the lack of coordination can be resolved by a process of social or group problem-solving. This process is needed for developing 'shared mental models, collective information processing, and team metacognition', which help to deal with individual and group needs.

An example found in business school projects illustrates the coordination dilemma. Teams of MBA students working on a project for an external company sponsor will typically share out the tasks required. The final team report, usually completed under intense deadline pressures, often reads as if it had been loosely connected from four or five individual contributions. There has been plenty of control, but not enough coordination. More successful teams share information about individual contributions, using processes which strengthen their shared POU and Zaccaro's 'social problem-solving'.

In real-world project teams, other dilemmas of coordination occur. There are well-known tensions between managerial and professional values (for example, in health teams 'juggling' budgets and medical imperatives). There are dilemmas of coordination between creative designers and accountants in design project teams. There are dilemmas of trade-offs of time, cost, and quality. Later in the book we will examine dilemmas of gender, and cultural differences and their reconciliation. These each play a part in making project leadership important. Box 3.3 examines two theories of dealing with such dilemmas.

In POU 3.2 the challenges of integrating individual requirements through project leadership were examined through the eyes of a German innovation scholar. Jürgen Hauschildt reported on a widely accepted European view that innovation (an important form of project work) requires not one but three leadership roles. The map implies that the roles are likely to be occupied by different individuals. This introduces us to a formalized enactment of the principle that leadership may be shared.

We saw how leadership could be *distributed* across several different leadership roles, each offering a means of promoting the primary project goal. Increasing project complexity and

---

Box 3.3: Team Composition: The Harmony versus Diversity Dilemma

A practical issue for action team leaders is the composition of the team. While technical and professional factors will largely determine composition, there is often scope for selection decisions. The dilemma may seem to lie between selection to achieve harmony through seeking like-minded individuals, or creative challenge through seeking constructive variety.

Two competing theories (maps) are known.[43]

- *Similarity theory* argues that homogeneous groups are likely to be more productive because of the mutual attraction shared by team members with similar demographics, and heterogeneous groups are predicted to be less productive because of inherent tensions between team members.
- *Equity theory* Team performance is enhanced by the tension that arises between dissimilar individuals within a group. If the individuals believe they are not being fairly rewarded, the theory predicts that the individuals will increase output to restore effort-to-reward equity.

Although both of these competing hypotheses predict performance based on team composition, their predictions lead to different conclusions . . . Similarity theory also predicts that those teams that are heterogeneous in ability will not perform as well as those teams with homogeneous ability composition. Equity theory predicts that performance in heterogeneous groups is dependent on the ratio of high performers to poor performers.[44]

uncertainties were suggested as factors leading to more distributed leadership. Included in these roles is the process-oriented leader, whose description is close to that of the facilitative problem-solving leader in Zaccaro's map. It is also similar to the creative problem-solving team leader described in the contextual materials.

The distribution of leadership roles was also reported in the contextual maps. Manz and Sims saw distributed leadership as a means of overcoming the central problems of unempowered workers. This concept reframes our understanding of leadership as a collective rather than an individual activity.

The concept of distributed leadership emerged again in our examples of sporting teams, in which the captain acted as the leader-in-action and the coach as a kind of boundary-spanning leader. Also in sports teams we had the concept of a coach assembling a sub-group of leaders-in-action (captain and other influential players as 'social architects').

This analysis of leaders of innovation teams connects the roles to the information flows across the boundaries of teams. This implies dilemmas concerned with coordination *between* a team and its environment and the role of boundary-spanning *within* project team work.

As has been shown, the project team finds its most common expression as a rational and structured means of achieving a desired and specified goal. The functionalist approach is acknowledged as less able to deal with contexts of complexity and ambiguity, which are acknowledged as becoming more critical to today's project leader.

In considering the development of a team, there may be emotional barriers between individuals at the beginning of working together. 'Hitting the floor running' may not always be possible, for behavioural reasons. Some teams fail to overcome behavioural challenges. The leader needs to have an understanding of the processes of conflict and conflict resolution.

One of the most widely known concepts within project management is the so-called Iron Triangle of constraints of cost, time, and quality (Box 3.4). The trade-offs are often discussed in a way consistent with logical analysis and problem-solving. However, they are also open to more creative efforts to deal with the constraints. These could involve a team leader in more behavioural considerations.

GETTING PERSONAL

Most readers engaged in today's work environments will have experience of project teams. Many will have become members of such teams, and eventually will occupy roles as team leaders.

This chapter has offered some maps to help you on the journey. We have seen how the most widespread accounts of projects tend to emphasize the tools and structures of a project in a 'one size suits all' kind of way. The accounts also tend to focus on the project leader as the

Box 3.4: Cost, Time, and Quality: The Iron Triangle of Project Management

Roger Atkinson has analysed the project management process as constrained by what is known as the Iron Triangle:

> After 50 years, it appears that the definitions for project management continue to include a limited set of success criteria, namely the Iron Triangle of cost, time and quality. These criteria, it is suggested, are no more than two best guesses and a phenomenon. A finite time resource is possibly the feature which differentiates project management from most other types of management. However, to focus the success criteria exclusively upon the delivery criteria to the exclusion of others, it is suggested, may have produced an inaccurate picture of so-called failed project management.[45]

Atkinson argues that the 'Iron Triangle' needs to be treated as provisional constraints which may have to be reinterpreted. This, he suggests, requires a new perspective in which project management is seen as 'the art and science of converting vision into reality'.[46]

The Iron Triangle challenges the decision-making of project leaders to deal with dilemmas involving trade-offs between the three functional constraints.

person who sees that a project is clearly specified and understood by the project team members according to pre-ordained criteria of success and resources constraints.

Experienced project leaders will have their unique experiences to reflect upon. Perhaps you have followed a highly structured and codified stage-gate approach, or perhaps you have developed your own approach, without a great deal of contribution from textbooks or from consultants. In either case, you may now wish to consider whether you have placed too great an emphasis on the functionalist approach (putting emphasis on those aspects of project work that can be precisely specified and monitored). If so, you may now consider how increasingly complex projects may require strategies for more distributed leadership and social problem-solving. You may also wish to review the outbursts and more emotional aspects of project life. Might this indicate a group that had engaged in the sort of dependency fantasies mapped by Bion and subsequent psychodynamic researchers?

'Wannabe' leaders are also advised to consider the kinds of leadership context they aspire to, before reflecting on the limits of a functionalist approach. Are you hoping to work in a team in which innovation, change, and uncertainties are central? If so, you should be more willing to review the ideas of distributed leadership. These views may also help you to take a more focused view of what kind of leader you see yourself becoming: an entrepreneurial leader, a change-centred process leader, or a technological product champion?

Whether you are an experienced or 'wannabe' leader, the maps and your examination of them should help you to approach the subject of project leadership in a way that takes more account of its generally ignored dilemmas of coordination and boundary management.

SUMMARY

This chapter has examined a wide range of activities in which leadership plays a part in the achievement of groups' desired ambitions and obligations. The focus has been on projects large and small, and the teams that can be found engaged in projects.

A dominant set of beliefs can be seen in the maps of projects. These derive from early notions of scientific management. Many professionals trained in technical and financial disciplines are comfortable with a rationale that is logical and rational. This helps to reinforce the dominance of a rational management ethos implied in the definition provided at the start of the chapter, that a project involves a unique set of coordinated activities, with definite starting and finishing points, undertaken by an individual or a team to meet specific objectives within defined time, cost, and performance parameters.

The strength of the rational model of management should not be overlooked in a critique of its weaknesses when applied unreflectively. Its pioneers, such as Taylor, helped to provide business with a map that permitted progress, enabling the rise of the modern economies of the twentieth century. However, as the study materials in this chapter indicate, scientific management helped to make the dilemma of coordinated action more acute. It provided theoretically based control systems which paid insufficient attention to the coordination required when groups of people were conscripted to address a shared task.

The model of rational decision-making favoured management control. Dealing with the requirements of different individuals required leadership to take into account more behavioural factors to achieve the formal and informal requirements in project work.

Furthermore, the styles that seemed most promising involved devolution of control and a shift toward distributed leadership, and attempts to deal with behavioural issues and dilemmas.

Exercise 3.2: Getting SMART

SMART is a widely used project management support system.[47] Many companies require personnel (including sub-contracted professionals) to be trained in a comprehensive set of procedures such as SMART before being permitted to work on company projects. The acronym stands for:

continued . . .

Exercise 3.2: Getting SMART ... continued

Specific
Measurable
Actionable
Relevant
Time-bound.

The basic assumption is that projects fail for lack of a well-defined structure. SMART offers such a structure at the early stage of identifying goals or objectives. Over time, the original acronym and even the words associated with it have changed. The basic principle remains, however, and the changes are refinements rather than radical ones.[48]

Exercise 3.2 Discussion Questions

1 Using information found in this chapter, evaluate the features of the SMART approach that illustrate the functional natures of maps of project management.
2 Suggest ways in which project leadership may overcome the weaknesses of an overemphasis on functional issues.
3 Can you think of reasons (suggested in this chapter) why projects may require skills that extend beyond those emphasized in the SMART approach?

[Exercise for individual reflection or classroom or tutorial discussion.]

NOTES

1 Project Management Institute (2004) *A Guide to the Project Management Body of Knowledge PMBOK Guide*, Penn: Project Management Institute, p. 5.
2 Definition from Office of Government Commerce, downloaded from www.jiscinfonet.ac.uk/p3m, 1 August 2010.
3 The Toyota story in 2009–10 is a case example of a successful company in danger of a serious decline. Various explanations were offered, including weak leadership, but a decline in operational standards was particularly noted. See http://leaderswedeserve.wordpress.com/2010/02/04/toyota-fights-to-preserve-its-global-brand/. The case was also evaluated and described as being part of a 'media circus'. Dushane, M. (2010) 'Toyota recall: Scandal, media circus, and stupid drivers – editorial', *Car and Driver*, February, p. 1, www.caranddriver.com/news/car/10q1/toyota_recall_scandal_media_circus_and_stupid_drivers-editorial.
4 Dejevsky, M. (2011) 'Goodwill alone can't fix the NHS troubles', *Independent*, 23 February, p. 23.

5 This is an important point in understanding the limitations of the dominant model of project management and needs to be better understood by project managers seeking to overcome unexpected difficulties of coordination and control.

6 http://news.bbc.co.uk/1/hi/world/americas/8639332.stm, downloaded 22 April 2010.

7 http://leaderswedeserve.wordpress.com/2008/09/17/lehman-bros-and-the-limits-of-leadership/, downloaded 30 April 2010.

8 F.W. Taylor (1911) 'The principles of scientific management', Harper & Brothers, now hosted online by Eldritch Press, http://www.eldritchpress.org/fwt/ti.html.

9 Taylorism (the principles of scientific management) and Fordism (its structures and philosophy in practice) are terms that are sometimes used synonymously.

10 Sun, G. (2011) *The division of labour in economics: A history*, Oxford: Routledge.

11 Larson, E. (2004) 'Project management structures', in Morris, P.W.G., & Pinto, J.K. (eds), *The Wiley guide to managing projects*, Hoboken, NJ: Wiley, pp. 48–66, at p. 48.

12 Clegg, S.R., Hardy, C., & Nord, W.R. (eds) (1996) *Handbook of organization studies*, London: Sage (2nd edn, 2006).

13 Hassard, J., Kelemen, M., & Cox, J.W. (2008) *Disorganization theory: Explorations in alternative organizational analysis*, London: Routledge.

14 Assiter, A. (1984) 'Althusser and structuralism', *British Journal of Sociology*, 35, 2, 272–296.

15 Larson, E. (2004) 'Project management structures', in Morris, P.W.G., & Pinto, J.K. (eds), *The Wiley guide to managing projects*, Hoboken, NJ: Wiley, pp. 48–66, at p. 52.

16 Wheelwright, S.C., & Clark, K. (1992) *Revolutionizing product development*, New York: Free Press; Kerzner, H. (2009) *Project management: A systems approach to planning, scheduling, and controlling*, 10th edn, New York: Wiley.

17 Atkinson, R. (1999) 'Project management: Cost, time and quality, two best guesses', *International Journal of Project Management*, 17, 6, 337–342.

18 Zaccaro, S.J., Rittman, A.L., & Marks, M.A. (2001) 'Team leadership', *Leadership Quarterly*, 12, 451–483.

19 Salas, T., Dickinson, T.L., Converse, S., & Tannenbaum, S.I. (1992) 'Towards an understanding of team performance and training', in Swezey, R.W., & Salas, T. (eds), *Teams, their training and performance*, Norwood, NJ: Ablex, pp. 3–29.

20 See also Ancona, D.G., & Caldwell, D. (1992) 'Bridging the boundary: External activity and performance in organizational teams', *Administrative Science Quarterly*, 37, 634–665.

21 Metcalfe, J., & Shimamura, A.P. (eds) (1994) *Metacognition: Knowing about knowing*, Cambridge, MA: MIT Press.

22 Edmondson, A.C. (2003) 'Speaking up in the operating room: How team leaders promote learning in interdisciplinary action teams', *Journal of Management Studies*, 40, 6, 1419–1452.

23 Pinto, M.B., Pinto, J.K., & Prescott, J.E. (1993) 'Antecedents and consequences of project team cross-functional cooperation', *Management Science*, 39, 10, 1281–1297; Tidd, J., & Bessant, J. (2009) *Managing innovation – integrating technological, market and organizational change*, 4th edn, Chichester: Wiley.

24 Hauschildt, J. (1999) 'Promotors and champions of innovation: Development of a research paradigm', in Brockhoff, K., Chakrabarti, A.K., & Hauschildt, J. (eds), *The dynamics of innovation: Strategic and managerial implications*, Berlin: Springer, pp. 167–182.

25 Schon, D.A. (1965) 'Champions for radical new inventions', *Harvard Business Review*, March–April, 77–86.

26 Chakrabarti, A.K. (1974) 'The role of the champion in product innovation', *California Management Review*, 17, 58–62.

27 Hauschildt, J. (1999) 'Promotors and champions of innovation: Development of a research paradigm', in Brockhoff, K., Chakrabarti, A.K., & Hauschildt, J. (eds), *The dynamics of innovation: Strategic and managerial implications*, Berlin: Springer, p. 172, citing Ancona, D.G.,

& Caldwell, D. (1992) 'Bridging the boundary: External activity and performance in organizational teams', *Administrative Science Quarterly*, 37, 634–665.

28 Manz, C.C., & Sims, H.P. Jr. (1987) 'Leading workers to lead themselves: The external leadership of self-managing work teams', *Administrative Science Quarterly*, 32, 106–128; (1991) *The new superleadership: Leading others to lead themselves*, San Francisco: Berrett-Koehler.

29 The 'Great Man' theory of leadership is attributed to Thomas Carlisle. See Hirsch, E.D. (2002) *The new dictionary of cultural literacy*, 3rd edn, Boston, MA: Houghton Mifflin; Carlyle, T. (1888) *On heroes, hero-worship and the heroic in history*, New York: Fredrick A. Stokes.

30 Manz, C.C., & Sims, H.P. Jr. (1987) 'Leading workers to lead themselves: The external leadership of self-managing work teams', *Administrative Science Quarterly*, 32, 106–128; Manz, C.C., & Sims, H.P. Jr. (1991) *Superleadership: Leading others to lead themselves*, Englewood Cliffs, NJ: Prentice Hall.

31 Tuckman, B.W. (1965) 'Development sequence in small groups', *Psychological Bulletin*, 63, 6, 384–399.

32 Tuckman, B.W., & Jensen, M.C. (1977) 'Stages of small group development revisited', *Group and Organisational Studies*, 2, 419–427.

33 Ginnett, R.C. (1993) 'Crews as groups: their formation and their leadership', in Wiener, E.L., Kanki, B.G., & Helmreich, R.L. (eds), *Cockpit resource management*, San Diego, CA: Academic Press, pp. 71–98.

34 Rickards, T., & Moger, S.T. (2000) 'Creative leadership processes in project team development: An alternative to Tuckman's stage model', *British Journal of Management*, 11, 4, 273–283.

35 Rickards, T., & Moger, S.T. (1999) *Handbook for creative team leaders*, Aldershot, Hants: Gower.

36 For an insightful popular view, see Eriksson, S.-G., Railo, W., & Matson, H. (2001) *Sven-Göran Eriksson on football*, English translation, London: Carlton Books.

37 Trist, E., Emery, F., & Murray, H. (1997) *The social engagement of social science*, Vol. 3, *The socio-ecological perspective*, Philadelphia: University of Pennsylvania Press.

38 Lippett, R., Watson, J., & Westley, B. (1958) *The dynamics of planned change*, New York: Harcourt Brace.

39 These principles were incorporated into the Manchester Method, an approach for enhancing experiential learning within team projects, initially within MBA programmes at Manchester Business School. See Drinkwater, P.M., Adeline, C.M., French, S., Papamichail, K.N., & Rickards, T. (2004) 'Adopting a web-based collaborative tool to support the Manchester Method approach to learning', *Electronic Journal of E-learning*, 2, 1, 61–68, http://www.ejel.org/volume-2/vol2-issue1/issue1-art23-drinkwater.pdf, downloaded 25 September 2008.

40 Back, K.W. (1987) *Beyond words: The story of sensitivity training and the encounter movement*, New Brunswick, NJ: Transaction; Cooper, C.L. (1980) 'Risk factors in experiential learning groups', *Small Group Research*, 11, 3, 251–278.

41 This may be seen as a form in which there is some self-management, within a more complex system in which leadership is distributed within the team and across levels in the wider sporting organization.

42 Strictly speaking, Zaccaro used the terminology of action teams, although the researchers make it clear that project teams may be considered a significant sub-set of action teams.

43 Bowers, C.A., Pharmer, J.A., & Salas, E. (2000) 'When member homogeneity is needed in work teams: A meta-analysis', *Small Group Research*, 31, 3, 305–327.

44 Ibid., p. 313.

45 Atkinson, R. (1999) 'Project management: Cost, time and quality, two best guesses', *International Journal of Project Management*, 17, 6, 337–342, at p. 341.

46 Turner, J.R. (1996) 'Editorial: International Project Management Association', *International Journal of Project Management*, 14, 1, 1–6.

47 Doran, G.T. (1981) 'There's a S.M.A.R.T. way to write management's goals and objectives', *Management Review*, 70, 11.

48 See, for example, www.prince2.com/prince2-structure.asp for the recommended system, PRINCE2®, from the Office of Government Commerce of the United Kingdom.

CHAPTER LEARNING OBJECTIVES

Learning focus
- How charisma survived into a 'post-charismatic' era

Key issues
- Charismatic leadership
- Transformational leadership
- Level 5 leadership
- The dark side of charisma

Dilemmas
- The popularity of the charismatic leader
- Succession problems of charismatic leadership
- Following the ego-driven charismatic leader

Platforms of understanding
- POU 4.1 A History of Charismatic Leadership
- POU 4.2 From Charismatic to Transformational Leadership

Contextual materials
- CM 4.1 James MacGregor Burns on Empowerment
- CM 4.2 Bernard Bass and the Full Range Leadership Model
- CM 4.3 Beyond Charisma: The Fifth-Level Leader
- CM 4.4 Jay Conger and the Dilemmas of Charismatic Leadership

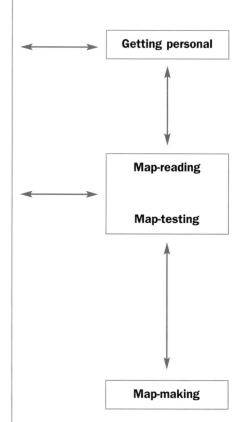

Getting personal

Map-reading

Map-testing

Map-making

4 CHARISMA
ANCIENT AND MODERN VERSIONS

The period after the charismatic leader is gone is always perilous, but in hypercompetitive, fast-moving industries, the loss becomes apparent much more rapidly.[1]

Last week in my small town of Leesburg, Virginia, an estimated 35,000 people turned out to see Barack Obama. Why is he drawing crowds like a rock star? It's a lot of things, of course – but don't underestimate the power of a largely misunderstood leadership quality – charisma.[2]

United repelled fluent moves from their opponents, cameras switching from time to time to Jose [Mourinho] on the touchline. . . . The crowd chanted 'You're not special anymore' but more with a mix of relief and black humour than of spite. We were witnessing the limits of charisma.[3]

Charisma is a tricky thing. Used wisely, it's a blessing. Indulged, it can be a curse. Charismatic visionaries lead people ahead, and sometimes astray.[4]

Charisma is a necessary ingredient of transformational leadership but by itself is not sufficient to account for the transformational process.[5]

LEARNING POINTS

The term 'charisma' is found in many popular accounts of leaders and leadership. It is almost always used with little in the way of even a working definition, as if the term requires no formal clarification. Take a little time to reflect on what you mean when you use the term, by tackling Exercise 4.1. This will provide you with an opportunity to compare your notes with any new understanding of charisma that you may have reached after studying the chapter.

Exercise 4.1: Your Working Definition of a Charismatic Leader

1 My working definition of a charismatic leader is . . .
2 My working definition mainly deals with exceptional people who are known for achieving exceptional results. *Agree/disagree.*
3 My working definition would include people in everyday life, such as my teachers, members of my family and friends, sports team captains and coaches, and politicians. *Agree/disagree.*

ORIENTATION

Why study charisma? A deeper understanding will help you to reach an informed view of whether there are aspects of the phenomenon which can be considered 'trainable', and also whether it is both possible and desirable to attempt to develop a charismatic style of leadership.

After reading this chapter you will have an understanding of the nature of charisma as implied in historical maps and of how modern maps appear to have modernized the concept, completely weakening its appeal to practical leaders as a means of achieving transformational change. You will be introduced to dilemmas associated with charisma. From the perspective of the leader, these include considering the dilemma of being regarded as so special that no one gets close enough to help to challenge a leader's understanding of what's going on. From the organizational perspective, dilemmas of governance include the question of how far a charismatic leader can be trusted to act primarily in the interests of stakeholders.[6]

POU 4.1 traces charisma from the ancient concept to its present-day forms. Then POU 4.2 takes an overview of contemporary mappings of transformational leadership. The two maps show that charismatic and transformational leadership processes are similar. The latter may be seen as a partially modernized revision of the former, which nevertheless retains considerable popular appeal.

The contextualizing materials take us into more specific aspects of empowerment, and to the dark side of charismatic leadership processes. We will follow the history of charismatic leadership from its pre-modern form. The influential work of Weber resulted in charismatic leadership being regarded as an appropriate means of contesting traditional institutional arrangements, while at the same time being replaced by more rational modes of organizational practice within modern industrialized organizations.

For over a century, spanning much of the twentieth century, the transactional form of leadership had been implicitly accepted. In the 1980s, the 'New Leadership' movement recognized the challenges posed by more complex and fast-changing business environments as requiring new approaches. Transformational leadership was being increasingly accepted as suited to modern industrial conditions.

However, transformational leadership struggled with questions about its relationship with the older and pre-modern ideas of charismatic leadership. This dilemma was partially resolved by giving charisma a modernist treatment, so that it re-emerged within the new transformational leadership mappings.

PLATFORMS OF UNDERSTANDING

POU 4.1: A History of Charismatic Leadership

The English term 'charisma' is a direct phonetic expression of χάρισμα, an obscure term found infrequently in Greek texts going back three millennia. Its precise meaning remains open to scholarly debate, but contemporary dictionary translations would link it with another and more familiar word in English, namely 'charity'. Both charity and charisma are to do with the widespread cultural notion of a gift. Charisma, on simple lexical grounds, is 'something to do with' a gift. We need to look more deeply to find out what sort of gift and how it is often (but not always) associated with leaders and leadership.

A comprehensive study of the history of the concept and term charisma was carried out in *A History of Charisma* by the Australian media scholar John Potts.[7] He traces the roots of the concept to early Jewish and Graeco-Roman cultures as referring to the widespread cultural concept of gifts bestowed on individual human beings from a spiritual world.[8]

Mythology tells of the beautiful goddess Charis, and how Athene bestowed *charis* or supernatural grace on a favoured mortal (Telemachus). The complex notions of various cultures offered supernatural gifts that were bequeathed on favoured individuals. Potts describes such concepts as proto-charismatic. The ideas can be found in accounts from ancient religious systems. Various cultures shared a view of the spiritual world in which gods and spirits communicated with identified humans. The chosen ones became

Table 4.1 Evolution of the Concept of Charisma[9]

Earlier related terms.	From the tenth century BC, Greek texts refer to *charis*, interpreted to mean a gift bestowed on chosen individuals. The context is that of early religious communities of faith across Asia Minor. Beliefs in faith healing, spiritual possession, clairvoyance and prophecy were widespread.
Early Christian church introduces the term 'charisma' in Greek texts. The texts are attributed to St Paul and become accepted as part of Christian orthodoxy within the Bible.	First century AD. Writing in Greek to the newly emerging Christian communities, St Paul explains the complex theological concept of spiritual grace, borrowing the well-known older term *charis*, meaning a spiritual gift, and introducing a more obscure and unfamiliar term, 'charisma', to signal the 'ownership' of the concept of *charis* made manifest in everyday life to believers. The writings attempt to establish an orthodox view of the new religion he was seeking to promote.
	Paul's messages ('Epistles') become part of the accepted canon of the Christian religion, retained through various translations to modern times.
	Early churches espouse variants of charismatic beliefs, drawing on practices from the older religious traditions (Minoan, Hebrew, Graeco-Roman).
Decline of early Christian practices drawing on Paul's charismatic theology accompanying 'the rise of bishops and the demise of prophets'.[10]	By the second century AD, the Christian church had established its rituals and hierarchy at the expense of the early heterodoxies. The early charismatic movement diminished. Some charismatic groups were considered to be engaged in heretical practices.
Christianity becomes established as a worldwide movement from a European power base.	Fourth century AD. Conversion of the Emperor Constantine to Christianity, and acceptance of Christianity as the official religion of the Roman Empire. Charismatic ideology and practices are side-lined but never eliminated.
Weber reinvents charisma as a means of explaining the nature of traditional religious movements.	Twentieth century AD. Max Weber's pioneering work in sociology becomes widely accepted as a secular orthodoxy. His critique reintroduces the notion of charisma as the means through which power and legitimacy were established in traditional cultures. Predicts its replacement by a rational mode of leadership more effective within modern organizations.
Charisma in a world of celebrity.	1960s. Mass media conflate fame, celebrity and charisma. Business courses offer routes to 'charisma for everyone'.
New Leadership movement 'tames' charisma as transformational leadership.	1980s. New Leadership movement provides a rationalistic reshaping of charisma, while retaining its 'vision making and giving' sense.
Post-charismatic movement.	21st century. Earlier maps of charismatic and transformational leadership challenged by social scientists from postmodern and critical perspectives.

'gifted' in various ways. Mystics such as shamans were believed to communicate with the spirits, often in a trance-like state. Shamans also occupied roles as prophets and religious leaders, but were not necessarily regarded as leaders.

Theologians suggest that earlier notions of gifts and giftedness were introduced into the early Christian church by the apostle Paul, who recognized the importance of communicating the theologically difficult aspects of the new religion. He chose to do this through a relabelling of older ideas.

Paul mobilized the obscure term 'charisma' to provide an explanation for abilities that could otherwise have been attributed to magic, miracles, gnosis and ecstatic manifestations associated with cults.[11] Later, the charismatic approach was to weaken in face of 'the rise of bishops, the demise of prophets . . . and transition from the rather free-wheeling Christian community of Paul's time to the structured ministry of the second-century'.[12] Charisma was to move to the margins of Christian dogma, often becoming associated with heretical views.

The term languished in the relative obscurity of theological debate until the writings of the great sociologist Max Weber, nearly two millennia later. What might have remained an obscure piece of scholarly work, written in the 1920s, was translated into English in the late 1940s.[13] By the 1960s it had become an influential scholarly text.

Box 4.1: Weber's Argument for the Decline of Charismatic Authority in Modern Institutions

Weber's famous analysis of the modern organizational form and its leadership provides one of the most influential conceptual maps within social science. He considered that the broad sweep of historical leadership could be studied as three theoretical or pure types of structure of authority:

- Traditional authority
- Charismatic authority
- Legal authority.

His analysis demonstrated how traditional structures had remained stable during long periods of history, through accepted power relationships (traditional authority). From time to time a traditional political or religious system was disrupted by a charismatic intervention which became the new orthodoxy.

More significantly for contemporary society and its organizations, he concluded that modern industrial societies had developed new institutional forms of organization. In these, leadership was associated with rationality and with a bureaucratic structure. Authority was derived through legal requirements.

Charisma was beginning also to acquire more secular connotations with the emergence of a youth culture and the first global rock stars, as well as retaining its significance in the analysis of political leaders. Potts examines towering figures from (Jack) Kennedy to Fidel Castro, Benazir Bhutto, Bill Clinton, Tony Blair, and Barack Obama.

Potts identifies the selling-power of charisma in the offerings of the self-help leadership literature. He points to the inherent contradictions within such popular texts. They indicate, on the one hand, that charisma is special, but on the other hand, that (almost) anyone can be special – and rather quickly so, if their advice is followed. He records how a so-called 'master of charisma' had been brought into the House of Lords in 1999 to inject some charisma into the peers' speeches, to make them a little more [Bill] Clintonesque.[14]

A term with such an extended history inevitably takes on different meanings over time. Its pre-modern applications fit with some difficulty into more modern maps of leadership. Weber argued that it was ineffective for leaders within the modern organizational form. Modern leaders worked rationally, within a bureaucratic structure.

Weber's work was compatible with the beliefs of rational action within the DRM. However, fresh challenges to charisma developed within the social sciences and came from scholars dissatisfied with dilemmas associated with the DRM. These challenges become increasingly important in maps covered in subsequent chapters.

POU 4.2: From Charismatic to Transformational Leadership

The contemporary use of the term 'transformational leadership' can be traced to an influential book written in 1978 by James McGregor Burns.[15] Burns, a historian, studied the characteristics of great political figures such as John F. Kennedy. One of his most significant observations was of leadership behaviours which *transformed* situations. He pointed out the difference between such transformational effects and *transactional* behaviours, which were the basis of the leadership studies of the modern era. The acceptance of Burns's insight was an important contribution to the emergence of the New Leadership movement of the 1980s.

His classification raises the question of why managers and researchers alike had accepted that leadership was grounded in transactional exchange processes. Why, in contrast, had transformational leadership been relatively ignored? It is plausible to suggest that they had been over-influenced by the DRM and had assumed that leaders deal with individuals who are motivated according to self-interest to act through a rational calculation of the outcomes of actions.

Transformational leadership was rather inconveniently close to the pre-modern form of charismatic leadership – a decidedly pre-modern form, according to Weber. Was Burns taking leadership back to an acceptance of pre-modern ideas? The dilemma was to be addressed by finding a modern mapping of transformational leadership which incorporated some of the pre-modern aspects of charismatic leadership. As we will see in CM 4.2,

Bernard Bass and his co-workers developed a metric through which a leader's transactional and transformational characteristics could both be studied.[16]

James G. (Jerry) Hunt, director of leadership programmes at Texas Tech, used a slightly modified vocabulary.[17] He proposed that leadership maps could be clustered into those treating leadership in a more traditional fashion ('transactionally oriented' skills) and those examining more recent ideas ('transformationally oriented' skills). In making this distinction, Hunt signalled that the emerging ideas required some way of resolving the ambiguities which appeared to surround the various concepts of transformational, charismatic, and visionary leadership processes.

Hunt described how other researchers were reorienting their maps towards more transformationally oriented perspectives. He cites the example of Robert House, who was reworking his Path-Goal model, which had become one of the best-known of the contingency approaches.[18] Its essential claim was that leadership effectiveness was contingent on the ways in which the leader behaves towards the paths and towards the goals of the employees. See Box 4.2 for more details of Path-Goal theory and its similarities with the contingency approach known as Situational Leadership.

Box 4.2: Path-Goal Theory of Leadership compared with Hersey and Blanchard's Situational Leadership Model

The New Leadership movement of the 1980s eventually led to revisions of contingency theories. Two such theories, by House and by Hersey and Blanchard, reveal their debt to a DRM of human behaviours. House, in particular, attempted to revise his earlier mapping.

In the 1970s, House studied leadership extensively as a process involving a leader seeking to achieve organizational objectives by supporting the path of employees in achieving goals. In its early form, the model had been based on the rational model of human behaviour known as valance theory. This proposes that individuals are motivated according to self-interest to act through a rational calculation of outcomes of actions. Thus, a leader is advised to attend to the perceptions of followers and to indicate how efforts directed towards wider organizational goals could align with calculations of follower self-interest.

The early version of the Path-Goal model can be seen as having similarities with Hersey and Blanchard's situational approach, one of the best-known commercialized products providing a schema for matching leadership style to specific situations.[19]

In each model, the most appropriate leadership style will thus be determined by situational factors. Typically, situations of ambiguity require more directional leadership; situations of repetitive work require more encouragement and consideration. The implication is that the leader knows the 'best' path for a follower, and is able to adapt a suitable leadership style.[20] The two models do not completely overlap, although shared characteristics can be seen:

Path-Goal leadership styles:

- Supportive leadership
- Directive leadership
- Participative leadership
- Achievement-oriented leadership.

Hersey and Blanchard leadership styles:

- Telling
- Selling
- Participating
- Delegating.

In the Hersey and Blanchard schema, attention is paid to a development path believed to be taken by groups towards a state of increased maturity.

House's earlier work had assumed people to be primarily rational and calculating in their decisions and behaviours. It was now being revised to take into account the emotional and non-conscious efforts of members of social groups and the symbolic significance of leader behaviours. His revised perspective was to consider charismatic leaders as differentiated by 'dominance, self-confidence, need to influence and strong convictions in the moral rightness of their beliefs . . .[whose] emotionally appealing goals motivate task accomplishment and arouse followers' needs for achievement, affiliation or power'.[21]

CONTEXTUAL MATERIALS

For our contextual readings in this chapter, we consider James MacGregor Burns's writing on empowerment (CM 4.1); Bernard Bass and his Full Range Leadership model (CM 4.2); Jim Collins examining the fifth-level leader (CM 4.3); and Jay Conger's treatment of visionary leadership and its drawbacks (CM 4.4).

CM 4.1: James MacGregor Burns on Empowerment

Regarded as the pioneer of transformational leadership, James MacGregor Burns also deserves attention for his insights into motivation and employee empowerment. In a review prepared under the Kellogg Leadership Studies Project, Burns describes the initiation of a change process as coming through the unexpected and individualistic action of an individual. Many such acts have transient impact. A few deeply touch and mobilize actions from others. The most famous acts are of political or military bravery: the unarmed student standing against the advancing tank; Nelson's 'blind eye' to orders. Burns further suggests that the consequences of the act rely on an intimate 'we' of future acts and relationships.

The acts involve so-called leaders and so-called followers. The manner in which each influences the others is problematic. He suggests that we reconceptualize the actors in such change processes. As well as the person identified as the transforming leader, there will be other actors. The action will reveal *opponents* to the change being initiated. There will be *passives*, a large group whose members are difficult to rouse, and the *isolates*. He further suggests that we think of leadership as 'made by the system' in ways comparable to parents being 'made' by their social circumstances – not least of which are their children. Here, Burns is arguing for a view of leadership roles as existing in a web of relationships.

If we take the perspective of a web of relationships, Burns argues, we find new insights into the way values impact on leadership. He reiterates his own understanding of values as being of three kinds. The first is of an ethical kind – chastity, sobriety, abstention, kindness to the poor; the second is social values such as honesty, trustworthiness, reliability, reciprocity, and accountability. The third kind is of normative or socially desired goals such as order, liberty, equality, justice, and community (fellowship). These are the elements from which a socially negotiated order emerges through acts of transformational leadership.

Burns points out that an initiating act triggers value-laden reactions from the people acting out the three kinds of role. The initiator triggers reactions from supporters and opponents. These reactions contribute to what may be called a first-order calculus of the trustworthiness of the initiator and his cause. But the reactions themselves become triggers for scrutiny, and second-order assessments of trustworthiness. Are the opponents trustworthy? He suggests that a dilemma in leadership studies has been recognized for some decades. Leadership-influencing processes appear to reduce freedom of choice in followers, regardless of whether the leadership is coercive or more positive in style. The argument that the leader is obliged to exercise awareness and self-restraint seems to Burns to be 'a weak reed'. However, if leadership is regarded as a social process, outcomes of change are better regarded as the outcomes of a social calculus: the outcomes are defined by the wider set of relationships.

Burns develops a similar argument in dealing with a well-known criticism of the vocabulary of empowerment. As he points out, the term invites the questions 'who empowers who[m]?'; and 'to whose purpose?' Parents lead their children to greater levels of development in what is a process of benign empowerment. However benign the intent, this is a top-down process. How should we regard similarly well-intentioned efforts of empowerment in the workplace? Burns considers that the conventional two-way relationship between a powerful leader and less powerful followers sets up a possibly irresolvable ethical dilemma.

Here Burns makes an interesting comment. In earlier work he had distinguished between power brokers and 'real' leaders. Power brokers mobilize their powerful resources regardless of the needs and values of their followers. In contrast, 'real' leaders mobilize resources in order to achieve mutually desired goals. He later came to regard several weaknesses in this formulation. In particular, he notes that there is still a top-down sense to it. He also concedes that he underestimated other roles, particularly that of the 'passives', in holding back change. He reached the conclusion that the term 'leadership' has become so intimately connected with an individual rather than a social collective process, that he would welcome the dropping of the term 'the leader' from the vocabulary if the concept were not so thoroughly embedded in popular and scholarly discourse.

CM 4.2: Bernard Bass and the Full Range Leadership Model

Bernard Bass and his co-workers were prominent among the early researchers exploring transformational leadership. They also found a way of integrating the transactional and transformational models into their Full Range Leadership model.

Bass summarizes transactional and transformational leadership as being based on two fundamentally different core assumptions. Transactional leaders essentially respond to their followers' immediate self-interests. Here we have the rational action assumption assumed within the DRM.

In contrast, the transformational approach is described as uplifting the morale, motivation and morals of a leader's followers. For Bass, transformational leadership is thus strongly connected with attempts to provide an empowering environment where autonomy, job satisfaction, and commitment flourish under challenging and motivating work conditions.

We see how transactional leadership involves exchanges rooted in self-interest. Transformational leadership involves a form of influence that moves followers to accomplish more than is usually expected of them. Leaders influence workforces to go beyond simple self-interest. The process is seen as one in which participants are enriched in ways that also enrich the wider group. The transformational business leader is assumed to promote the achievement of the economic goals of the organization and the development of socially desirable 'elevating' behaviours among its followers.

The full-range model of leadership proposed by Bass has been widely examined using the Multifactor Leadership Questionnaire (MLQ).[22] In factor analyses, two transactional factors consistently emerge:

- ■ *Contingent rewards* This style rewards followers for conforming to performance targets. The key responsibilities of the leader are the clarification through direction or participation of what the follower needs to do, and how he or she will be rewarded for achieving what is required.

■ *Management by exception* In this style, the leader takes action when task-related activities are found to be failing, such that procedural or task goals are not being achieved. The style may be further split to contrast *active management by exception*, in which the leader constantly monitors followers' performance and takes corrective action when necessary; *passive leadership*, where the leader waits for problems to arise before taking corrective action; and *laissez-faire leadership*, through which the leader makes no further interventions, having set the required performance procedures and goals. Recent studies have supported the factorization into active and passive forms of management by exception. However, such extended studies have cast doubt on the precise formulation of the sub-factors.

Transformational leadership was split into four sub-factors believed to assist in moving the follower beyond immediate self-interest, and elevates the followers' level of maturity and ideals, as well as concerns for achievement, self-actualization, and the well-being of others.

The factors became known as the 'Four Is':

■ Idealized influence (charisma)
■ Inspirational motivation
■ Intellectual stimulation
■ Individualized consideration.

Idealized influence is displayed when the leader envisions a desirable future, articulates how it can be achieved, and engenders pride, respect, and trust.

Inspirational motivation is associated with leaders who motivate by creating high expectations, set an example to be followed through setting high standards of performance, and show determination and confidence by modelling appropriate behaviour and using symbols to fuse the effort. Followers want to identify with such leadership.

Intellectual stimulation is displayed when the leader helps followers to become more creative and innovative, continually challenging followers with new ideas and approaches.

Individualized consideration is displayed when leaders pay personal attention to the developmental needs of followers, giving them respect and consideration.

Bass[23] reported that transactional leadership may induce more stress, and that transformational leadership enhances the commitment, involvement, and performance of followers and helps to deal with stress. He has also examined how transformational and transactional leadership may be affected by moral and personal development, training, and education. Mature moral development is required of the transformational leader, although there is still a need to learn more about the ethical factors that distinguish transformational leaders.

> ### Box 4.3: Transformational and Transactional Styles: A Common Misunderstanding
>
> Popular articles tend to focus on the differences between transformational and transactional leaders. This leads to the classification of leaders as *either* transactional *or* transformational. However, Bass and his co-workers have consistently indicated that leaders exhibit a mix of both styles. Research using the MLQ has shown that transformational leadership adds to the effectiveness of transactional leadership, yet does not substitute for it. Effective leaders are perceived as being strong on both transformational and transactional factors.

CM 4.3: Beyond Charisma: The Fifth-Level Leader

The charismatic business leader continues to hold considerable sway in the beliefs and assumptions of many people. The charismatic story, briefly, holds that great changes are achieved by exceptional people. More careful studies are beginning to reveal that the story is at best partial. At the very least, our image of the exceptional leader has been shown to ignore the contributions of people with characteristics of style and behaviour that are in many ways the mirror image of the larger-than-life charismatic.

This particular dilemma seems to be on the way to being resolved, at least in respect of the founders and leaders of the great American companies, thanks to research conducted by Jim Collins. Collins was a respected academic who subsequently turned thought-leader and guru, publicizing his ideas around the world. His work is a nice combination of well-grounded research and well-rounded stories easily communicated to a wider audience. His earlier work with Jerry Porras had revealed the secrets of exceptional companies, ones that survived and prospered. Collins and Porras called these companies ones that were *built to last*.[24] Now, with teams of experienced researchers, he went more deeply into the features of such companies. Although he wished to avoid the risks of over-celebrating the great leader, the results were unavoidable.

From over fourteen hundred companies studied, eleven achieved the kind of sustained excellence he was looking for. In these eleven companies, the strongest differentiating factor was what Collins called *level five leadership*. The various levels were summarized as follows:

Level 1 leadership is that of individual talent individually applied. In teams and groups, the individual may be an isolated but valued technical or professional expert.
Level 2 leadership is leadership in the sense of collaborative team efforts, and may include specialized professional or personal talents.
Level 3 leadership is that of the competent manager, effectively organizing people toward pre-determined goals.

Level 4 leadership is that of the effective leader, who promotes commitment to and pursuit of a compelling vision, together with high performance standards.

Level 5 leadership is that of the level-five executive, who builds great companies through exercise of personal humility and great will-power.

Collins compares level-five leaders with those at other levels, particularly those who had been hailed as 'the greatest' in recent times and yet, on their departures from the organizations they had 'transformed', were subsequently found to have left no lasting legacies. Level-five leadership implies the acquisition of capabilities found in the other four levels. In vivid and, at times, in harshly judgemental tones, Collins lists the might-have-beens. His point is that cultural stereotyping of leaders permits the continued elevation of 'non-level fives' to top positions. And the characteristics of level-four leaders are too often incompatible with his recipe of *humility with strong resolve*. The descriptions of modest leaders of steely resolve help us understand some of the features that were previously concealed. Interestingly, as he points out, the leaders were never celebrated in the media in the way in which some of their level-four counterparts were.

He cites Darwin E. Smith of Kimberly Clark as having many of the characteristics of level-five leaders. A Spartan upbringing reinforced no-nonsense attitudes to life's problems (including a battle against a life-threatening illness). For Collins, this is the modest yet iron-willed characteristic of an Abe Lincoln. Smith saw the necessity for Kimberly Clark to get out of its core business of coated paper. The implication was entry into the highly competitive consumer products markets against such big hitters as Procter & Gamble. The consequence was the painful closure of paper mills and a risky repositioning of the company. The financial institutions reviled the strategy and the share price plummeted. The strategy eventually succeeded. Inevitably, the company, rather than the leader, became the hero of the tale.

Similar stories were told of the other relatively unheralded level-five leaders. Mockler, CEO of Gillette from 1975 to 1991, was 'a reserved, gracious man with a gentle almost patrician manner . . . who fought off three bitter take-over attempts'. George Cain, of Abbott laboratories, did not have an inspiring personality, but he had 'inspired standards', which led him to deal ruthlessly with nepotism in his family business, resulting in its ultimate transformation. Charles Walgreen was another quiet but strong-willed leader, whose gentle 'invitations to act' were as effective as more strident approaches. Again, through his leadership, unwelcomed transformation occurred, taking a food-service company into over-the-counter medicines.

With some enthusiasm, Collins contrasts two contemporary figures: Darwin Smith of Kimberly Clark with Al Dunlap of Scott Paper. 'Chain Saw Al' had become a business celebrity for his exploits in companies, primarily through ruthless downsizing. After less than two years at Scott Paper, Dunlap (not known for his modesty) announced that he was leading what would be one of the greatest and fastest corporate turnarounds. In his autobiography, he had described himself as a corporate Rambo. This particular morality tale ends with Dunlap's Scott Paper collapsing, and eventually being taken over by Smith's Kimberly Clark.

According to Collins, in roughly two-thirds of the comparison companies, continued mediocrity of performance was associated with leaders whom he described as having 'gargantuan egos'. That is not to say these leaders were unsuccessful. On the contrary, many were lauded for their instant success and their dynamism. The same leaders perpetrated the myth through their enthusiasm for self-publicity ('in the interests of their company', they might have believed). The fifth-level leader offers insights into leadership (and perhaps not a little comfort) to many leaders and researchers.

CM 4.4: Jay Conger and the Dilemmas of Charismatic Leadership

Jay Conger helps us to appreciate the importance of empowerment, and also the dilemmas associated with the concept. For example, he acknowledges that empowerment contradicts the stereotype of a leader as having to demonstrate an omniscience which includes a sort of all-powerful influence over his followers.

He illustrates this in a study of leaders of major business organizations who have been nominated for their exceptional qualities. He observes the growing emphasis, in writings on change, on the importance of instilling people with a sense of power. Put simply, the theory suggests that the first step is to establish self-fulfilling mind-sets: *'you can if you think you can'*. Conversely, *'and if you think you can't, you probably can't'*.

Conger offers a theoretical rationale from work on social learning theory, predicting that individuals feel more self-determined when they encounter four kinds of experience:

- *Evidence (feedback) that they are actually being successful.* This justifies the emphasis placed by many effective leaders on breaking down large goals into achievable smaller tasks. This is the most significant of the four kinds of personal experience.
- *Recognition of progress, by words of encouragement.*
- *General emotional support*, which becomes particularly important under conditions of high stress.
- *Powerful role models.*

At times, the leaders *jolted their followers out of a debilitating sense of negativity and behavioural impotence.*

The leadership jolts are highly specific to the situations, so that attempts to blindly follow the examples may be utterly counter-productive. For example, Conger tells of a newly installed leader facing a demoralized group of young employees. Shortly after his appointment, the leader takes part in a miserable meeting, with sullen indications of low morale from the participants. There seemed to be widespread disbelief that the new leader would be able to change anything. The leader, in what was described as a playful manner, pulled out a squirt-gun (a water pistol) and squirted its contents over one of the employees. This served to shock them into realizing that he was not just another boss expected to be the same as all the others. The shock appeared to work.

Conger considers that the leader's action was effective only if it is understood in terms of the situation. Specifically, it was an action completely different from those associated with the (disliked) previous leader, who kept a psychological distance from his employees.

However, he warns of the dangers of charisma. Such leaders may earn admiration, yet they may work on the frailties of others through effective communication- and impression-management skills. Conger presented evidence of various leaders who were at first hailed as exemplary and charismatic and later decried as misguided and, in some instances, worse. His examples are now only of historical interest. He suggested that these leaders had exceptional skills in anticipating a future opportunity and articulating it in a way that convinced and inspired others.

He has also pointed to a pattern of dysfunctional behaviours suggesting a pathological sense of invulnerability which becomes more evident over time.[25] For successful leaders, the diet of adulation and unconditional respect reinforces belief in the rightness of their 'vision'. Thomas Edison, for example, pioneered direct electrical current (DC) for urban power grids, and this seems to have blinded him to the benefits of alternating power (AC) systems.

Three mutually reinforcing factors are described as contributing to the downfall of the charismatic leader. The first is the leader's relationship with the vision.[26] The second is the manner in which the leader communicates, including communications connecting with the vision and its corporate impact. Finally, there are aspects of the style of charismatic leaders.

The leader's utter commitment to the vision (which he or she may have created) risks the shift from single-mindedness to obsessive behaviours. Conger refers to the ancient tale of Pyrrhus, the general who remained true to his military objective and eventually won a military victory – at a devastating ultimate cost to his cause. We still refer to a pyrrhic victory in which a battle was won at an overwhelming cost to longer-term goals.

The communication skills of the visionary leader are widely acknowledged. As the vision becomes less grounded in available evidence and more an extension of the leader's personality needs, the communications become less authentic. Techniques that gain commitment and dependence become exaggerated. They may depend increasingly on distortions of the evidence and on stereotyping of the enemy (within, or without). The process is one that is often accepted as necessary and legitimate for leaders whose progress remains acceptable. For example, it is common for a charismatic leader to pour scorn on outsiders. The insiders are 'people like us'.[27] In his early days at Apple, Steve Jobs achieved a highly motivated team working on his own projects, while belittling other groups.

The thrust of Conger's analysis is that visionary leadership may be associated with a dark side. Some leaders may remain vigilant to deal with the dangers of self-aggrandizement, for example. Others may have their egotistical style reinforced by the adulation of and dependence exhibited by their followers.

Important studies of the dark side of charismatic leadership have been made by the Dutch social scientist Manfred Kets de Vries[28] and by Barbara Kellerman at Harvard.[29]

Kets de Vries points to the psychological weaknesses that often accompany the traits associated with enormous energy, ingenuity, and commitment. These may have a dark side that is revealed as obsessional or narcissistic behaviours. Nevertheless, driven by a sense to prove their self-worth, the charismatic leader may create innovative products and businesses, to the benefit of society.[30] Kellerman's work provides a taxonomy of dysfunctional leadership, from the milder forms of narcissism to the behaviours associated with the pathologically disturbed.

INTEGRATION

The fundamental story told in this chapter is that of charismatic leadership and its re-emergence within New Leadership thinking. Charismatic leadership, and its newer form, transformational leadership, regardless of the differences between them, both stand in contrast with earlier transactional forms of leadership. The fundamental difference is that transactional leadership is essentially a means of economic exchange. One feature of such theory is the ultimate rationality of transactional exchanges. It is possible to conceive of the system without the intervention of leaders who 'make a difference'. Indeed, the basic economic principles taught in business schools remain wedded to transactional processes. Leadership remains taught largely as a specialized elective, or implicit within such core modules as strategy, technology and project management, and organizational behaviour.

Charisma in its earliest forms was rooted in ideas of mystical and religious 'super heroes'. This mapping became a target for modernizing thinkers and the shift to transformational leadership, with its preference for psychologizing the concept through accurate measurement of leadership features. The readings in this chapter suggest the numerous dilemmas that can be derived from their ideas and implications.

- *The extrapolation dilemma* Our models of leadership began with studies of political leaders. How far can we extrapolate our understanding of historical figures like President John Kennedy or Prime Minister Margaret Thatcher to gain insights into leaders in contemporary business organizations? In what ways might different cultures and contexts influence the practice of transformational leadership?
- *The inclusion dilemma* Charisma and transformational leadership are 'top-down' theories. What 'space' do they leave for leaders at other organizational levels? Does this imply 'transformation at the top, transaction below'?
- *The maverick dilemma* To whom is the 'pure' charismatic leader accountable? Is it to the proposed 'vision'? If so, how does the leader remain accountable within complex constituencies (for example, in public service organizations)?
- *The tyrant dilemma* Conger and others warn of the consequences of charismatic styles as reinforcing leaders' feelings of invincibility. Petty tyrants, as well as dictators, are vulnerable to a belief in their own invulnerability. Yet Burns, Bass, and Conger are among the scholars who accept the dark side of charismatic leadership while promoting the new-leadership belief that transformational leadership shifts followers from narrow self-interest to wider ('loftier') and more socially coherent perspectives.

GETTING PERSONAL

The various readings offer many opportunities for connecting them with personal leadership challenges. The following points are based on classroom and internet discussions around the topics of charismatic and transformational leadership. The issues are posed in the conversational format in which they took place (Box 4.4).

Box 4.4: Discussions on Charisma and Transformational Leadership

- In my culture it is impolite to be a certain kind of leader. It is difficult for me to speak up loudly in teams, from my early days. I want a career in an international organization. What can I do to become a transformational leader?

  A transformational leader does not have to be a dominating personality. Indeed, the fifth-level leaders described in this chapter are quiet but of firm resolve. Also, cultures differ, and some cultures are more collectivist, so that their leaders are more often modest rather than extrovert.[31]

- I have been a successful leader in several different jobs and have worked hard at my career. Now I am in charge of a large national institution. I know that I am good at influencing my people and gaining their loyalty and motivation. In most of the jobs, I have found politics and opposition to my ideas, and I have even been accused of being too loyal to my own department or team.

  Your description seems to be of actions associated with transformational leaders outlined in the chapter. Did you study the dilemmas of such a style (for example in Conger's work in CM 4.4)?

- I am in charge of a group of highly qualified scientific professionals. They are motivated to succeed scientifically, but respond only to scientific logic. They are particularly resistant to any attempt to play on their emotions. Transformational leadership, and particularly a charismatic style, does not seem appropriate in my role.

  Transformational leadership is not the only show in town for all leaders at all times. You may find it worthwhile to re-examine the contingency maps of leadership described in Box 4.2.

- Can you be transformational without empowering your people?

  You may be able to introduce changes which transform the organization by concentrating on expressing your strategy clearly and communicating it. The maps of charismatic leadership are full of examples. Henry Ford is more known for 'Fordism' than for empowering his employees. The New Leadership movement in the 1980s introduced the idea that transformation of structures goes hand in hand with transformation of people. The pioneers of transformational leadership would argue strongly that the great transforming leaders transformed the values of individuals beyond self-interest. See Burns (CM 4.1) for a thorough examination of the dilemmas of empowerment.

■ I sometimes wonder if I have what it takes to be a leader. [A medical professional]

I understand from colleagues that this has become an important issue for medical staff who are expected to show leadership capabilities as part of their professional development. You will already have had experience of one of the dilemmas of leadership, in finding ways of dealing with anxious people needing professional reassurance without misleading them. The ambiguities of the relationship produce what has been called the mask of command.[32] One consolation is that in broader leadership decision-taking you do not have to present the mask of command in quite the same way. Note also that leaders do not have to be charismatic (e.g. CM 4.3).

SUMMARY

In this chapter we have seen how the early explanations of charisma invoked mythological beliefs. The concept was revived by Weber, but remained somewhat peripheral in the dominant theories of scientific management. It was to be rediscovered and modified during the rise of New Leadership theories in the 1980s.

Nevertheless, the older ideas persisted and became embedded in popular use to describe a style of leadership which is regarded as 'special'. Furthermore, the more limited situations, essentially in religious transformations, became extended to modern political contexts, and then to business and sporting environments. Such popular notions of the 'special one', while retaining Weber's idea of an individual considered to be 'extraordinary',[33] and becoming powerful in times of distress or crisis.[34]

Within New Leadership, the idea of transformational leadership became an important element, following the work of Burns. Bass and his co-workers provided a full-range model of leadership. The model was supported with methodologically sound inventories which could be factor analysed into leadership styles. This work presents leaders as having a range of styles, transformational modes being an *addition* to transactional ones, rather than a replacement for them.

The New Leadership maps presented leadership as occurring throughout organizations. It was a shift away from top-down control, and popularized leadership development programmes for employees (such as team leaders) of lower organizational status.

The New Leadership theories have also tended to associate transformational leadership ('new charisma') with follower empowerment. Such a view is a particular point of difference from older maps of charisma. The so-called dark side of leadership poses particular problems to the New Leadership position of moral rectitude and ethical values. These issues tend to have been ignored in biographies and autobiographies of leaders, which have tended to emphasize the virtues of transformational leaders in achieving change. As we have shown, the approach throws up challenging dilemmas of theory and action. The evidence of modest yet deeply committed 'fifth level' leaders helps us to broaden our understanding of leadership excellence.

Exercise 4.2 invites you to reflect on your personal view of charisma. You may find it useful to complete the exercise after revising the notes you made in Exercise 4.1.

Exercise 4.2: Big C and Little C Charisma

In Chapter 10 you will come across the concepts of Big C creativity and Little C creativity.[35] Children are creative in a 'Little C' way; great scientists are creative in a 'Big C' way.

Exercise 4.2 Discussion Questions

1 How might this sort of distinction apply to explaining different ways of mapping charisma?
2 Can you explain how the maps have been influenced by different theoretical perspectives on human behaviour?

[Exercise for class discussion or personal reflection.]

NOTES

1 Jay Conger, quoted in www.bloomberg.com/news/2011–01–20/apple-after-steve-jobs-less-charismatic-more-corporate-commentary.html, downloaded 8 May 2011.
2 Arneson, S. (2009) 'The power of charisma', *Leadership Examiner*, 26 October, downloaded 11 May 2010, www.examiner.com/x-652-Leadership-Examiner~y2008m10d26-The-Power-of-Charisma.
3 http://leaderswedeserve.wordpress.com/2009/03/12/no-mourinho-magic-in-manchester/.
4 http://money.cnn.com/magazines/fortune/fortune_archive/1996/01/15/207161/index.htm, downloaded 11 April 2010.
5 Bass (1985) *Leadership and performance beyond expectations*, New York: Free Press, p. 31.
6 See Froud, J., Johal, S., Leaver, A., & Williams, K. (2006) *Financialization and strategy*, Oxford and New York: Routledge, pp. 49ff. for a discussion of this.

7 Potts, J. (2009) *A history of charisma*, Basingstoke, Hants: Palgrave Macmillan.

8 Strictly speaking, the more widespread and linguistically related term for the gift in Greek texts was *charis* (χάρισ). Charisma (χάρισμα) was a more obscure term which was to lead to much theological debate when it was appropriated into the doctrines of the early Christian church.

9 The table is developed from Potts (2009) but draws also on Bryman (1992) and MacCulloch, D. (2009) *A history of Christianity*, London: Allen Lane.

10 Ibid., p. 53.

11 Potts, J. (2009) *A history of charisma*, Basingstoke, Hants: Palgrave Macmillan, p. 50.

12 Ibid., p. 53.

13 Weber, M. (1947) *The theory of social and economic organization*, Henderson, A.M., & Parsons, T. (trans.), Parsons, T. (ed.), New York: Free Press (original work, 1924); Giddens, A. (1971) *Capitalism and modern social theory: An analysis of the writings of Marx Durkheim and Max Weber*, Cambridge, UK: Cambridge University Press.

14 Potts, J. (2009) *A history of charisma*, Basingstoke, Hants: Palgrave Macmillan, p. 195.

15 Burns, J.M. (1978) *Leadership*, New York: Harper & Row.

16 Avolio, B.J., & Bass, B.M. (1991) *The full range of leadership development: Basic and advanced manuals*, Binghamton, NY: Bass, Avolio, & Associates.

17 Hunt, J.G. (1991) *Leadership: A new synthesis*, Newbury Park, CA: Sage.

18 House, R.J. (1971) 'A path-goal theory of leader effectiveness', *Administrative Science Quarterly*, 16, 321–339.

19 Hersey, P., & Blanchard, K. (1988) *Management of organizational behavior*, 4th edn, Englewood Cliffs, NJ: Prentice Hall. See also Chapter 2.

20 House, R.J., & Mitchell, T.R. (1974) 'Path-goal theory of leadership', *Contemporary Business*, 3, Fall, 81–98. A good summary can be found in http://changingminds.org/disciplines/leadership/styles/path_goal_leadership.htm, downloaded 11 August 2010.

21 Hunt, J.G. (1991) *Leadership: A new synthesis*, Newbury Park, CA: Sage, p. 187. The motivational model draws on McClelland, D.C. (1985) *Human motivation*, Glenview, IL: Scott, Foresman.

22 Avolio, B.J., & Bass, B.M. (1991) *The full range of leadership development: Basic and advanced manuals*, Binghamton, NY: Bass, Avolio, & Associates.

23 Bass, B.M. (1998) *Transformational leadership: Industrial military and educational impact*, Mawah, NJ: Lawrence Erlbaum.

24 Collins, J.C., & Porras, J.I. (1994) *Built to last: Successful habits of visionary companies*, New York: Random House.

25 Festinger, L. (1957) *A theory of cognitive dissonance*, Stanford, CA: Stanford University Press.

26 Conger takes for granted that the process of charismatic leadership is bound up in the vision and impact it has within the organization. This has become New Leadership orthodoxy.

27 Margaret Thatcher had a fondness for the description of insiders as 'people like us', with its implied rejection of outsiders. But the quote can be traced to Rudyard Kipling: www.transition-dynamics.com/weandthey.html, downloaded 12 August 2010.

28 Kets de Vries, F.R. (1994) 'The leadership mystique', *Academy of Management Executive*, 8, 3, 73–93.

29 Kellerman, B. (2004) *Bad leadership: What it is, how it happens, why it matters*, Cambridge, MA: Harvard University Press.

30 For reasons we leave our readers to explain, a disproportionate number of highly disturbed individuals seem to find their way to the top of the creative industries.

31 Claims can also be made that extraversion is a general trait more associated with leadership than is introversion. Fortunately for introverts, contrary examples can be found. It may be accurate to say that there are more extraverts than introverts in leadership positions, although this will be subject to contingent factors.

32 http://leaderswedeserve.wordpress.com/2009/10/12/authentic-leadership-and-the-mask-of-command/.

33 Weber, E.S. III, cited in Bryman, A. (1992) *Charisma and leadership in organizations*, Newbury Park, CA and London, UK: Sage, p. 24.

34 Weber, E.S. III, in ibid.

35 Beghetto, R.A., & Kaufman, J.C. (2007) 'Toward a broader conception of creativity: A case for mini-c creativity', *Psychology of Aesthetics, Creativity, and the Arts*, 1, 2, 73–79. [doi: 10.1037/1931–3896.1.2.73].

CHAPTER LEARNING OBJECTIVES

Learning focus
■ Socially constructed knowledge as an alternative reality to the DRM

Key issues
■ The management of meaning
■ Sense making
■ Symbolic leadership

Dilemmas
■ The reality of socially constructed knowledge
■ The continued appeal of 'essentialism'
■ Dilemmas of multiple realities
■ Dilemmas of the return of archaic mythological beliefs

Platforms of understanding
■ POU 5.1 The Management of Meaning: Smircich and Morgan's Map
■ POU 5.2 Symbolism and Leadership (Turner's Map)

Contextual materials
■ CM 5.1 Paths of Change: McWhinney's Study of Mythic and Other Leadership Realities
■ CM 5.2 Organizational Culture and Leadership: Ed Schein's Contributions
■ CM 5.3 Weick and Sense-making
■ CM 5.4 The Symbolism of a Business Leader: The Case of Peter F

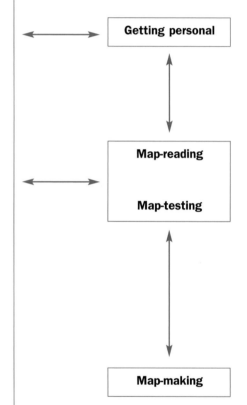

Getting personal

Map-reading

Map-testing

Map-making

5 SHARED MEANINGS AND WHY MYTHS MATTER
MAPPING THE SYMBOLIC AND THE CULTURAL

The symbolic leadership concept assumes that reality, created and lived by employees in companies is a social construction, with leadership being a part of this reality.[1]

Albert Einstein once stated: 'Concerning matter, we have been all wrong. What we have called matter is energy, whose vibration has been so lowered as to be perceptible to the senses . . . in other words, "Perception is Reality".'[2]

Barack Obama was at one time the symbol of hope to the post-baby boomers. The President, however, has lost this position of symbolic leadership, perhaps irretrievably, due to a worsening economy and an incoherent foreign policy.[3]

Madame President, speaking here in Dublin Castle it is impossible to ignore the weight of history, as it was yesterday when you and I laid wreaths at the Garden of Remembrance.[4]

The quotations at the start of this chapter show the importance attributed to symbolic leadership. But they do not offer clear indications about its nature. Before examining the topic in more detail you are invited to record your own working definition and understanding of symbolic leadership by completing Exercise 5.1. If you have no recollection of coming across the term before, you are challenged to put into your own words what sense you make of the term, based on the quotations above. You are advised to complete this exercise rapidly, without searching for further information from this chapter or seeking information from other sources.

Exercise 5.1: Your working definition and understanding of symbolic leadership

Without further reference to the contents of this chapter or referral to other texts or authorities:

1 Write down your personal working definition of symbolic leadership.
2 Can you think of an action carried out by President Obama which you believe had a powerful symbolic impact on those witnessing it?
3 What sense do you think might have been made of his actions by people who witnessed them?

[Exercise for personal reflection or for classroom or tutorial discussion.]

The questions raised in Exercise 5.1 will be easier to answer after you have studied the contents of this chapter. All three questions are concerned with examining symbolic leadership. They indicate how sense-making is an important aspect of understanding its map.

ORIENTATION

Chapter 5 suggests that concepts such as leadership may be thought of as social constructions based on interpretations and 'reading' of situations. This approach has become part of a scholarly movement critical of what is regarded as an overemphasis on the rationality of individuals and organizations. It differs profoundly from the dominant maps based on theories and practices within the natural sciences.

One of the most fundamental differences is the abandoning of the rational idea of a correct way of understanding a social 'world'. It is replaced by the ambiguities of a world of multiple meanings that draw on perceptions.

Earlier chapters have shown the impact of dominant rational beliefs about human beings and their relationships to the natural world. Emphasis was placed on the valued and scientific status of facts and the rational processes through which facts are evaluated and justified. These ideas contributed to an accepted world-view of economic and cultural progress across successive eras, through scientific advances and technical innovation. The view is so powerful that it tends to dismiss alternative perspectives in pejorative terms such as irrational, emotional, or primitive.

Unreflective acceptance of the DRM made it difficult for alternative perspectives to emerge. Attempts to deal with dilemmas of leadership resulted in new ideas, but these were found to be strongly influenced by the DRM. In Chapter 4 we saw how even some aspects of the New Leadership maps of the 1980s were addressed through methods which drew on DRM beliefs of rational action and transactional exchanges.

Nevertheless, alternative ways of seeing and understanding our world had been recognized as having well-developed and coherent underpinnings which were distinct from the DRM. The approaches were gaining credibility within a wide range of studies in the social sciences long before the 1980s watershed in leadership research.

A ferment of ideas had begun to be introduced into organizational theory, drawing on a range of disciplines and paradigmatic maps favoured among social scientists. They came under various labels such as post-structuralism, symbolic interactionism, social constructivism, sense-making, critical theory, and postmodernism. A working definition would cover elements that are important in understanding the concept and that will be found consistent with the texts and maps you will come across in this chapter:

> Symbolic leadership concerns itself with *communicating* a *story* whose *meaning* is assessed through *interpreting* its *symbolic* aspects.

From earliest times, cultural beliefs were captured and conveyed in stories which were passed on through artefacts such as paintings, poems, and written texts. Such accounts are now regarded as mythological representations explaining the nature of an experienced world.

Our working definition should not be taken to assume that a story has only one meaning. As will be shown, a leader's intentions are open to various interpretations. Indeed, even the leader may be struggling with different perspectives in arriving at a coherent story or narrative. The shift will provide a further way of understanding charisma, and particularly the symbolic processes associated with it. We see more clearly the nature of leadership visions, how they become shared within an organizational culture, and what happens if they are not shared. The more formal terminology is that organizational reality is socially constituted, or socially constructed.[5]

For readers with a technical or professional training, this will appear both new and, perhaps, suspect. This chapter may be particularly important in introducing you to a deeper understanding of perception and reality. You may also find yourself broadening your beliefs about leadership to include a willingness to consider reality as constructed by the words and actions of the leader and the wider group involved in the situation. Emphasis shifts from a belief in rationality as the only way of approaching questions and dilemmas about truth, to a socially constructed reality, with emphasis on meanings and symbolism. This shift helps us to understand that visions may arise, and their significance for organizational leadership.

Our first platform of understanding, POU 5.1, deals with a study by Smircich and Morgan.[6] It is based on the concept of leadership as the *management of meaning*, popularized by the writings of Karl Weick (covered in CM 5.3).[7] It immediately confronts us with a challenge. Social sense-making processes result in the production of shared meanings created jointly by leaders and followers. An important implication of this work is the possibility of multiple meanings. The management of meaning removes the possibility of there being one correct way of understanding a social 'world'.

POU 5.2 is based on the work of the sociologist Barry Turner. He argues for the need to understand organizations through sensitivity to their symbolic and cultural environments.[8] Turner suggests that such an approach reveals what remains hidden if organizations are understood only through their structures and functions. In this, he shares with Smircich and Morgan opposition to the DRM. They also agree in seeing the merits of analysis through examining multiple perspectives rather than claiming a new dominant mapping to replace the DRM. Turner considers that new forms of understanding of organizations will tend to be more participative and sensitive to cultural aspects of change.

The theme of symbolic leadership is continued in the contextual materials. CM 5.1 explores a typology proposed by Will McWhinney. He suggests that symbolic leadership or myth-making is one of the most powerful of the general paths (life journeys) taken by leaders as they change and attempt to bring about change.[9]

CM 5.2 summarizes Ed Schein's view of corporate culture and how it is created, embedded, developed, manipulated, managed, and changed. He considers that culture is at least partly determined through leadership, and that culture defines leadership, which in turn contributes to the processes of culture change.[10]

CM 5.3 examines Karl Weick's much-cited work on sense-making as the process which shapes beliefs about social reality.[11]

CM 5.4 outlines the (anonymous) reflections of an industrial business leader. It shows the importance he attributes intuitively to the symbolic impact of his actions throughout his extensive leadership career.

PLATFORMS OF UNDERSTANDING

POU 5.1: The Management of Meaning: Smircich and Morgan's Map

Smircich and Morgan wrote an influential paper which appeared in the 1980s, at a time when interest was growing in the New Leadership ideas discussed in Chapters 2 and 4.

Their work was developed within a network of researchers who considered that symbolism and organizational culture could be powerful means of understanding organizational life.[12]

Their approach constituted a fundamental shift away from the rationality dominating business school courses. The new perspective provided a way of examining important aspects of organizations, such as the stability of beliefs, acceptance of the authority of leaders to lead, commitment to, or resistance to, change. The cultural theorists believed that prevailing maps of organizational life placed too much emphasis on rational and individualistic structures and processes. Organizational symbolists often acknowledged the influence of Berger and Luckmann, and their much-quoted text *The Social Construction of Reality*.[13]

Smircich and Morgan brought to a wider management audience the conception of organizations as socially constructed systems. The social perceptions of individuals within groups are regarded not as 'mere' subjective beliefs to be contrasted with objective reality. Rather, the concept is that perceptions create the reality. Smircich and Morgan departed from formal sociological terminology, preferring Weick's vocabulary of *the management of meaning*. Using illustrations from empirical studies of unstructured, and apparently leaderless, group situations, the two researchers suggest that the management of meanings plays an influential role in shaping the reality maps of their colleagues and staff. There may be a struggle for formal leadership to evolve.

The authors suggest that in such situations:

■ Leadership is a social process defined through interaction.
■ Leadership involves defining reality in ways that make sense to followers.
■ Leadership inevitably requires that some individuals give up their power to interpret and define reality to others.
■ Formal leadership roles emerge, and with them the rights and obligations of the leaders to define the system of shared meanings are recognized.

Smircich and Morgan accept much of Weber's broad analysis of modern business as constituted through formal rules and procedures provided to employees. Authority patterns and work practices become accepted influences through which an individual makes sense of working life. A pattern of unconscious dependency relationships is thus established. In particular, this institutionalization specifies that organizational reality is defined by a boss, or manager or leader, acting on behalf of 'the organization'. Leaders set and direct the rules, and followers comply with them.

Leadership actions may be seen as (more or less conscious) attempts to shape and interpret situations, influencing a common interpretation of reality for followers. Smircich and Morgan conceptualize the formal leadership process in terms of a relationship between what they term figure and ground – the person and the context. Leadership or 'leading' is seen as a form of action that seeks to shape its context.[14]

This is illustrated by an ethnographic ('fly on the wall') study carried out within a large insurance company. The president had taken personal charge of responding to evidence of the functioning of the sales function. His goal was to eliminate a backlog of orders and motivate the staff. The authors analysed how the project led to different and competing interpretations of reality. The leader, a Mr Hall, believed that his interventions would provide a meaningful way for the company to make progress.

At the start of the initiative, Mr Hall was impressed by the efforts of which he became aware as he became involved himself in the day-to-day activities arising. He saw that his plan was working. Unfortunately, his senior management team saw things very differently. They doubted whether the plan would succeed in addressing either the short-term or longer-term issues. The plan was ultimately unsuccessful.

This case example reveals how Mr Hall's attempts to lead a change programme were carried out on the assumption that change is primarily a matter of planning and executing a plan. A management-of-meaning perspective, as indicated above, suggests that he had been insensitive to the possibility that his perception of reality made little sense to followers. Perhaps, as Smircich and Morgan suggest, the leader needed to redefine his 'reality' in ways that made sense to his colleagues, giving up his presumed leadership entitlement to having the 'right' way of seeing things.

The case example illustrates the nature of multiple perceptions of reality. The issue is not that employees were wrong in the way they saw their world, or had wrongly misunderstood Mr Hall's perspective. It is, rather, that there is no right or wrong perspective. Each defines itself, and 'owns' its reality. The general point is that the management of meaning removes the possibility of there being one correct way of understanding a social 'world'. It is replaced by the ambiguities of a world of multiple meanings.

As shown in Box 5.1, the management-of-meaning approach has much in common with the processes of learning and change.

Box 5.1: The Management of Meaning as an Alternative to the Dominant Rational Model for Understanding Organization Processes

Smircich and Morgan drew on earlier contributions in constructing their map of the management of meaning in POU 5.1. Some years earlier, Gareth Morgan had drawn attention to alternative sociological paradigms which were being excluded through the dominant sociological paradigm of objectivity and control.[15] Morgan later simplified the theoretical treatment into a book of *Images of Organization* which replaced the vocabulary of paradigms with one of everyday symbols to represent socially constructed organizational cultures.[16]

Morgan argues that 'our theories and explanations of organizational life are built on metaphors that lead us to see and understand organizations . . . by using different metaphors . . . we are able to design and manage organizations in ways we may not have thought possible before'.[17]

Morgan provided the machine metaphor to illustrate the DRM way of thinking. His other maps included organizations as cultures, as psychic prisons, biological organisms, and information-processing networks. Other researchers have drawn directly or indirectly on Morgan's work to offer alternative maps and metaphors helpful in the symbolic analysis of organizations.[18]

POU 5.2: Symbolism and Leadership (Turner's Map)

Barry Turner, in his work on the symbolic understanding of organizations,[19] acknowledges his debt to the Jungian concept of *archetypes*[20] as culturally shared symbol systems. Jung placed great emphasis on the ancient and mythic as residual and psychologically important influences on individuals. Turner examines attempts to address the nature and significance of symbolism in organizational studies. He recognizes the contribution of cultural theorists (as described in POU 5.1) in raising the profile of symbolism, although largely outside established organizational theory.

He points out that, for organizational leaders and employees alike, considerations of the nature of reality do not intrude directly into their daily work or thoughts. The nature of reality has been a concern of philosophers down the centuries, through to a generation of contemporary social theorists. If we wish to associate leadership with the management of meaning we need some indications of a higher-level conceptualization of 'the meaning of meaning'.

He suggests that the organizational culture movement has largely ignored the wider debate, which he refers to as the *structural allegory*. This is a shorthand expression to indicate the schools of cultural thought whose work has disputed the notion that the social world is best explained as having a reality that can be established beyond doubt. This movement includes those who have been labelled postmodernists, structuralists, and post-structuralists. The varied and pluralistic ideas to be found depart from dominant models of reality, and beliefs in scientifically or rationally grounded evidence:

- Structuralists place great importance on interpretation of the codes within cultural life. Thus they are said to be concerned not so much with meaning, but with the way in which meaning is produced.[21]
- Structuralist ideas indicate the absence of a specific and unique relationship between the elements of a text (or images within a visual 'text' such as a poem, a story, or a painting) and some absolute reality.
- Post-structuralists deny any possibility of an authoritative explanation within a text.[22]

Citing the postmodernist Baudrillard, Turner suggests that meanings are created, but that they have the nature of illusions. Their reality lies in the beliefs of people in the (observed) sign. He presents us with the concept of a simulacrum – that which has *cultural reality* and is believed in, and is replicated although there was no original physical entity. In such a treatment, concern for 'what is real' is replaced by awareness that cultural life is moving to a form of reality shaped by symbols.

Turner suggests that treatments of the symbolic need not inevitably return us to mythic and mystical interpretations of the social world. He speculates that understanding culture offers escape from the dominance of powerful but mythological symbols. He is indicating that the escape is likely to come from participatory cultural forms.

Metaphoric thinking helps in the process of sense-making. Metaphors of animals seem to connect us to very early ways in which humans made sense of their environment. Box 5.2 illustrates this with the metaphor of the mandrill.

Box 5.2: Mandrill Management: Examining Its Symbolic Significance

Animals have been worshipped within many religious traditions, and leaders have long been associated with the courage and strength of a lion, or fleetness of foot of a cheetah, or the great vision of an eagle, surveying the world coolly from a lofty vantage point. We think of foxes as 'cunning', and perhaps 'cruel' if they break into a henhouse. We also often describe humans in terms of animals (which may, in a complicated way, be no more than projecting back onto humans those human properties used to describe animals). One recent species that has been studied is the mandrill, which has been identified as exhibiting behaviours associated with tyrannical human leaders.[23]

In this case study we examine the evidence and test the map with information on symbolic leadership processes.

1 *A visit to the zoo*

A visit to the zoo reveals different leader behaviours in different species. Some species, such as the chimpanzees, engage in a complex mix of violence and collaboration, with the leader appearing to display both kinds of behaviour. One animal, the mandrill, captures the imagination of visitors in a particularly powerful way. Regardless of the sophistication of the observers, their discussion quickly reveals the powerful symbolic impact of the experience.

The leader of a troupe of mandrills demonstrates dominance through highly confrontational and physical means. The leader is the physically strongest animal, and has the brightest displayed colouring, in particular, its vivid scarlet nose. Mating is a violent, non-consensual process.

One particular feature of the behaviour of mandrill leaders leaves a particular impression on visitors. A great deal of interactions of the leader with troupe members seem directed towards maintaining the leadership position. The battle for leadership, once lost to a younger contender, is rarely regained. As another symbolic consequence, a deposed leader loses its status. It even loses its colouring, the bright-scarlet nose of the troupe leader biologically linked to testosterone levels.

The story of the mandrill leads to considerable discussion among managers. Some find it a powerful metaphor to help them to understand behaviours of leaders with which they were familiar.

2 The anthropomorphic assumption

Socio-biologists warn us against attributing human characteristics to animals (the anthropomorphic assumption). They point out that perceptions of cruelty are based on human values and ethical standards. These judgements should not be mapped onto animal species.

3 Social identity and sense-making approaches

Animals, as indicated above, have long provided symbolic ideas from which we derive insights into human behaviour. Identity theorists ask corporate executives which animal best describes their organization, and which animal best describes its ideal future form. In one course, an executive stated that he believed it to be most like a mole, unable to sense much that was going on in the world above its subterranean home. Contrastingly, executives from the same organization subsequently nominated a hawk as the creature they would most prefer to identify their company with. The search for identity is assisted by comparisons of self and others. From the earliest cultures, humans have attempted to explore such questions by reference to the natural world. We make more sense of our identities as individuals and as members of a social group when we compare the 'otherness' of people and of projections.

4 The symbolism of cruelty and the psychopathic leader

The story observed within the mandrill community makes sense to employees across a wide range of organizations. The mandrill stands for or symbolizes the violent, competitive, and bullying leader. The story ends with the confrontational deposing of the leader, accompanied by loss of status.

5 What can we learn from the mandrill leader?

The mandrill story (or map) may be tested against the concerns of comparing the animal world with the world of human experience. Are we comfortable with the idea that we are no more than another species of ape in our social behaviours? One resolution might be to accept the story as a metaphor in which sense is made of the mandrill leader as a morality tale in which a drive for power has inevitable consequences.

At the start of the chapter a working definition was suggested for symbolic leadership as concerning itself with *communicating* a *story* whose *meaning* is assessed through *interpreting* its *symbolic* aspects. The story of mandrill management can serve as a way of making sense of behaviours experienced in the workplace which we may choose to explore and communicate with others.

The story might suggest that followers of such a leader may find themselves preoccupied with surviving, or with scheming to depose the leader. One dilemma is to find a way of confronting dysfunctional leadership without reinforcing the culture of violence and aggression that accompanies such leadership and organizational politics.

CONTEXTUAL MATERIAL

CM 5.1: Paths of Change: McWhinney's Study of Mythic and Other Leadership Realities

McWhinney developed a theory of change based on a classificatory scheme of four personality styles. The approach was tested by McWhinney and colleagues at IBM in the 1990s.[24]

The approach offers a means of personal development and includes ways of identifying 'ways of seeing' which are based on beliefs about reality. Conflict arises when initiation of change is resisted through different perspectives. McWhinney was still working on his theory of change when he died.[25]

His model identified four types of leadership maps indicating four archetypal leaders. Far from claiming these as newly discovered, he considered them to be related to very widespread categorizations of human differences found in many cultures, and with different names. McWhinney considered that an overreliance on one of the 'maps' hinders effectiveness in life, and particularly attempts to relate to and influence others. His own life's project may be seen as an exploration of the importance for an individual to carry out map-reading, map-testing, and map-making to achieve a personal 'path of change' and influence the paths of others. We will concentrate on the form most associated with mythology.

McWhinney's typology of leaders is:

- Idealists
- Realists
- Social relativists
- Mythics.

An account of the four forms can be found in Box 5.3, McWhinney's Four Leadership Forms.

Box 5.3: McWhinney's Four Leadership Forms

Will McWhinney's model outlined in his book *Paths to Change* (1972) is a relabelling of fundamental differences in human behaviours and beliefs.[26]

McWhinney and colleagues suggest that a four-fold characterization of differences in individual mapping of reality is found across cultures. The model has been found to relate to a range of other concepts, including the work of Myers and Briggs (developed from Jung).

■ *Idealists* hold unitary beliefs and are willing to be guided by notions that the world is of a single, pre-ordained nature; the future can be predicted from understanding of the 'true' nature of the past, and (logically) cannot be influenced by human intervention. These leaders believe in the ultimate guidance offered by a unified philosophy of leadership.
■ *Realists* hold sensory beliefs, and place their faith in knowledge whose elements can be empirically observed. The observable elements have been analysed or decomposed ('scientifically'). Sensory leaders put their faith in dealing as well as possible with the observable 'facts'.
■ *Social relativists* accept the possibilities of more than one 'truth' ('my way is my way, not the way'). Social relativists may be seen as sharing beliefs with social scientists with maps of postmodern thinking.
■ *Mythics* combine a perspective that a 'one true view' exists with a belief that a reality is what you choose to make of it. 'My way is the way'.

Extreme mythic leaders found religious or social movements. They are unshakeable in their belief in the rightness of their new belief system. For McWhinney, the charismatic leader falls into the mythic reality. However, he suggests that charismatics may be distinguished by their impact on the realities of the other domains, under which circumstances he considers them to be the most powerful agents of change. More directly relevant for business leaders is the leader whose mythic beliefs become mixed with other realities. He gives examples of prophetic charismatics such as Winston Churchill, Ronald Reagan, Mary Baker Eddy (founder of Christian Science), and (Disney's) Michael Eisner.[27] Entrepreneurial charismatics are found among impresarios and innovators. Facilitative entrepreneurs charm the members (of a team or group) into a feeling of co-ownership in the symbol's creation and propagation.[28]

Cultures are more likely to accept a charismatic leader and a symbolic view of reality when conditions are unclear and threatening. These are also circumstances in which willingness to hate and attack any 'unbelievers' becomes easier. After the banking crisis of 2007–8 several disgraced leaders were described as having charismatic personalities.[29]

McWhinney's approach has acknowledged similarities to Jung's work, particularly as this has been applied by Isabel Briggs, applying the Myers-Briggs inventory.[30]

CM 5.2: Organizational Culture and Leadership: Ed Schein's Contributions

Edgar Schein has gained an international reputation for his capacity to communicate his ideas on culture change and the symbolic. His text *Organizational Culture and Leadership*[31] stands as one of the most influential management books of the last decades of the twentieth century. In it, he provides a frequently cited theoretical definition of culture:

> A pattern of shared basic assumptions that the group learned as it solved its problems of external adaptation and internal integration, that has worked well enough to be considered valid and, therefore, to be taught to new members as the correct way you perceive, think, and feel in relation to those problems.[32]

Schein summarizes his view of corporate culture as an all-embracing phenomenon which reveals itself in terms of how it is created, embedded, developed, manipulated, managed, and changed. He considers that culture is at least partly determined through leadership, and indeed he states that culture defines leadership. Schein's map treats culture as the secret to understanding leadership and organization. Schein urged those who would understand and influence change to take an anthropological approach. This implies that there are important, perhaps unique, aspects of each organizational culture that have to be considered and discovered by any outsider ('anthropologist'), or indeed by any insider seeking deeper understanding. Such an approach involves attention to the customs and rites of the organization.

Culture is seen very much as a social construction within which meanings are established, negotiated, and retained or suppressed. The approach sits well with the view of the leader as manager of meaning. At the very least, leaders should be conscious of culture and its consequences.

Schein has provided widely accepted advice on change programmes for practitioners. His commitment to interpreted meanings sits well with a cultural perspective. He is also, nevertheless, reinforcing the unitary cultural view that was challenged by Smircich and Morgan in POU 5.1. In this respect, Joanne Martin and Peter Frost described Schein as being among those for whom culture is 'an internally consistent package of cultural manifestations that generates organization-wide consensus, usually around some set of shared values. Sub-cultures are noted only as a secondary consideration, if at all.'[33] The critique implies that he is among the many leaders and consultants who see a strategy for culture change through the formation of a coherent culture, These beliefs were popularized by Peters and Waterman in their best-selling management book, *In Search of Excellence.*[34]

CM 5.3: Weick and Sense-making

Karl Weick may be regarded as one of the main protagonists in introducing sense-making as a key issue in the field of work and organization. He argues that people are constantly trying to make sense of the contexts in which they find themselves. Thus, an understanding of leadership from the sense-making perspective requires us to examine how individuals see things rather than to seek explanations for organizational issues in terms of structures or systems (e.g. initiating structure and consideration for people).[35]

Weick is keen to differentiate sense-making from interpretation, arguing that sense-making is clearly about an activity or process, that is, it is about how individuals generate that which they interpret. Among his most-cited concepts is the notion of sense-making. According to Weick, there are at least seven characteristics that distinguish sense-making from other explanatory processes, such as understanding and interpretation. Sense-making is:

- *Grounded in identity construction* An important part of making sense of a situation concerns a person's sense of who he or she is in a setting; what threats (to this sense of self) the setting contains; and what is available to enhance, continue, and render efficacious that sense of who one is. These considerations all provide the basis for judgements of relevance.
- *Retrospective* The perceived world is actually a past world, in the sense that things are visualized and seen before they are conceptualized. Sense-making is influenced by what people notice in elapsed events, how far they look back, and how well they remember what they were doing.
- *Enactive of sensible environments* Sense-makers create their own environments for future action.
- *Social context* Sense-making is influenced by the presence of others. Sensible meanings tend to be those for which there is social support, shared relevance, and consensus.
- *On-going* The experience of sense-making is constrained not only by the past, but also by the speed at which interpretations become outdated. It is one in which people are thrown into the middle of things, and forced to act.
- *Focused on and by extracted cues* Sense-making is about the resourcefulness with which people elaborate cues into stories that selectively support initial views.
- *Driven by plausibility rather than accuracy* Sense-making is about coherence, how events hang together with a certainty that is sufficient for present purposes and credibility.

These properties of sense-making are proposed as influential in enabling people to disengage from, discard, or walk away from their initial interpretations and to adopt a newer story that they find 'makes more sense' of their circumstances. Sense-making placed in a leadership perspective might be seen as following a sequence. People concerned with identity in the social context of others (e.g. the leader and others in the situation) engage with on-going events, extracting salient cues to make plausible sense of the situation, taking into account their actions past and present. The sense-making also directs future actions.

The processes of sense-making are distinguished from interpretation and problem-solving. Weick considers interpretation to be more a matter of unfolding and revealing, whereas sense-making deals with the ways in which people achieve their interpretations. Problem-solving provides specific episodes within which sense-making occurs. Weick offers sense-making as influenced by theories of symbolism and meanings attached to objects. However, he does not consider prevailing theories to capture the essence of sense-making, which he offers as an emerging and promising set of ideas.[36]

CM 5.4: The Symbolism of a Business Leader: The Case of Peter F

Peter F is an English businessman and entrepreneur. When speaking to other executives or business students, he reveals a deeply symbolic style. He is a popular presenter at leadership electives, admired for his convincing ways of bringing his leadership experiences to life in the classroom.

He presents a commanding physical figure. He attaches considerable importance to the symbolic impact he has as a leader in as many situations as possible. He is alert to signals of weakness and untrustworthiness in others, and presents himself as someone who is emotionally robust, decisive, physically imposing, reliable, and honest. He believes that he occupies a place in which such attributes are necessary to impress, influence, and sometimes to deceive.

His story begins as he sets out on a career without formal business qualifications. At first he worked in a family firm which manufactured products for the printing and textile industries. He acquired considerable technical expertise before moving on, often obtaining jobs over more qualified applicants. He eventually became an international business manager with global financial responsibilities before becoming self-employed (reasons not given). For the first time in his life, at the age of 53, he had begun the process of writing a CV to support future career initiatives.

In the classroom, he shows that he reflects on various formative incidents in his working life. He tends to recall these as a series of leadership stories and lessons learned. His views tend to be expressed as certainties, 'Never ask for more money because you have just done a good job', rather than as the more cautious academic 'Be careful you do not lose more than you gain by the way you seek to capitalize on doing a good job'.

Peter's tips are accompanied by vivid specific examples, which are evidently significant episodes in his working life. For example, he conveys a view that leaders tread a path beset with dangers. These can be triggered by failure to follow those leadership beliefs captured in his tips. Here are some of his stories:

1 'Don't attempt a rebellion'

Once, faced with a headstrong CEO who he believed was following a faulty policy, Peter set about launching a challenge to the CEO and his views. 'I had found the main spokesman who would start the attack. I was to follow him. Other directors were then to speak, or indicate their intention to vote down the chairman. After the first rebel had his say, the chairman asked if anyone else agreed. Somewhat nervously I said I had some similar misgivings. The chairman then played his next card. "Does anyone else agree? This is a resignation matter." But no one else stepped forward although I had their agreement in advance. The first speaker was forced out of the company. I survived – just because I was doing something the company needed doing. But I was finished too, and I left a few months later.'

2 'Don't ask for more money immediately'

'I mean, don't do a good job on some project and then immediately use it to put in a pay claim. You lose out later, when you are not in that sort of position.'

3 'Look at the toilets'

'I had to go around looking at progress in thirty subsidiary companies. That doesn't give a lot of time for detailed financial studies. I worked out my own short-cuts. For example, they may tell you they are big on people management. Check that out by looking at how their workers eat and take breaks. And look at the toilets. That tells you what's really going on.'

4 'Why not just use your name [on business cards]?'

'That's what you want to be remembered by isn't it?' [Several of his 'leadership tips' indicate how sensitized Peter is to status symbols. He talks disparagingly of the widespread use of cars as status indicators. He is far from impressed by someone's title. Grand titles on business cards are the subject of his scorn.]

5 'Look behind the boasts'

'I have become suspicious when someone tells me "I don't want to be surrounded by yes-men". Usually that's the sort of person who hates it if someone disagrees with them. Then there's the person who says "I'm telling you this in confidence". Do you trust that sort of person? I don't.'

6 'Democracy and leadership'

'Democracy. It's a lovely idea, in principle. But often you can't have it as a leader. Everything is slowed up. But also, you look weak. Sometimes you have to show what's needed. What must be done.'

7 'Make a good first impression'

'When I arrive at a reception area, I never sit down. However long I'm kept waiting. Why? Because you must make a good first impression. If you sit down, what happens when the person you are visiting arrives? He's standing over you. If you are sitting down, you are at a disadvantage.'

8 'The fate of the leader'

'The fate of the leader is to be vilified eventually. Particularly by your successor, who's got to mobilize the company and show that things are changing for the better. So anything you have achieved has to be done down.'

9 'Keep your expenses honest'

'Never cheat the company you work for. It's stupid. It gets noticed. I was entertaining a client once. We stopped for me to buy petrol. I paid for the petrol on my company card, and bought some firewood, which I paid for in cash. The client told me much later that he saw then I was someone to be trusted. That was how we got the first contract with his firm.'

10 'Share bad news'

'Of course, clear communications are important for good leadership. Don't be afraid to share bad news. Sometimes there are legal reasons you have to withhold some things. But share what you know, and say what you can't announce yet. That way, your people will trust you.' Peter's views have the strength of being based on direct experience in a variety of business and leadership roles. They offer much that is worth examining. That is not to say that they have universal applicability, regardless of the situation and the culture. You can explore this further by attempting Exercise 5.2.

Exercise 5.2: Do you agree with Peter's 'Tips for Leadership Success'?

Peter gave ten tips for leadership, based on his wide experience as a leader. To what degree do you share Peter's views? To what degree might the views be universally applicable?

Use the information provided by Peter to rate each item (strongly agree to strongly disagree). Use a very high rating (5) if you believe the suggestion has universal applicability. Use a very low rating (1) if you believe the view expressed is an opinion held by Peter, but has very low generalizability across cultures and situations.

If possible, compare your ratings with those of someone from a different cultural and professional background.

	Your rating	Other rating
1 'Don't attempt a rebellion'		
2 'Don't ask for more money immediately'		
3 'Look at the toilets'		
4 'Why not just use your name [on business cards]?'		
5 'Look behind the boasts'		
6 'Democracy and leadership' [nice idea in theory]		
7 'Make a good first impression'		
8 'The fate of the leader' [to be vilified]		
9 'Keep your expenses honest'		
10 'Share bad news'		

[Exercise for individual or group work.]

INTEGRATION

The readings examined in this chapter show how leadership processes may be studied for the symbolic implications of actions. A more formal definition is offered by the theorist Ingo Winkler, who defines symbolic leadership as 'leadership which refers to, and is based on, the category of meaning'.[37]

The processes are also those through which a culture is generated and maintained. Culture consists of common values, norms, and fundamental ideas about the organization – an organization's expressive and affective dimensions, forming part of a system of shared and meaningful symbols, manifested in myths, ideology and values, and in multiple cultural artefacts (rites, rituals, metaphors, language, etc.). We have seen in POU 5.2 how leadership activities control in symbolic ways. The symbols in the executive suite and the corporate car park are constant reminders of executive power.

Smircich and Morgan, in common with other organizational researchers, suggest how constructions of reality (managing meaning) affect organizational behaviours. They set out to develop a theoretical understanding which emphasizes the sense or meaning that followers attach to the actions and articulations of the leader. To understand these processes better is to understand how the leader frames social reality and exercises influence through the followers' interpretations of their behaviour.

McWhinney develops the notion of shared meanings through his idea of leadership and myths. Myths represent institutionalized meaning structures where thought and action are related in a purposeful way. In modern organizations meaning is derived mainly from its strategic orientation. Strategy serves to develop a shared understanding of the environment through the communication of mission and vision statements.

Box 5.4: Symbolic Leadership

Leadership theorist Ingo Winkler traced the theory of symbolic leadership back to work on corporate culture as found in Schein's treatment (found here in CM 5.2).[38] Symbolic leadership is defined as leadership which refers to, and is based on, the category of meaning. Meaning becomes tangible and therefore can be experienced in the form of symbols. The concept assumes that reality, created and lived by employees in companies, is a social construction, with leadership being a part of this reality.

Symbolic leadership 'concentrates on studying values, meaning, interpretation, history, context, as well as other symbolic elements in the leadership process'.[39] It provides a promising alternative way of understanding leadership compared with what Winkler sees as more dominant rational treatments.

The leader who is aware of the symbolic content of actions and the likely sense that will be made of them is able to develop practical approaches, for example, in effective communications.

One important message is that an organization can be interpreted as having various different 'ways of seeing'. This contrasts with a popular belief that a strong leader succeeds in creating a coherent and unitary culture. In practice, symbolic leadership theory (backed up by empirical studies) suggests there may be competing realities or sub-cultures. These will resist efforts by a leader to impose changes in order to achieve a unitary culture and a shared set of beliefs. This may be one of the most important dilemmas facing an organization and its leadership.

GETTING PERSONAL

Some experienced leaders may feel that they have already been aware of the importance of the symbolic at work, even if they had not labelled it as such. Peter, in CM 5.4, was unaware of any such labelling of his actions. Yet he appears to have attributed considerable weight to the symbolic aspects of his behaviours.

Perhaps in the past you shared the view that your leadership role needed to concentrate on the factual and the rational. The maps of this chapter offer another view. Leadership is what people perceive to be the most important aspects of the leader's behaviours and actions. The actions are those of symbolic significance.

You may also find yourself shifting your understanding of leadership away from a property of the leader, and more toward the property of a reality constructed by the words and actions of the leader, and the wider group involved in the situation. The most immediate implication is that leadership is more than being allocated the role or label of leader. Simply acting out the roles of being a leader makes sense to the workforce only if the map is that of the classical, scientific management world of leaders giving orders and followers obeying them.

It may help you to understand why a leader like Peter is sensitive to the status decisions of car-parking arrangements. Should the most senior director get the best car-parking location? If so, the very recognizable vehicle reinforces its symbolic significance every time employees pass by, every day of the week. Should the directors get executive toilets, while permitting unhygienic conditions for other employees? We are not suggesting that there is a 'right' answer to such questions, although we have our preferences. Our point is that you, as a leader, may benefit from understanding why such actions are not trivial and are possibly highly significant, and how they set up recurrent patterns of behaviour within which actions shape and reinforce beliefs.

The texts in this chapter indicate ways of understanding how a leader's acts may or may not have impact through the sense made of those actions. Note that 'speech acts' are among the most common sorts of action through which symbolic interpretations become significant.

Box 5.5: Speech Acts: How to Do Things with Words

This chapter has been concerned with the management of meaning. Something said may be taken for its truth or falsity, according to some external reality. Some statements are better studied for their social intentions. We have to seek sense and intentions. A good example is what is known as 'speech acts'.

Linguist Professor Katharine Perera explains the work of philosopher J.L. Austin on such speech acts:

> As a philosopher [Austin] wanted to be able to look at uses of language that had traditionally been ignored by other philosophers. They had typically taken statements and considered them in terms of whether they were true or false. So a sentence like 'It is raining' can be judged to be true or false in relation to some external reality.
>
> He was interested in what he called 'performative utterances' ie utterances that in themselves perform an action (a speech act) . . . In these utterances it is not usually appropriate or particularly relevant to think in terms of their truth or falsity. What matters is that the speech (or writing) creates the action and that without the speech (or writing) the action cannot be effected. Speech acts are a part of social interaction because they depend upon a hearer hearing the words, so 'I apologise' has to be uttered in front of the person to whom the apology is due for it to be a true speech act.
>
> This is the definition that David Crystal gives: 'An utterance defined in terms of the intentions of the speaker and the effect it has on the listener, eg a directive.'[40]

SUMMARY

Chapter 5 represents a major shift from the content of maps studied in the first four chapters of *Dilemmas of Leadership*. It may be helpful at this stage to review the key aspects of chapters 1 to 4 as shown in Box 5.6. It illustrates the manner in which more ancient maps were modified in an attempt to find explanations more in tune with modern rational beliefs. It also shows that changes in the dominance of a map did not eliminate its influence. Ancient beliefs persist. A good example is the way in which charisma remains an important aspect of everyday maps of leadership and is accorded mysterious and even supernatural aspects. This has survived the 'New Leadership' treatment and its integration into a more modern transformational form.

Chapter 5 covers maps which draw on radical challenges to the DRM. The DRM rests on a belief in a reality that is objective and independent of individuals. The challenges treat reality as being constructed by perceptions, which are in part individual and in part shared.

A powerful element within a shared and constructed reality is its symbolism, revealed by 'reading' stories or narratives. Leaders help to establish a socially constructed reality by the symbolic potency of the stories they tell, including its visionary content.

One way of understanding the symbolic power of a story is through the process of sense-making, popularized by Karl Weick. It is also known as the management of meaning (POU 5.1).

Maps of reality as socially constructed have been influential in the social sciences and in theories of knowledge management, including those of cultural theorists such as Smircich and Morgan. They can be subsumed under two general and related schools of knowledge: postmodernism and critical theory. These maps are not without dilemmas. Turner shows how organizational beliefs may be too influenced by archaic symbolism embedded in myths that have little to offer as a means of sense-making in organizational life.

The sense-making approaches introduce alternatives to a view of social reality grounded in the DRM. We will come across further examples in subsequent chapters.

Box 5.6: Review of Leadership Maps of Chapters 1–4

1 Ancient beliefs (maps) of leadership proposed leaders as heroic figures who were granted special status and special powers.

2 Later, these maps were considered to be based on primitive belief systems and became classed as pre-modern.

3 Modern societies and modernity were believed to be better served by leaders whose actions were based on rationality and logic.

4 The rise of modern and 'enlightened' thinking was believed to be through discarding earlier beliefs and replacing them with modern methods of thinking and acting, which was to become the basis of the Dominant Rational Model (DRM).

5 The DRM was seen as central to understanding and developing modern society, and other beliefs were ignored or dismissed as pre-modern.

6 Leadership studies applied the DRM to establish 'scientifically' the fundamentals of leadership.

7 Attempts to discover the 'essence' of leadership led to further work, but retaining the belief as to the nature of the reality of the DRM, as well as retaining its methods of investigation. Failure of a map led to the emergence of a new map that retained its adherence to the DRM.

8 New Leadership appeared to move away from the DRM. Its fundamental novelty was a shift away from leadership as a rational transaction process and towards leadership as including the possibility of transformational change processes.

9 By the twenty-first century, New Leadership came to be seen as derived from the older maps, including the DRM. Transformational leadership was evaluated as a revival of the pre-modern idea of charismatic leadership, 'tamed' through the use of a modern methodology consistent with the DRM.

10 Although charisma could be said to have been tamed by these developments in leadership thought, the concept retained its popularity in the accounts (maps) of outstanding leaders in business, sport, military, and political arenas.

NOTES

1 Summarized from Winkler, I. (2009) 'Enhancing the understanding of the complexity, subjectivity and dynamic of leadership', in *Contributions to management science: Contemporary leadership theories*, Berlin: Springer-Verlag, pp. 59–63.
2 http://timberwolfhq.com/perception-is-reality/, downloaded 20th May 2010.
3 www.newjerseynewsroom.com/commentary/vice-president-chris-christie-could-be-the-ticket-for-2012, downloaded 14 August 2010.
4 Queen Elizabeth II, speech, 17 May 2011, on her first State visit to Ireland, downloaded 18 May 2011.
5 Berger, P.L., & Luckmann, T. (1966) *The social construction of reality: A treatise in the sociology of knowledge*, Garden City, New York: Anchor.
6 Smircich, L., & Morgan, G. (1982) 'Leadership: The management of meaning', *Journal of Applied Behavioral Science*, 18, 257–273.
7 Weick, K.E. (1995) *Sense making in organizations*, Thousand Oaks, CA: Sage.
8 Turner, B. (1992) 'The symbolic understanding of organizations', in Reed, M., & Hughes, M. (eds), *Rethinking organization: New directions in organizational theory and analysis*, London: Sage, pp. 46–66.
9 McWhinney, W. (1992) *Paths of change: Strategic choices for organizations and society*, Newbury Park, CA: Sage.
10 Schein, E.H. (1985/1992) *Organizational culture and leadership: A dynamic view*, San Francisco: Jossey-Bass.
11 Weick, K.E. (1995) *Sense making in organizations*, Thousand Oaks, CA: Sage.
12 Pondy, L.R., Frost, P., Morgan, G., & Dandridge, T. (eds) (1982) *Organizational symbolism*, Greenwich, CT: JAI.

13 Berger, P., & Luckmann, T. (1967) *The social construction of reality*, New York: Anchor.

14 This is a concept that can be traced to the work of the gestalt school of psychologists. E.g. Wertheimer, M. (1959) *Productive thinking*, Chicago: University of Chicago Press. I am indebted to Susan Moger for pointing out the preference in executive development programmes for focusing on active 'leading' processes rather than on the abstractions which often accompany discussions of 'leadership'.

15 Burrell, G., & Morgan, G. (1979) *Sociological paradigms and organisational analysis: Elements of the sociology of corporate life*, London: Heinemann.

16 Morgan, G. (1986) *Images of organization*, Newbury Park, CA: Sage.

17 Ibid., pp. 10–11.

18 Winter, M., & Szczepanek, T. (2009) *Images of projects*, Farnham: Gower.

19 Turner, B. (1992) 'The symbolic understanding of organizations', in Reed, M., & Hughes, M. (eds) *Rethinking organization: New directions in organizational theory and analysis*, London: Sage, pp. 46–66.

20 Jung, C.G. (1981) *The archetypes and the collective unconscious, collected works*, 9, 2nd edn, Princeton, NJ: Bollingen.

21 Lacey, N. (2009) *Image and representation*, 2nd edn, Basingstoke, Hants: Palgrave Macmillan gives a basic introduction to Saussure and Pierce in the context of media studies.

22 Rosenau, P.M. (1992) *Post-modernism and the social sciences: Insights, inroads, and intrusions*, Princeton, NJ: Princeton University Press; Hollinger, R. (1994) *Postmodernism and the social sciences: A thematic approach. Contemporary social theory*, Vol. 4, London: Sage.

23 http://www.independent.co.uk/student/postgraduate/mbas-guide/can-we-learn-from-the-apes-562335.html, downloaded 29 August 2010.

24 McWhinney, W. (1992) *Paths of change: Strategic choices for organizations and society*, Newbury Park, CA: Sage; McWhinney, W. (1993) 'All creative people are not alike', *Creativity and Innovation Management*, 2, 1, 3–16; McWhinney, W., & Webber, J.B. (1997) *Creating paths of change: Managing issues and resolving problems in organizations*, Thousand Oaks, CA: Sage.

25 See http://coachingcommons.org/inventing-the-future-of-coaching/what-does-legacy-mean-for-you/ In memory of WMcW; http://hans.wyrdweb.eu/paths-change-how-change-organization-starting-changing-your-self/.

26 http://hans.wyrdweb.eu/paths-change-how-change-organization-starting-changing-your-self/.

27 Stewart, J.B. (2005) *DisneyWar*, New York: Simon & Schuster.

28 Richard Branson appears to be a more recent example of such a leader.

29 http://corpgov.net/?p=4895; http://leaderswedeserve.wordpress.com/2008/09/17/lehman-bros-and-the-limits-of-leadership/, downloaded 12 May 2011.

30 Myers, I., & Briggs, M.I. (1980) *Gifts differing: Understanding personality type*, reprint edn (1995), Davies-Black Publishing, ISBN 0–89106–074-X.

31 Schein, E.H. (1985/1992) *Organizational culture and leadership: A dynamic view*, San Francisco: Jossey-Bass.

32 Ibid., pp. 373–374.

33 Martin, J., & Frost, P. (1996) 'The organizational culture war games: A struggle for intellectual dominance', in Clegg, S.R., Hardy, C., & Nord, W.R. (eds) *Handbook of organization studies*, London: Sage, p. 602.

34 Peters, T., & Waterman, R. (1982) *In search of excellence*, New York: Harper & Row.

35 Weick, K.E. (1995) *Sense making in organizations*, Thousand Oaks, CA: Sage.

36 See Rickards, T. (1997) 'Book of the quarter', *Creativity and Innovation Management*, 6, 65–67, for an evaluation of Weick's (1995) text on sense-making.

37 Winkler, I. (2009) 'Enhancing the understanding of the complexity, subjectivity and dynamic of leadership', in *Contributions to management science: Contemporary leadership theories*, Berlin: Springer-Verlag, pp. 59–63.

38 Ibid.
39 Ibid., pp. 58–59.
40 Perera, K., Personal correspondence, July 2011.

CHAPTER LEARNING OBJECTIVES

Learning focus
- To understand the nature of trust-based leadership

Key issues
- The changing nature of trust relationships in modern societies
- The breakdown of trust and its restitution
- Trust, vulnerability and exploitation

Dilemmas
- Trust and rationality
- Trust and loss of leadership control

Platforms of understanding
- POU 6.1 Trust in Leadership: A Meta-analysis
- POU 6.2 Trust and Identity (Anthony Giddens)

Contextual materials
- CM 6.1 Trust, Conflict, and Collaboration: Tjosvold's Model
- CM 6.2 Trust in a World of Social Media
- CM 6.3 Trust-based Leadership: Lessons from the Horse-pen?
- CM 6.4 Fukuyama's Analysis of Trust

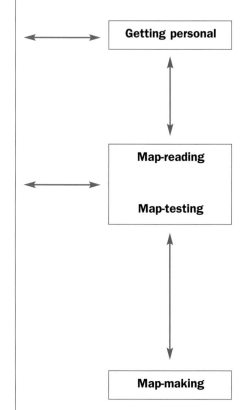

Getting personal

Map-reading

Map-testing

Map-making

6 DILEMMAS OF TRUST, COMPETENCE, AND VULNERABILITY

Trust tends to be somewhat like a combination of the weather and motherhood; it is widely talked about, and it is widely assumed to be good for organizations. When it comes to specifying what it means in an organizational context, however, vagueness creeps in.[1]

Humans have a basic drive to bond, to trust and care for others and a basic drive to make some sense of our lives.[2]

The financial crisis [2008–9] started with a burst housing bubble . . . Pervasive loss of trust in banks, including on the part of other banks, reinforced the vicious circle.[3]

Collaboration at a distance requires good leadership, and a sense by all participants that decisions are made fairly and clearly . . . As Charles Handy has claimed, 'trust takes touch'.[4]

A verbal contract isn't worth the paper it's written on.[5]

ORIENTATION

Trust and its breakdown are important considerations for any leader. The quotations at the beginning of the chapter illustrate the variety of contexts in which trust has broken down, with damaging consequences for leaders, corporations, and political parties.

Attention to the trustworthiness of business and political leaders was heightened in the first decade of the twenty-first century. The challenges arose from economic crises and various financial scandals, heightened by the impact of social media and the speed at which stories threatening corporate reputations were transmitted around the world. Live images of leaders answering to government committees were rapidly converted into damaging videos seen by vast audiences. A flippant remark may have been a significant episode contributing to the downfall of BP's Tony Hayward during the Gulf of Mexico oil-spill disaster.[6] These experiences help in understanding the moral and behavioural components of the trust relationship.

'Am I trusted by people around me? Do I need to be trusted in order to be an effective leader? Can I do anything about it?' These are practical questions which, once asked, take on importance to many in leadership positions. There are no easy answers, although there are several theoretical maps which help in understanding the way in which leadership, trust, and effectiveness may be interrelated.

Informally, many leaders assume that, in practice, it is helpful for followers to have trust in a leader, and that loss of such trust is a bad thing. Unfortunately, most of the theoretical ideas we have come across in earlier chapters make little reference to trust as a central concept. Research which does refer to trust (defined in various ways) suggests that the authors start from a position that accords with the practical beliefs of leaders. However, as indicated in the quotations above, more specific answers require further and deeper examination of the theories of trust-making and trust-losing.

Before exploring the texts dealing with leadership and trust you are invited to examine your personal views by tackling Exercise 6.1. The quotations at the start of the chapter may have started you thinking about trust. We would like you to reflect on these and consider your personal map of trust in leadership processes. You may have taken the topic for granted, in which case it is particularly worthwhile to spend a few minutes at this stage to reflect on your beliefs. You may already have been influenced by your study of chapters 1 to 5.

If you tackled Exercise 6.1, you may have become aware of an interesting point. There is no well-established map of trust as it applies to business and leadership. This may have also suggested that the subject may not fit particularly well into the assumptions of rational behaviours expected in relationships in organizational life according to the DRM. This starting-point prepares us for dilemmas and for approaches to human relationships that are not totally determined by rational transactions.

Trust is frequently mentioned in leadership texts. In recent times, interest in trust has increased with the New Leadership ideas of the 1980s. Northouse, in his examination of

Exercise 6.1: The Trust Challenge

1 From what you have read and experienced, would you consider trust to be important or even necessary for successful leadership?
2 Why do you reach the conclusion you have reached?
3 Can you think of situations in which the level of trust in a leader might be particularly important?
4 Can you think of situations in which the level of trust in a leader might be relatively less important?

[Exercise for individual reflection or classroom or tutorial discussion.]

transformational leadership,[7] refers to trust-building as one of its attributes. Similarly, Bennis and Nanus,[8] in a much-cited study, collected the views of nearly a hundred leaders, and identified trust as a differentiating attribute of transformational leaders.[9] Goleman suggests that people will not automatically trust one other with sensitive information.[10] A leader has to be trusted in order for followers to be prepared to open up regarding their fears and vulnerabilities. As will become even clearer, trust is a process with emotional and behavioural components. Rationality and professional competence are utterly interlinked, which leads to dilemmas of loyalty and professional responsibilities. As also might be expected, many scholarly studies have built on approaches taking a DRM perspective which, when tested, reveal dilemmas associated with trust, in theory and in practice.

POU 6.1 is a meta-analysis of studies of trust, conducted by two American psychologists, Dirks and Ferrin.[11] It reveals the importance of vulnerability within many of the trust studies, and indicates the conditions influencing followers in developing high or low levels of trust in their leaders.

POU 6.2 is drawn from the sociological perspective taken by Anthony Giddens. It explains his concept of modernity and its consequences. He proposes that the nature of trust relations has changed in consequence of the conditions of modern life. Individuals, now more separated in time and space, have to come to terms with technological systems that are more remote and unknowable. Giddens argues that trust provides psychological protection against deep anxieties of identity and existence. It is constantly challenged and renewed through personal processes of reflection.

The contextual materials offer further examples of trust and its dilemmas. In CM 6.1, Tjosvold concludes that, at the level of the organizational team, cooperation and trust are important, and have been mistakenly ignored in comparison to processes that encourage competition as factors influencing team effectiveness.

CM 6.2 is a case revealing how adverse stories can become publicized almost instantaneously through the internet. This increases the vulnerabilities of organizations to a rupture of trust in a world of social media.

CM 6.3 examines trust-based leadership from the perspective of the metaphor of 'horse-whispering' methods of horse management. This form of trust-based leadership will later be seen to be consistent with creative leadership as explored in Chapter 10.

CM 6.4 is a macro-perspective of trust at the level of society, provided by the work of Francis Fukuyama.[12] His work suggests that trust involves various dilemmas which cannot be explained entirely by a Dominant Rationality world-view. Employees may withhold their labour on grounds of social justice and fairness rather than for economic considerations. Succession to leadership in family firms may pose the dilemma of trust in the family over mistrust of other stakeholders in the firm in the new leaders and succession plan.

PLATFORMS OF UNDERSTANDING

POU 6.1: Trust in Leadership: A Meta-analysis

Dirks and Ferrin[13] examined research on trust in leadership conducted over four decades (1960s–1990s). They compare the various studies in a meta-analysis. As indicated in Chapter 2, a meta-analysis simplifies and brings order to what might otherwise be a complex and confusing body of work. The authors offered a definition of trust that, in their view, captured much of the variety of the work they had studied and its multiple definitions:

> a psychological state comprising the intention to accept vulnerability based upon positive expectations of the intentions or behaviour of another.[14]

The literature was classified according to the focus towards which trust is directed. This is known as the referent. Two kinds of referent are identified. The first is trust in a *direct leader*. The second concentrates on trust in *organizational leadership*. This distinction, they argue, has important practical and theoretical implications. For example, if research shows that trust is most strongly associated with direct reports, organizations should focus, in their trust-building, on establishing trust in personal ways. If the more significant referent is organizational leadership, the processes of trust development require more indirect methods and symbols.

Studies examining trust often fail to clarify whether they are concerned with direct or indirect referents. This is made the more confusing because they also introduce two perspectives, which appear to be connected with, but cannot be totally identified with, one rather than the other referent.

Direct leaders appear to be a particularly important referent of trust. This supports the need to view leadership as an important concept at all levels of organization, and the potential pitfalls of simply concentrating our efforts on understanding leadership through the actions of the top leadership team or the edicts of the chief executive officer.

The relationship-based perspective focuses on the followers' perceptions of the relationship with the leader. Trust is studied as a social exchange process. Social exchange deals with individual willingness to *reciprocate* care and consideration expressed within a relationship. Such a style takes account of the vulnerabilities of followers, and (according to the definition) of the propensity to trust.

The *character-based perspective* focuses, as it implies, on perceptions of the leader's character.[15] Followers attempt to draw inferences about the leader's characteristics such as integrity, competence, and openness. In everyday terms, we may consider the relationship-based approach to be one in which considerations of benevolence (and its converse, malevolence) are core.

The character-based approach is more concerned with considerations of fairness.

The relationship perspective would consider that trust may be stronger if the leader has a transformational leadership style (see Chapter 4). It shows evidence of the factors of idealized influence, or individual consideration.

Box 6.1: Trust in Leadership: Key Concepts from Dirks and Ferrin

Dirks and Ferrin (POU 6.1) provide a widely accepted definition of trust as 'a psychological state comprising the intention to accept vulnerability based upon positive expectations of the intentions of behaviour of another'.[16]

They suggest that two perspectives or maps are to be found in the literature of trust: the *leader–follower relationship* and the *character-based perspective*.

Both perspectives have taken a perceptual approach consistent with the sense-making ones found in Chapter 5. Trust is based on perceptions and beliefs. Both suggest that trust derives from inferences – in the one case drawn about the leader–follower relationship, and in the other about the leader's character.

The character-based perspective 'seems to be logically associated with cognitive definitions of trust and the relationship-based perspective . . . with affective definitions'.[17]

Dirks and Ferrin's analysis permitted an estimate of the 'antecedents' (possible causal factors) influencing trust. The highest correlation was with transformational leadership, followed by transactional leadership, which was only marginally weaker.

Transactional leaders put more emphasis on character-based issues of integrity and fairness. For example, a transactional leader is able to operate by virtue of followers' trust in the leader's capability for delivering a contractual arrangement.

The diamond traders of Hatton Garden exist within a social world in which transactional integrity is taken for granted. Similarly, the transactional leader in an industrial context promises rewards and punishments. The emphasis is on integrity, fairness, and dependability ('that's not a threat, that's a promise').

Dirks and Ferrin conclude that research on trust in leadership has tended to treat the two perspectives (relationship-based and character-based trust theories) as functional equivalents, presuming a similar conceptual model of factors initiating trust and being assessed by the same consequences. The authors suggest that the two theoretical perspectives have been too mixed together (conflated). Confusions may be resolved if this is addressed in future research.

Significantly, they also suggest that their study reveals trust in leadership as being significantly related to performance outcomes. Transformational leadership was found consistently to have a substantial relationship with trust. However, the meta-analysis fails to identify the precise causal processes involved. That is to say, there is no clear mechanism through which leadership actions influence trust, and trust becomes translated into organizational effectiveness.

Exercise 6.2: A Fistful of Diamonds

1 Two diamond traders in London's Hatton Garden examine a handful of precious stones. They agree a sale. The buyer says he needs three days to obtain the finance for the cash transaction. The deal is agreed. There has been no discussion of the authenticity of the information provided about the origins and specification of the stones. By tradition, such deals have been conducted with no legal or written exchange. Their bedrock is the intangible bond of trust between the two traders.
2 The motto of the London Stock Exchange: 'My word is my bond'.[18]
3 'A verbal contract isn't worth the paper it's written on.'[19]

Exercise 6.2 Questions

1 Which of items 2 and 3 is easier to explain using the DRM reasoning? Why?
2 Which of items 2 and 3 is easier to explain using a trust-based map of human behaviour? Why?
3 Which map helps to explain item 1? Why?

Organizational research has demonstrated a lack of clarity in the trust construct.[20] This study hypothesized that trust in direct leaders (i.e. trust by workers in their direct report 'leaders') shows stronger relationships with job performance, satisfaction, and altruistic organizational behaviours, than does a generalized trust placed in organizational leadership. Definitions of trust, it was argued, may seem to have a common conceptual core. However, researchers have attempted to measure trust along different and multiple dimensions, and often from different conceptual mappings. Overall, the meta-analysis helps in clarifying different perspectives on the development and consequences of trust in leadership.

POU 6.2: Trust and Identity (Anthony Giddens)

Anthony Giddens has written extensively and profoundly about the importance of trust in the social world. He considers that trust is a social necessity and has changed its essential character under conditions of modernity. By modernity, Giddens implies a world dominated by the perspective of rational thought and of rationally informed behaviour.[21] He defines modernity as 'a first approximation . . . to modes of social life or organization which emerged in Europe from about the seventeenth century onwards and which subsequently became more or less worldwide in their influence'.[22]

Taking a historical perspective, Giddens contrasts pre-modern and modern environments. Pre-modern societies had a localized and immediate environment of trust. In a modern environment, technological changes have contributed to a shift in the nature of trust. This has been brought about by a different set of relationships concerning time and space experienced by individuals around the world. It is an example of a consequence of modern life or modernity. The globalization of organizations and markets accentuates the conditions about which Giddens writes.

Trust under the conditions of modernity takes on a different meaning. We trust our bank and our various investing institutions to protect our savings. The infrequent instances of loss of trust and a 'run' on the banks serve to illustrate the far more typical trust relationship.

Even in earlier days, banking required trust in unfathomable relationships and tokens of exchange beyond physical artefacts such as gold or precious metals. Electronic banking puts even greater demands on our trust of a mysterious and intangible system. Concerns about the security of our savings also surface from time to time. The financial crisis of 2007–8 demonstrates the most recent episode when the normal trust relationships broke down. Each story of financial corruption or governmental malpractice disturbs our taken-for-granted trust beliefs, as we relate it to personal circumstances.

To take another example, we trust the technology of aircraft in order to believe that our holiday flight will transport us safely to our destination. That is not to say that we remain in a permanent and unconcerned condition of trust. Fear of flying persists.

Modernity operates through a process of 'disembedding' symbolic tokens such as money, which have becoming increasingly abstract (*what* is an e-bank? *where* is my money located?).

Also, there is the increasingly abstracted set of relationships that is implied by our intimate involvement in expert systems such as airlines. Trust exists as a concept that, in part, lies beyond rationality in a world in which the dominant beliefs prize logic and reason.

Giddens summarizes his analysis in the following way. Loss of trust is related to personal absence in space and time, which, together with a lack of relevant information, produces what he calls *distantiation*. He considers trust to derive from faith (belief) in an individual, such as a leader, or in a social system. When it comes to trust through faith in abstract systems such as banks and airlines, we are concerned with not their moral but their functional reliability. That is to say, there is a *moral* basis of the trust we place in people, and a *functional* basis of trust in systems, including organizations and institutions of government and control. Giddens notes:

> Trust may be defined as confidence in the reliability of a person or system, regarding a given set of outcomes or events, where that confidence expresses a faith in the probity or love of another, or in the correctness of abstract principles (technical knowledge).[23]

Trust involves psychological risk. In pre-modern societies, trust might be no more than the fatalistic acceptance of destiny. Modernity offers the individual a philosophy of free-will, so that our actions contribute to personal destiny. This is one example of the consequences of modernity and the conditions through which trust itself has taken on a different context.[24]

How do we cope with such anxieties inherent in modernist societies? Giddens, writing in the last decade of the twentieth century, refers to late-modern society, within which the more stable processes of identity formation enacted in traditional societies have been eroded. The consequences of modernity include a heightened interest in, and willingness to challenge the legitimacy of, beliefs and a far greater tendency to consider future possibilities. Giddens argues for presuming the modern condition to be one in which every facet is open to revision. The revision arises through the processes of actions and personal monitoring of actions. Trust is considered as a fragile and universal human condition, yet recurring in differing forms under changing circumstances.

Giddens draws on sociological writings, as well as a range of psychological theories, to explain his understanding of trust. One of his specific contributions is the importance of a person's sense of identity and security in the realities of existence. For this, he coined the term *ontological security*. 'The phrase refers to the confidence that most human beings have in the continuity of their self-identity and in the constancy of the surrounding social and material environments of action.'[25]

Why are people not overwhelmed with the uncertainties of life in general, and particularly of those differentiating modernist society? Giddens cites developmental psychologists such as Erik Erikson, who consider trust as being involved in developing self-identity.[26] A religious upbringing contributes a further powerful means of developing and sustaining a sense of faith and trust in the ultimately unknowable.

Learning to trust others is an important part of learning to trust ourselves. Trust, from this perspective, is a necessary protection against deepest doubts, not just in another person, but in one's basis for self-understanding and, therefore, identity. The betrayal of trust opens the psychological floodgates to anxieties of the deepest kind.

For a leader, then, the possibilities become clearer. In relationships, the leader plays a part in the development of trust, the containment of uncertainties (Giddens prefers the term ambiguities).

Today's business leader can no longer expect the form of trust from his followers that would be granted to the clan leader of earlier societies. The fragility of trust derives from increasingly delocalized experiences (distantiation) and more complex and ambiguous social relationships. An appeal to 'trust me' can unintentionally trigger conscious awareness of deeper concerns and anxieties.

When trust has to be 'worked at', an openness or self-disclosure by the leader becomes vital as part of a developing process of mutual understanding. For Giddens, trust remains a fundamental feature of today's social and organizational life, always open to scrutiny, and therefore always a source of psychological tension.

The analysis is of particular interest to anyone interested in leadership. It presents a treatment of a renewable dynamic process that differs from psychological treatments of trust. It points to a phenomenon that is constantly under reflective review by social actors. It may be compared with the processes of sense-making examined in Chapter 5.[27]

This differs somewhat from the common-sense view that trust takes a lot of building but is something that can be destroyed for ever in a single act perceived as untrustworthy. ('After that, I was never able to trust him again . . .') It offers a theory relevant for exploring the 'irrational' condition of unconditional trust associated with followers of the charismatic kind of leader.

A charismatic leader, even in an enlightened age of rationality, is still able to weaken and even turn off the customary vigilance of followers. As with other acts of dramatic performance, there is a suspension of disbelief. The leader's capacity to induce a suspension of reflexivity and rational thought provides an important and different way of understanding the processes of charismatic leadership.

CONTEXTUAL MATERIALS

CM 6.1: Trust, Conflict, and Collaboration: Tjosvold's Model

A model addressing tensions in work groups has been developed over a period of years by the researcher Dean Tjosvold. His work presents a map of the processes he believes are important in a team's leadership and performance. He suggests that trust operates in tension with competitive and individualistic actions. Neither competitive behaviour nor trust-supporting behaviour is an adequate basis for group effectiveness.

Tjosvold captures his experience and research findings in the book *Team Organization: An Enduring Competitive Advantage*.[28] He suggests that cooperation has been considered inefficient from a dominant economic perspective, with evidence of productivity losses against more Darwinian efforts of competing individuals.

He contends that such a view neglects the synergy arising from collaborative (and trusting) relationships.

Tjosvold argues that, since Taylorism and the rise of scientific management as a dominant philosophy, considerations of productivity have had an individualistic bias. This has contributed to the down-playing of what he considers to be an overwhelming body of evidence that *collaboration* has considerable merits within teams. He acknowledges the potential of teams to engage in self-limiting behaviours through being too preoccupied with collaboration.[29] Yet, he insists that groups working in a collaborative mode can be more productive than those in which individuals work competitively.

He draws on the historical work of Morton Deutch[30] to arrive at his cooperation maxim. Nevertheless, conflict may even be necessary, so that minority opinions can be tested and effectively integrated. Evidence for this has been found among a range of working teams, including engineers, customers, and technical sales teams. Indeed, it is the *avoidance of conflict*, rather than conflict itself, that is more likely to reduce a group's effectiveness.

Tjosvold develops a model in which a team engages in visualization of goals, developing a shared perspective, thus achieving more committed (empowered) members, working in innovative ways, reflecting and learning from their actions. These processes interact, although not necessarily in a simple stage-by-stage fashion. The leader directs a great deal of effort towards the manner in which the teams operate on each of the components.

The model avoids a simple dichotomy of 'conflict is bad, cooperation is good'. It offers a sophisticated basis for indicating how the dilemma of cooperation versus conflict can be resolved, trust being one of the benefits of cooperative group arrangements.

CM 6.2 Trust in a World of Social Media

An incident occurred in February 2010 in which the filmmaker Kevin Smith was removed from a Southwest Airlines flight. Smith responded immediately by communicating to 1.6 million people via the social networking site Twitter, claiming that he had been victimized for being 'too fat'. According to social media commentator Greg Ferenstein, the story rapidly became news.[31]

> Filmmaker Kevin Smith sent a series of exasperated Tweets this weekend claiming that he'd been kicked off a Southwest Airlines flight for being 'too fat'. Proving, perhaps, the speed at which Twitter can spread messages about your brand. The Tweets were picked up by the Wall Street Journal, USA Today, ABC and other major outlets.

The incident (13 February 2010) resulted in dozens of tweets on Smith's account. A brief sampling of the tweeted exchanges is shown below:

Dear @SouthwestAir – I know I'm fat, but was Captain Leysath really justified in throwing me off a flight for which I was already seated?

Dear @SouthwestAir, I'm on another one of your planes, safely seated & buckled-in again, waiting to be dragged off.

Southwest, which also has over 1 million Twitter followers, using Twitter to convey personal concern for its customers, replied rapidly:

Hey folks – trust me, I saw the tweets from @ThatKevinSmith I'll get all the details and handle accordingly! Thanks for your concerns!

I read every single tweet that comes into this account, and take every tweet seriously. We'll handle @ThatKevinSmith issue asap.[32]

Ferenstein wanted to find out how the case might be explained by theories of trust. He sought out Professor Judy Olson at the University of California at Irvine, who with a team of researchers are investigating communication and scientific collaboration across virtual groupings.[33]

Olson's studies have led to the conclusion that when only text is available (as in web-based social media) participants judge the trustworthiness of the people or corporations involved based on speed of response. Even acknowledging that you received the message contributes to assessments of trustworthiness.

Among their important findings is the manner in which 'distance matters' (cf. Giddens' distantiation concept in POU 6.2). As virtual group working increases in importance, leadership and trust become increasingly relevant for the effective functioning of groups that have to communicate globally. Collaboration at a distance requires good leadership, and a sense by all of the participants that decisions are made fairly and clearly. The researchers highlighted three kinds of significant issues:

- ■ *Time zones* When the participants are in different time zones, coordination can be extremely difficult.
- ■ *Culture* Variations in national cultures, and in corporate cultures, place demands on collaborative working.
- ■ *Trust* As Charles Handy (1995) has claimed, 'trust takes touch'. This implies that it can be difficult to establish or maintain trust among participants who are geographically distant.

CM 6.3 Trust-based Leadership: Lessons from the Horse-pen?

Contextual reading CM 6.3 introduces work on a trust-based method of leadership. At its core is the concept of gaining trust through appropriate communication skills. Its map shares a belief in the moral basis for trust-building as identified by Giddens in POU 6.2.

The basic methodology was developed by the American 'horse whisperer' Monty Roberts. His ideas were popularized after the fictionalized version in the film *The Horse Whisperer* and have subsequently become part of a worldwide movement towards pain-free horse management. The approach is a challenge to traditional approaches to working with horses that rely on 'breaking' the horse into a condition of compliance. It is based on recognition of a horse's instinctive desire to be part of the herd. From a study of such behaviours over a period of many years, Roberts developed a method that he demonstrates regularly in his exhibitions. Regardless of the 'troubled' horses brought to the event, he illustrates techniques that permit him to win the trust of a horse rapidly. Previously unridden animals accept saddling and being ridden ('trustingly') by a human rider within half an hour. Such demonstrations have convinced thousands of knowledgeable spectators of the merits of the approach. Queen Elizabeth the Queen Mother of England was among influential and knowledgeable individuals who have endorsed the method and encouraged its wider use.[34]

The case against using the 'intelligent horsemanship' metaphor is that it risks the charge of anthropomorphism discussed in Chapter 1. Although the principles may be seen as consistent with a person-centred leadership,[35] some scholars find it offensive and perhaps dehumanizing of the leader–follower relationship. A second objection is that the methods are not yet accepted by many in the horse-breeding and horse-managing worlds. Monty Roberts argues his case eloquently:

> If you want to pursue [trust-based leadership] as a concrete practice, you must give up what I call 'the myth of the gentle'. There is a prevailing, virtually worldwide belief that equates gentleness with weakness, slowness and lack of discipline. When [in a tough situation] I am calm because I have learned that any other state of mind is detrimental . . . It is also *knowledge* that keeps me calm and free of any desire to dominate through fear. I am a willing partner. Gentleness is the true strength of the world. Violence always comes back in the form of more violence.[36]

CM 6.4 Fukuyama's Analysis of Trust

Francis Fukuyama, former deputy director of the US state department, wrote several influential books exploring the nature of capitalism. He describes his work[37] as understanding the human historical process as an interplay between two forces. The one force is that of rational desire, the other a striving for freedom as moral beings.

He suggests that conflicts are widespread, found in the refusal of individuals to operate in strictly economic fashion in a variety of contexts. Fukuyama proposes that a worker withdrawing from a working contract may be striking as much for economic justice as for economic gain. Similarly, the entrepreneurial leader is motivated by need for recognition as well as the anticipation of disposable wealth.

Primitive societies sought recognition through physical conflicts, which later were largely displaced into economic struggles. Fukuyama sees the process more as leading to the spiritualization of economic life. Thus, in Japan, he sees the energies of the earlier *samurai* or warrior class as displaced into business. In other cultures a similar transformation has occurred, so that energies directed towards war became displaced towards entrepreneurial actions. Fukuyama traces trust in the workplace to its cultural origins. A culture's economic organizations develop out of an interplay between the culture's family and state arrangements. He suggests that there are three elements to consider in the emergence of organizations: the family, voluntary arrangements outside the family, and state-owned or sponsored institutions. His principal thesis is that a strong, family-based culture (such as in China) tends to have weak, voluntary, extra-familial arrangements, and strong state influences. Family values, then, are not necessarily connected with economic success for a society. The combination produces differentials in the trust relationships found in different cultures.

We can take from Fukuyama the notion that leaders will find cultural conditions strongly influencing their attempts to engender trust among their followers. He illustrates the cultural shaping with numerous examples, such as leadership in the high-technology multinational corporation Wang Computers. Its founder, An Wang, automatically assumed that his successor would come from within the family. In contrast, American employees and financial analysts found this an unconvincing rationale and did not trust the proposed successor. An Wang responded by replacing his son with a more credible figure, one more easily able to command and retain the trust of these important stakeholders.

INTEGRATION

From the meta-analysis of Dirks and Ferrin, we see how understanding of trust in leadership has been hindered by an absence of integration of the research findings of the many and varied studies involving the construct. Their attempt at integration was to define trust as a psychological state comprising the intention to accept vulnerability based upon positive expectations of the intentions or behaviour of another.

The definition, and the theoretical constructs on which it draws, suggest that leaders need to be alert to the dilemmas of gaining trust through claims which play to the vulnerabilities of others. Where trust is unconditional, betrayal leads to feelings of rejection by the individual, which converts to the rejection of the person or organization involved. Their work also indicated that the strongest empirical relationships involving trust derived from leaders taking a direct (as opposed to a distant) process of trust-building.

The second distinction made in the meta-study was between two perspectives on trust, one termed relationship-based and the other character-based. Clearly, the remote leader is forced towards being trusted through a character-based approach associated with fairness; for a more relationship-based approach, the leader has to overcome the remoteness, perhaps through adapting a more direct style (popularized as 'leading by walking about').

POU 6.2 also addresses the nature of trust, but makes fewer direct references to leadership. Giddens considers that trust is a fundamental characteristic of a person's identity. He considers that trust in two ways: either in the probity or love of another, or in the correctness of abstract principles. Here we have overlap with the two referents of trust identified in the Dirks and Ferrin study. Giddens also indicates how trust in a leader has changed fundamentally under so-called conditions of modernity, which provide settings of increasing complexity and ambiguities. Leaders have become remote (distantiated), and less able to interact directly. Dirks and Ferrin arrived at a similar conclusion through their finding that local leaders had stronger trust relationships than did spatially distant ones.

In both POUs, trust is seen as having explanations that are grounded in beliefs in a rationalistic culture, and yet having important behavioural features that require further explanation. These concern the vulnerabilities and anxieties of individuals in social environments. Giddens suggests that trust is fragile, always under scrutiny through personal processes of reflection. In a crisis, trust is not so much lost as temporarily set aside. This is contrary to the popular belief that trust, once lost, can never be regained. The evidence is that dishonoured leaders are reinstated and deceivers are forgiven.

Trust and loss of trust are constructs for which fully rational behaviours are inadequate explanations. That is to say, the willingness of an individual or social group to trust a leader is not only influenced by the compelling rational logic of its ideas.[38]

Giddens notes that our world of late-modernity retains dilemmas that go beyond the perspective of rational thought and of rationally informed behaviour.

The maps of trust offered by Dirks and Ferrin's meta-analysis and Giddens' sociological treatment are compared in Table 6.1.

Table 6.1 Two Maps of Trust Compared

	Dirks and Ferrin	*Giddens*
Definitional core	'[A] psychological state comprising the intention to accept vulnerability based upon positive expectations of the intentions or behaviour of another'	'confidence in the reliability of a person or system, regarding a given set of outcomes or events, where that confidence expresses a faith in the probity or love of another, or in the correctness of abstract principles (technical knowledge)'
Distinctions	Vulnerabilities and willingness to trust. Willingness to reciprocate care and consideration (relationship with direct leader). Willingness to enter transactional arrangements based on assessment of character-based virtues of a distant leadership (fairness, integrity, competence, and openness).	Insecurities at deep level of self-identity and beliefs. A *moral* basis of trust in people with confidence (faith) in the probity or love of another. A *functional* basis of trust in systems with confidence (faith) in the correctness of abstract principles.

The contextual maps also offer scope for map-testing. Fukuyama (CM 6.4) explains the dynamics of trust as arising through cultural and individual interplay between two forces, one of rational desire and the other a striving for freedom as moral beings. Again we have the dilemma of trust as one of reconciling rational and non-rational impulses.

For Monty Roberts, the strongest relationships are trust-based, whether they be someone's relationships among humans or with other sentient creatures such as horses. The core aspect of any relationship is voluntarism and cooperation rather than influence in its other formats. This was found to approximate to creative or invitational leadership approaches.

Tjosvold develops a theory of cooperation in groups that is counter-intuitive, perhaps a dilemma, for many leaders who hold taken-for-granted beliefs that human behaviours are innately competitive and, under modern conditions, inherently rational.

GETTING PERSONAL

The chapter began with a few anecdotes involving trust, indicating how important it could be for a range of leadership situations. Then the maps, and much of the contextual materials, took us a long way away from the real-life challenges that face business leaders. We can move towards these practical dilemmas following our advocated procedures of working out our own journeys, and our own maps, with assistance from the general maps provided.

Is Trust Exploitative?

We are aware of several dilemmas of widespread concern. They emerge as we 'get personal' in our leadership courses. One is whether the very concept of trust is to be trusted! For many leaders and 'wannabe' leaders, the maps of trust take them into very alarming territory. Some express it forcefully. 'There's no chance that trust works in our company . . . trust is a way of exploiting the gullible . . . to survive, you have to say one thing and mean another.'

In effect, the leader who makes disparaging remarks about the company's products is implying that the customers are foolish and gullible, failing to understand the realities of commerce. Giddens follows developmental psychologists in suggesting that our core beliefs are an important part of our self-identity, perhaps learned from our earliest family and cultural experiences.

The dilemmas for a leader are particularly acute in unpromising circumstances. Sometimes painful dilemmas arise, as illustrated in Box 6.2. The issue of trust is here connected to issues of ethical behaviour, examined in Chapter 9.

Box 6.2: A Dilemma of Loyalty and Trust

As a leader, you are in possession of information that a business unit and associated manufacturing facilities will be closed down. The information has been decided at corporate headquarters and an announcement will be made in ten days' time. Any premature announcements could have legal consequences. The director of human resources tells you that she is considering leaving for a better-paid post in another company. She is partly influenced by the uncertainties, and could be persuaded to stay with appropriate reassurances. You know that she could be very helpful in managing the close-down procedures. What do you do? Do you try to dissuade her from moving? You could tell her that you hope to have some interesting new changes to tell her about shortly. Or you may take her into your confidence. In which case, would you want her to guarantee her silence, either verbally or, more legalistically, in writing?

These approaches have different implications and consequences. Taking her into your confidence shows how trust occurs in a two-way relationship. She needs to trust your assurances; you need to trust her with sensitive information. However, it may well be that in real life you have already undertaken a commitment not to pass on the information. These are the extra dimensions that produce hard-to-resolve dilemmas in real life. Furthermore, in real life you will always find pressures of time to reach a decision. 'Buying time' (although often necessary) is rarely enough to constitute a complete strategy.

Even when you find yourself in a condition where trust seems absent, there may be possibilities, as a leader, for a trust-based approach. Anything you say is open to the cynical response 'Why should we trust you?' Trust refers to the condition of *vulnerability* that influences expectations. The leader may have to signal vulnerability – and by actions as well as by words. It is a relationship-based response. The leader 'goes at risk'. It is the tradition of the leader 'falling on the sword', or offering resignation as a demonstration of trustworthiness and honourable acceptance that trust cannot be restored.

SUMMARY

Detailed consideration has been given to the notion of a trust basis for leadership and, significantly, the idea that trust is the essential ingredient for effective leadership. As noted in earlier chapters, the emerging dilemmas often are based on the differences between a rational model of human behaviours and more behavioural mappings.

You may be better placed now to reach some conclusions about the workings of the Hatton Garden diamond traders in Exercise 6.2.

Dirks and Ferrin addressed the complexities and ambiguities involved in trust examined as a psychological mechanism for understanding leadership effectiveness. Trust was mapped as having a widely accepted definitional focus, based on notions of vulnerability. Such a process remains a potential source of psychological tension for the leader as well as for followers. Charismatic leaders may, arguably, be understood as individuals who are able to gain the trust of followers, who become vulnerable to the wishes of the leader.

Giddens offers an approach to the analysis of trust from a sociological perspective. His mapping of the contemporary world is of a technologically complex, globalizing environment that requires new forms of trust in technologies that cannot be fully understood and therefore have to be trusted. He argues that trust in people (rather than in technological systems) is a means of protection against deep anxieties of identity and existence. It is constantly renewed through personal processes of reflection, although it remains vulnerable to disruption and betrayal. Giddens draws on developmental psychologists such as Erik Erikson to map trust as a component in the development of a sense of self.

Trust-based leadership offers a map that differs profoundly from many leadership maps that imply leadership as a control process. Trust-based approaches encourage cooperative behaviours. These approaches address the dilemmas of rationality and control by introducing leadership maps that give preference to empowerment over control, accepting the leader's vulnerability to the values and needs of others within organizational groups.

The chapter has focused on the nature of trust-based leadership and has explored it from perspectives that have revealed dilemmas of trust, rationality, and loss of leadership control. Specifically, trust-based leadership places the leader in a vulnerable position where traditional control has been set aside in the interests of empowering relationships.

Applying the vocabulary of mapping, it might be concluded that trust-based methods are contrary to the DRM assumptions regarding the rationally based actions of agents in modern organizations. Similar difficulties are to be found in other concepts, such as power, diversity, and ethics, which will be examined in subsequent chapters.

Such considerations suggest that alternative maps are worth examining for concepts that are difficult to deal with within the DRM's focus on the rational.

Trust-based leadership goes beyond the strictly rational, to address the behavioural and emotional components of relationships. Loss of leadership control, a possible dilemma for those accustomed to DRM approaches, becomes an accepted vulnerability as a way of empowering others towards higher-order priorities.

Trust addresses the dilemmas of leadership encountered in other chapters. Exercise 6.3 is an opportunity for you to integrate the materials on trust with the various maps of leadership that you have encountered in earlier chapters.

Exercise 6.3: Leadership Theories and Their Trust Implications

Leadership Theory	Trust Implications	Notes
Great Man (Trait theory)	Born to lead; trust assumed	
Leadership Development	Skills for trust-building may be developed	
Situational leadership	Trust may be important in some situations	
Project leadership	Trust not central but may be assumed, mainly through the project structure and task clarity	
Charismatic leadership	Trust transcends rationality, e.g. through symbolism and vision	
Transformational leadership	Trust developed through 'Four Is' factors	
Transactional leadership	Trust in 'exchange' mechanisms	
Symbolic leadership	Trust through sense-making of symbolic information	

[Exercise for personal reflection, or tutorial or classroom discussion.]

NOTES

1 Porter, L.W., Lawler, E.E., & Hackman, J.R. (1975) *Behavior in organizations*, New York: McGraw-Hill, p. 497.
2 Lawrence, P.R. (2010) *Driven to lead: Good, bad, and misguided leadership*, San Francisco: Jossey-Bass, p. 3.
3 Paul Krugman writing in the *New York Times*, 10 October 2008, www.khazanah.com.my/docs/KMF2008_krugman_nytimes.pdf, downloaded 21 November 2010.
4 Charles Handy quote is from Handy, C. (1995) 'Trust and the virtual organization', *Harvard Business Review*, 73, 3, quoted on http://research.microsoft.com/pubs/78697/Olson9370.pdf, downloaded 2 November 2010.
5 Attributed to Sam Goldwyn, www.imdb.com/name/nm0326418/bio, downloaded 2 November 2010.
6 See, for example, http://leaderswedeserve.wordpress.com/2010/07/26/bp%E2%80%99s-hayward-goes-how-we-get-the-leaders-we-deserve/.
7 Northouse, P.G. (2004)) *Leadership theory and practice*, 3rd edn, Thousand Oaks, CA: Sage.
8 Bennis, W.G., & Nanus, B. (1985) *Leaders*, New York: Harper & Row.
9 Trust was identified together with developing a clear vision; being 'social architects'; and having positive self-regard. The other three factors have been covered in earlier chapters.
10 Goleman, D. (1995) *Emotional intelligence*, New York: Free Press.

11 Dirks, K.T., & Ferrin, D.L. (2002) "Trust in leadership: Meta-analytic findings and implications for organizational research', *Journal of Applied Psychology*, 87, 4, 611–628.

12 Fukuyama, F. (1992) *The end of history and the last man*, New York: Free Press.

13 Dirks, K.T., & Ferrin, D.L. (2002) "Trust in leadership: Meta-analytic findings and implications for organizational research', *Journal of Applied Psychology*, 87, 4, 611–628.

14 Dirks & Ferrin, ibid., who cite this nice example of a theoretical definition as coming from Rousseau, D.M., Sitkin, S.B., Burt, R.S., & Camerer, C. (1998) 'Not so different after all: A cross-discipline view of trust', *Academy of Management Review*, 23, 393–404, at p. 395.

15 Mayer, R.C., Davies, J.H., & Schoorman, F.D. (1995) 'An integrative model of organizational trust', *Academy of Management Review*, 20, 709–734; Clark, M.C., & Payne, R.L. (1997) 'The nature and structure of workers' trust in management', *Journal of Organizational Behaviour*, 18, 205–224.

16 Dirks, K.T., & Ferrin, D.L. (2002) "Trust in leadership: Meta-analytic findings and implications for organizational research', *Journal of Applied Psychology*, 87, 4, 611–628, at p. 612, drawing on Rousseau, D.M., Sitkin, S.B., Burt, R.S., & Camerer, C. (1998) 'Not so different after all: A cross-discipline view of trust', *Academy of Management Review*, 23, 393–404.

17 Ibid., p. 616.

18 www.londonstockexchange.com/about-the-exchange/company-overview/our-history/our-history. htm, downloaded 2 November 2010.

19 Attributed to Sam Goldwyn, www.imdb.com/name/nm0326418/bio, Downloaded 2 November 2010.

20 Clark, M.C., & Payne, R.L. (1997) 'The nature and structure of workers' trust in management', *Journal of Organizational Behaviour*, 18, 205–224.

21 Giddens, A. (1990) *The consequences of modernity*, Cambridge: Polity.

22 Ibid., p. 1.

23 Ibid., p. 34.

24 Giddens refers to such anxieties as a condition of ontological insecurity, implying that modernity has rejected the ultimate grounding of beliefs offered in the past through faith in a higher being.

25 Ibid., p. 92.

26 Erikson, E.H. (1965) *Childhood and society*, Harmondsworth: Penguin; Winnicott, D.W. (1974) *Playing and reality*, Harmondsworth: Penguin.

27 Weick, K.E. (1995) *Sense making in organizations*, Thousand Oaks, CA: Sage.

28 Tjosvold, D. (1991) *Team organization: An enduring competitive advantage*, Chichester, UK: Wiley.

29 Steiner, I.D. (1972) *Group process and productivity*, New York: Academic Press.

30 Deutch, M., (1985) *Distributive justice*, New Haven, CT: Yale University Press.

31 Ferenstein, G. (2010) http://mashable.com/2010/02/24/social-media-trust/, downloaded 24 Oct 2010.

32 Material draws on the tweets reported in ibid. as downloaded 24 October 2010.

33 The seminal study can be found in Olson, G.M., & Olson, J.S. (2000) 'Distance matters'. *Human–Computer Interaction*, 15, 139–178. For update studies see: Olson, G.M., Zimmerman, A., & Bos, N. (eds) (2008) *Scientific research on the internet*, Cambridge, MA: MIT Press; Olson, J.S., Hofer, E., Bos, N., Zimmerman, A., Olson, G.M., Cooney, D., & Faniel, I. (2008) 'A theory of remote scientific collaboration', in Olson, G.M., Zimmerman, A., & Bos, N. (eds) *Scientific research on the internet*, Cambridge, MA: MIT Press, pp. 73–97; http://research.microsoft.com/pubs/78697/Olson9370.pdf.

34 Rickards, T. (2000) 'Trust-based leadership: Creative lessons from intelligent horsemanship', *Creativity and Innovation Management*, 9, 4, 259–266.

35 McGregor, D. (1960) *The human side of enterprise*, New York: McGraw-Hill. See also (no author given) (2002) 'Douglas McGregor: Theory X and Theory Y', *Workforce*, 81, 1, 32.

36 Roberts (2000) *Horse sense for people*, London: Harper Collins, p. 208.

37 Fukuyama, F. (1992) *The end of history and the last man*, New York: Free Press.

38 One business leader-turned-television-celebrity regularly demonstrated the non-rational side of the process of trust-building. Playing the role of a corporate trouble-shooter, his approach to winning trust involved declaring passionate and utter belief in the change he was urging on the organization while signalling his warmth towards the executives with whom he was dealing. The style is as charismatic as it is rational.

CHAPTER LEARNING OBJECTIVES

Learning focus
- Understanding the dominant map found in strategy textbooks

Key issues
- Formulation and implementation
- Top echelon research
- Emergent strategy

Dilemmas
- Is strategy rationally determined or is there leadership choice?
- Formulation and implementation dilemma

Platforms of understanding
- POU 7.1 Strategic Leadership: Nahavandi and Malekzadeh's Investigation
- POU 7.2 Boal and Hooijberg's Important Themes in Strategic Leadership

Contextual materials
- CM 7.1 Twenty-first-Century Strategic Leadership: Ireland and Hitt's Analysis
- CM 7.2 Tipping-point Leadership: Bill Bratton
- CM 7.3 An Information-based Leadership Strategy
- CM 7.4 Sun Tzu and Business Strategy

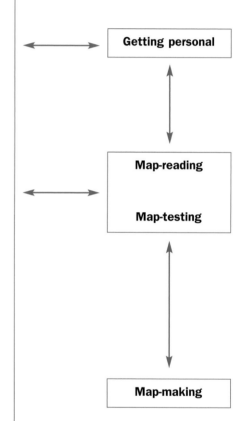

Getting personal

Map-reading

Map-testing

Map-making

7 STRATEGIC LEADERSHIP
DO STRATEGIC LEADERS MATTER?

Have I got what it takes to be a strategic leader? Do strategic leaders matter? Some do, some don't, and a lot more could.[1]

The first book on business strategy I ever read was by Igor Ansoff. Recently I re-opened it, and understood how much has changed in the way we think about business strategy – and how much remains the same.[2]

While certainly extreme and clearly over the line, it appears unlikely the Enron cover-up began as a widespread conspiracy to commit fraud. Rather it seems mostly a case of a business strategy not delivering expected results (quickly enough) and a short-term solution getting totally out of hand.[3]

In today's environment, we no longer view the defining role of the CEO as master-strategist or expect a single mind to do all of the thinking for our organisations. The role of the CEO is just as concerned with shaping the organisational context within which a compelling vision, moral purpose and creative strategy are most likely to emerge.[4]

ORIENTATION

As in previous chapters, readers are first invited to reflect on their existing POUs of leadership to provide an initial benchmark or map for later comparative purposes. Most practitioners and students of business will already be familiar with some concepts of strategy, and with techniques to support it. Exercise 7.1 should be completed before further study of the contents of the chapter.

In this chapter we examine the nature of strategy as it is taught in executive programmes through a POU shared by consultants, practitioners, and many management scholars. We also see how the approach has marginalized the role of leadership. The elevated position of strategy in formal business education conceals dilemmas which we will explore.

One dilemma was revealed by a provocative question posed by Donald Hambrick, a distinguished scholar of business studies. He was writing as guest editor of an issue of the influential *Strategic Management Journal* in 1989. In his introduction, he suggested it was time to 'put top managers back in the strategy picture'. His shocking question was 'Do strategic leaders matter?'

Strategy is an ancient discipline, perhaps first studied and executed by military leaders.[5] It has been taught for at least two millennia in military academies and administrative staff colleges. Its formal study took a modern turn with the emergence of business schools in the twentieth century. There it became an essential component of the curriculum of MBA courses around the world. Such a modern business education was seen as a means of bringing more rigour to understanding organizational behaviour in order to assist the untutored efforts of pioneering business leaders. It reinforced the merits of the prevailing

---

Exercise 7.1: What Do I Understand by the Term Strategic Leadership?

You have been asked to write an essay about strategic leadership. Compose a short paragraph outlining what you understand by the term. Mention one or two most important experiences and/or more formal contributions to your understanding that you intend to expand upon in your essay. If you are completing a formal business course, you may want to split your remarks into 'before course' and 'during course' aspects.

1 Early influences
2 During course influences.

[Exercise for personal reflection, or tutorial or classroom discussion.]

scientific approach to management, and was to contribute to the acceptance of a DRM as necessary for effective corporate decision-making.

In an examination of the history of strategic leadership, Leavy and McKiernan suggest that in its early days, strategy was grounded within a business policy perspective.[6] They traced its origins to work at the Harvard Business School in the 1950s–1960s. Roland Christensen and colleagues had developed a case-based approach to the teaching of strategy, which has been retained to the present day.[7] These pioneers regarded corporate strategy as 'a simple practitioner's theory . . . a kind of Everyman's conceptual scheme [to deal with] unstructured, complex and unique situations'.[8]

By the second half of the twentieth century, the centrality of the Harvard view of strategy for the effective management of the modern business enterprise was widely accepted. It added to the credibility and mystique of leading management consultancies such as McKinsey & Co.,[9] which were to grow into global enterprises. Harvard Business School was to supply leading consulting firms with many of their own graduates, in a mutually beneficial relationship.[10]

By the start of the new millennium, however, serious questions were being asked about the theory and practice of corporate strategy as it had been traditionally taught.

Newer ideas were being discussed to address what were seen as increasingly turbulent and unclear business conditions.[11] New industries offered promise, but only through creative strategies.

One recent reformulation suggested that the old realities have been replaced by two strategic possibilities: 'One to find and develop markets where there is little or no competition – blue oceans – and the other is to exploit and protect blue oceans.'[12]

This re-examination was the more urgent in the wake of the credit implosion of 2007–8 which swept around the world from its US origins. Lessons from the Enron scandals of the early 2000s had appeared to have been forgotten or ignored. Had there been a collective failure of strategic leadership in many firms? Might existing models of strategy need re-examining in light of these experiences?

Has the business landscape of the twenty-first century changed so much that we should discard the most respected theories of the latter half of the twentieth century? In this chapter, it is suggested that drastic rejection of well-established theoretical maps is premature. Nevertheless, their re-evaluation against breakdowns of strategic leadership is timely in what is becoming known as the post-Enron era of business practice.

An additional consideration is the significance of environmental uncertainties. These are perceived as producing a more complex and turbulent operating environment, impacting on firms from the largest global enterprise to the smallest of local businesses. For such reasons, the post-Enron era is often characterized as having high-velocity turbulent conditions that weaken the potential for effective strategic forecasting and planning.[13] The shocks of the economic crisis of 2007–8 help to bring into focus the contemporary dilemmas of strategy and help us to test them against the conventional wisdom suggested in its historical maps.

Readers may reflect on these issues by tackling Exercise 7.2.

Exercise 7.2: What They Don't Teach You at Harvard Business School

Mark McCormack pioneered the business of sports sponsorship. He founded International Management Group, a multimillion-dollar, worldwide corporation, and is credited as the single most important influence in turning sports into big business. In 1984, he wrote a dismissive critique entitled 'What they don't teach you at Harvard Business School'.[14] He argued: 'Business demands innovation. There is a constant need to feel around the fringes, to test the edges, but business schools, out of necessity, are condemned to teach the past.'[15]

Exercise 7.2 Questions

1 How would you assess McCormack's assertion that business schools fail to provide instruction about innovation?
2 Can you think what McCormack was implying in his assertion that business schools 'out of necessity are condemned to teach the past?'
3 Can you suggest how working in team projects for corporate clients helps to address his criticisms?

ORIENTATION

One of the defining features of business schools is the way strategy became one of its core elements within the MBA curriculum. By the 1970s, MBAs were introduced to the subject through the contents of a slim volume entitled *Corporate Strategy*, written by Igor Ansoff.[16] In the 1980s, this had been replaced by more substantial texts, such as *Competitive Advantage* by Michael Porter.[17] By the turn of the century, corporate strategy was studied as a capstone course, with even weightier textbooks of readings and strategy cases.[18] The materials in the most popular texts showed a remarkable convergence in both content and treatment. 'What they teach you' at Harvard had become 'What they teach you in any business school'.

Strategy textbooks have tended to be grounded firmly in the DRM. Little emphasis is placed on the dilemmas of leadership, although, as we will see in this chapter, the dilemmas were addressed by strategy scholars. For example, strategy was largely presented as being determined by objective factors in the competitive environment. This poses the question of whether the strategic leader can initiate creative change beyond adhering to the prescriptions provided by leading authorities for identifying the objectively correct strategic option or options.

This dilemma became known as the question of strategic choice. Or, as strategy scholar Donald Hambrick put it: 'Do strategic leaders matter?' If the question challenged strategy theorists in the 1990s, it was to become a matter of practical concern in the subsequent financial scandals culminating in the global economic crisis of 2007–8.

Exercise 7.3 invites you to reflect on your own views of the dilemma of strategic choice.

Exercise 7.3: The Strategic Challenge: Do Strategic Leaders Matter?

The importance of strategy hides a dilemma for strategic managers. If strategy is a matter of analysis that identifies the best strategic choice, the importance of leadership vision diminishes. Strategy is essentially a matter of information processing. If, on the other hand, there is scope for imagination and creativity to shape the internal structures and strategy, the effective strategic leader makes a profound difference.

Exercise 7.3 Discussion Questions

1 Can you think of circumstances when strategic choice is likely to be limited?
2 Can you think of circumstances when strategic choice is likely to be less restricted?
3 Has anything you have come across in earlier chapters contributed to your conclusions about the importance of a strategic leader for organizational change?

Igor Ansoff claimed to have invented the discipline of corporate strategy, a claim contested by Peter Drucker, among others.[19] Ansoff's *Corporate Strategy* taught a generation of business leaders the techniques of SWOT analysis, weighing up the tensions between a company's internal strengths and weaknesses, and its external environment's threats and opportunities, exposing the strategic dilemmas facing the company.[20] Michael Porter developed a series of conceptual models that analysed the forces present in competitive environments as a way of revealing appropriate strategies. Executives have become aware of his ideas, and terms such as competitive advantages, niche strategies, and strategic entry barriers have entered professional discourse, popularized through his work although traceable to earlier industrial economic theories.[21]

It has been suggested that research focus in strategy has swung like a pendulum.[22] In the 1960s, the emphasis was at the level of the firm and its internal structure. The work provided rich, case-based accounts of interest to industrial leaders and management teachers and researchers. In the 1970s and 1980s, the pendulum swung, with appreciation of the under-explored strategic implications of industry structures. The push on the pendulum came from the efforts of researchers drawing on the economics literature. The swing took the emphasis away from concepts of direct relevance to strategic leaders, such as the tools and techniques developed by the corporate-level writers. Unsurprisingly, the role of the business leader was less central (except as a player in the drama known as the strategic-choice debate: could leaders and their actions make a significant difference to the strategic choices open to a company?).

In the 1990s, the pendulum was pushed back towards internal structural issues for gaining competitive advantage through deployment of the firm's resources. A range of themes relevant to strategy was emerging, under the generic title of resource-based theories of the firm. The role of the leader was back on the research agenda as a means of knowledge capture and exploitation. The leader was seen increasingly as one possible influence, rather than as a major initiator of change.[23]

Box 7.1: Strategic Leadership Maps and Dilemmas

Strategy as a business subject has been grounded in several perspectives or maps. The early maps applying the strategy case were often written as leadership dilemmas to draw in and inspire potential business leaders.[24] The writings of Chandler also credited leadership actions in the historical development of the new international structures (the M-form).[25] Much emphasis was placed on the relationships between strategy formulation and implemented structural innovations.

More recent maps have turned their attention to corporate competences and to identifying how such competences may be converted into competitive advantages. Prahalad and Hamel argued that, in fast-changing and uncertain (turbulent) environments, leaders will be judged by their skills in identifying and exploiting core competences.[26] A broader theoretical debate has developed around the firm as a means of managing such resources. This has become known as the *resource-based theory of the firm.*

One extended debate is whether leaders have scope for influencing strategy effectively. This amounts to a dilemma of determinism against the possibility of a leader creating new possibilities encapsulated in a strategic vision.

A study of research themes in the *Strategic Management Journal* listed six broad maps over the period from the 1980s to the 2000s:[27]

■ *Strategy and top management* Involving leadership, methods of planning and modelling strategic decision-making and change.
■ *Strategy and its environment* Including and extending the early strategic-fit ideas.

- *Strategy and performance* Often including studies at the level of strategic groups, corporate strategy, and financial measures.
- *Growth and market entry* Including entry processes, and strategic advantage models.
- *Industry and competition* Competitive and industry analysis, and the theory of strategic groups sharing strategic characteristics.
- *Resource-based theory of the firm* A firm's distinctiveness is embedded in its unique resources or core competences.

PLATFORMS OF UNDERSTANDING

Our platforms of understanding explore two maps of the historical territory of strategic leadership. The first is by Afsaneh Nahavandi and Ali Malekzadeh, of Arizona State University.[28] The chronological focus of their study is the period of New Leadership's emergence (1970s and 1980s).[29] Their work helps us to understand the dilemmas of strategy formation and implementation during this period. The second map is that of Kimberly B. Boal and Robert Hooijberg, who examined theorizing of what is known as top-echelon theory at the end of the twentieth century.[30]

Both maps indicate that top-level leaders can make a difference. However, a leader's influence is only one factor involved in effective strategy formation and implementation. This provides some support for a strategic-choice view of leadership, as opposed to the view that strategy is essentially deterministic. The two POUs also indicate the complexities of multi-level theoretical modelling. The impact of top leaders tends to be emphasized in strategy *formulation*, and that of lower-level leaders/supervisors as moderating factors in strategy *implementation*.

POU 7.1: Strategic Leadership: Nahavandi and Malekzadeh's Investigation

Nahavandi and Malekzadeh carried out a thorough investigation of empirical studies of the impact of leadership and strategy on performance.[31] They showed how the literature gave some comfort to two opposed viewpoints on the impact of leadership in addressing the critical question 'Do strategic leaders matter?'

This is the debate which examines strategic determinism and strategic choice. The determinists propose that strategy is a process of identifying factors determined by environmental, structural, or cultural factors. The strategy is thus not *created* by insight on the part of a leader but *discovered* by analytical processes. Non-determinist views propose that the leader has strategic choice, which eventually influences the corporation's success.

Some of the confusions can be explained by looking at the studies in closer detail. The studies have tended to examine two different levels of influence: top leaders, and leaders throughout the organization, thus including team leaders and first-level supervisors. Much of the work has focused on individuals who would not have been considered leaders in the early, trait-based era of leadership research.

For leaders outside the top leadership cadre, there has been little scope traditionally for influencing strategy *formulation* in practice. Even strategic choice advocates would consider that the impact would be through a lower-level leader influencing the *implementation* of strategy. For top leaders, the strategic choice advocates would consider that the most significant influence a leader can bring to bear is in strategy formulation.

The majority of studies have focused on implementation. The widely accepted view is that leaders are unable to modify behaviours and beliefs so as to be more effective in implementing a strategy. Consequently, in line with the dominance of contingency theory for several decades, an impact arises if the leaders are *matched* to the strategies. (Compare contingency theory.) If a new strategy is brought in, new leadership practices, and probably new leaders responsible for implementation, have to be introduced.

The general thrust of this analysis is that leaders influence implementation as one among a range of so-called intervening or contingent variables. However, different styles and functional backgrounds may be needed at different stages of implementation, and for different kinds of strategy. For example, entrepreneurial and pioneering strategies require leaders at all levels with greater capabilities for dealing with uncertainties and with risk management; cost leadership may require process-engineering orientation and skills.

A relatively minor proportion of studies examined the role of leader in strategy formulation. Here, the leader is studied as a main factor impacting on strategy and performance. Three broad classes of factor have been given particular attention:

- leader's personal values (which may extend to the personal values of the top management team)
- demographic characteristics
- personality constructs.

Various studies have identified demographic, personality, personal values, and inter-personal factors as having an impact on the choice of strategy, giving support to the strategic choice perspective.

As in most attempts to develop a meta-analysis in the social sciences, the identification of factors suggests that their influence varies according to circumstances. The conclusion is that any mapping reveals a contingency view ('it all depends . . .') of the importance of a particular factor in influencing leadership performance.[32]

Box 7.2: How Leaders Make a Difference

Nahavandi and Malekzadeh offer an easy-to-understand integrative framework of strategic leadership. The researchers suggest that the strategic leader may be considered to provide a 'main effect', or may operate to provide moderator or intervening variables between strategy and outcomes. They suggest that challenge-seeking orientation and the need for control are dimensions that discriminate the strategic orientation of leaders. High challenge-seeking leaders are innovative in their strategic choices. High control leaders wish to retain control over decisions and actions. This gives a typology of four strategic types:

- A *high challenge/low control* leader seeks change within a process of delegating and sharing responsibilities.
- A *high challenge/high control* leader would seek challenges but expect more conformity to his or her prescribed strategy, retaining control. Innovation, for example, would be 'micro-controlled' for costs.
- A *low challenge/high control* leader would advocate centralization and seek stable environments.
- A *low challenge/low control* leader would encourage participation under conditions in which major change is unlikely. Most often found in organizations not facing tough competitive challenges, or fast changing environments. Some cooperatives, communes, and social clubs operate under such conditions (although these groups may also have high-challenge leadership).

Such typologies simplify the realities of organizational practices. Leaders may have a preferred or dominant style, and yet behave differently, according to situational circumstances.

POU 7.2: Boal and Hooijberg's Important Themes in Strategic Leadership

Kimberly B. Boal and Robert Hooijberg reviewed the field of leadership and arrived at the view that the 1980s and 1990s were decades of substantial changes in leadership thinking.[33] They suggested that the changes involved three themes. These are essentially:

- strategic leadership research
- new leadership
- emergent leadership.

They also suggested that strategy had swung between an interest in a dominant chief executive and leadership at supervisory levels of operational teams, and was moving back to its earlier focus under the rubric 'Upper Echelon theory'. Strategic theories of leadership were rediscovering the importance of leadership *of* organizations rather than leadership *in* organizations.[34]

In an influential article in the mid-1980s, Hambrick and Mason proposed that strategy in organizations reflected characteristics of its top executives ('upper echelon'). The impact of their contribution was to help redirect attention towards strategic-level issues. Hambrick and Mason highlighted aspects in the way the leader(s) thought, and the values they held. Essentially, they were proposing that leaders within an upper echelon 'made a difference' through their cognitive styles and belief systems.

At the time when upper-echelon leadership research was developed, one of the influential theories of strategy widely taught in business schools was that of Michael Porter. Specifically, his method of identifying an organization's optimal strategic 'position' indicated that, with correct analysis, there was no need for leadership intervention in setting strategy. (Strategy could be carried out by well-trained MBAs.) A related debate was that between the earlier rational school of strategic planning and ideas of emergent strategy, advocated by Henry Mintzberg.[35]

This again raises a dilemma of strategic choice: 'Can I, as a leader, create a unique strategy for my organization, or is it a process best left to a team of strategic planners?'

Hambrick and co-workers found a way of dealing with this dilemma. They identified *leader discretion* as a critical component of effectiveness,[36] describing the idea as a bridge between two kinds of theory, one claiming priority for leadership creativity, the other claiming priority for environmental forces. This theory neatly side-steps the 'either/or' debate of strategic choice. It indicates that creativity may be possible as a form of leadership option. Based on the perception of the increasing turbulence of organizational work,[37] Boal and Hooijberg argued that the essential features of concern for strategic leadership are *absorptive capacity*, *adaptive capacity*, and *managerial wisdom*.

- ■ *Absorptive capacity* has become a central concept within knowledge management theory and involves a capability for knowledge capture and utilization (learning).
- ■ *Adaptive capacity* is the potential for change, and has been linked to what some researchers call strategic flexibility.[38]
- ■ *Managerial wisdom* manifests itself in a sensitivity to change in the environment and to the behavioural patterns of others. The former involves what is sometimes referred to as environmental scanning or discernment.[39] The latter has become the focus of attention for researchers into social intelligence and the related concepts of emotional intelligence. It is suggested that a strategic leader's skills in such knowledge management processes are significant through their influence on her/his actions throughout the organization.

CONTEXTUAL MATERIALS

CM 7.1: Twenty-first-century Strategic Leadership: Ireland and Hitt's Analysis

Strategic leadership has often been more implicitly covered than explicitly examined in textbooks on corporate strategy.[40] A review by American scholars Ireland and Hitt in the 1990s for the *Academy of Management Executive* was reprinted as a 'classic' in 2005.[41] It represents a perspective of two distinguished experts in the field and has been widely cited. It also provides an excellent reference source on contemporary studies into strategic leadership.

According to Ireland and Hitt: 'Strategic leadership is defined as a person's ability to anticipate, envision, maintain flexibility, think strategically, and work with others to initiate changes that will create a viable future for the organization.'[42] The broad thrust of the article is that changing environmental conditions in the late decades of the nineteenth century were met with a shift in the behaviours of organizations and organizational leadership. Furthermore, the authors argue that

> being able to exercise strategic leadership in a competitively superior manner facilitates the firm's efforts to earn superior returns on its investments . . . [In] the new competitive landscape . . . in the twenty-first century, the ability to build, share and leverage knowledge will replace the ownership and/or leverage of assets as a primary source of competitive advantage.[43]

As a consequence, a shift was occurring away from the earlier view of the 'The Great Leader', 'The Lone Ranger', or, as Bennis termed it, 'The Corporate Hercules'.[44] They argue that the shift will be from the Great Leader to the Great Group.

The vocabulary of the Great Group was introduced by Warren Bennis.[45] Ireland and Hitt argue that

> [Great groups] usually feature managers with significant profit and loss responsibilities, internal networkers . . . Top managers . . . have shifted the locus of responsibility to form adaptive solutions from themselves to the organization's full citizenry.[46]

The authors write of corporations becoming learning communities, a view shared by learning theorists such as Etienne Wenger[47] and organizational experts such as Peter Senge and Charles Handy.[48] They list six components of the emerging strategic leadership approach:

- ■ *Strategic vision* Here the quotes suggest wide acceptance of the importance of establishing a creative vision through a Top Management Team (a special kind of Great Group), although some role-model leaders quoted are rather reluctant to depart from the older 'Lone Ranger' view.

- *Developing core competences* Particularly important is privately owned knowledge. Viable firms are increasingly dependent on nurturing their knowledge base through encouragement of innovative enquiry.
- *Human capital* This is a broader version of the assets within the firm's 'entire workforce or citizenry'.[49] The efforts of the Top Management Team (a very important Great Group) will be increasingly directed to nurturing the talents of all employees.
- *Sustaining culture* Successful firms are associated with a culture that enhances positive reactions to challenges of change.
- *Ethical practices* The importance of establishing ethical norms is noted, and some ethical pitfalls are anticipated, prior to both the Enron and the 2007–8 financial crises.
- *Balanced controls* The older idea of top-down control through objective financial demands is replaced by a more complex balance of strategic and financial controls. The new conditions call for strategic 'information based exchanges . . . with emphasis on actions rather than outcomes [which] encourage lower-level managers to make decisions that incorporate moderate and acceptable levels of risk'.[50]

The general treatment of the 'Great Group' has much in common with writers on distributed leadership as outlined in Chapter 3. Ireland and Hitt provide a valuable integrative analysis of views of the successful twenty-first-century organization embedded in its fast-changing, turbulent, and global environment. Their review provides a road map for strategic leadership into the future. Some of the exemplary leaders cited for their practices are no longer considered role models. One commentator argued that the rise and fall of a leader's reputation 'in a curious way supports as much as weakens the broader conceptualization provided in the article'.[51]

CM 7.2: Tipping-point Leadership: Bill Bratton

The concept of a radical point at which old ideas are rapidly and irreversibly shifted was known to management theorists for decades, derived from the studies of paradigms and paradigm switching by Kuhn. It was popularized more recently by Malcolm Gladwell in one of his best-selling books, *The Tipping Point*. He reported the work of two management scholars, Chan Kim and Renee Mauborgne.[52]

Gladwell, in one interview, explained his own model:

> One of the things I'd like to do is to show people how to start 'positive' epidemics of their own. The virtue of an epidemic, after all, is that just a little input is enough to get it started, and it can spread very, very quickly. That makes it something of obvious and enormous interest to everyone from educators trying to reach students, to businesses trying to spread the word about their product, or for that matter to anyone who's trying to create a change with limited resources.[53]

According to Kim and Mauborgne, strategic transformations occur where there is a rapid shift (they talk of a hurdle crossed) in strategy orientation and strategy implementation.[54] There are four hurdles (or tipping-points): two of re-orientation, and two of implementation. Implementation of strategy results in unexpected outcomes. The process is more of a series of tipping-points, rather than a single, linear sequence of four stages.

The re-orientation of strategy involves a shift in assumptions and beliefs – *the cognitive hurdle* – and a shift in resources – *the resource hurdle*. The implementation involves a shift in *motivational* and *political* factors. These are the four steps of the model, the 'what' of strategic change. The authors indicate the 'how' of strategic change, illustrating with the rapid and transforming changes that have been achieved and credited to the strategic leadership of New York Police Chief Bill Bratton.

New York City is famous for the scale of its buildings, its pace of life, and for its rich cultural contribution in the shaping of modern America. It is also famous for its social problems, and the challenges of policing. The city suffered its greatest single catastrophic event in the World Trade Centre attack of 11 September 2001. His leadership at the time of crisis contributed to the reputation of the mayor, Rudolph Giuliani. Our story links Mayor Giuliani with his redoubtable police commissioner, Bill Bratton.

Bratton has a track record of achieving impressive and sustainable strategic change, initially in Boston at district level, then as chief of the Massachusetts Bay Transit Authority ('the terror train'), and eventually as superintendent of the Boston Metropolitan Police. In each of his assignments, Bill Bratton developed a strategic style exemplifying the four stages of the tipping-point model.

Prior to Bratton's appointment at the New York Police Department in 1994, the city faced a crisis of confidence in the safety of its citizens in public places. There was increasing movement out to the suburbs, leaving whole areas derelict. Drug crime and vandalism were on the increase. Bratton had already been credited with the one bright spot, the highly visible improvements to the infamous New York Transit Authority (NYTA), within a few years after his arrival from Boston. In New York, his strategic plans were credited for the clear progress made in addressing and dealing with the major sources of social discomfort and danger. In the media, Bratton's achievements were simplified as the success of his controversial *zero-tolerance* strategy.

'Winning hearts and minds' has become a leadership cliché. Bratton developed several powerful approaches, which he modified to meet each new set of circumstances. One might be termed '*back to the shop floor*'. Managers 'see' their jobs differently after they (re-)encounter the realities of the shop floor or the front line. Policing permits many opportunities for introducing this strategic shift plan. At the NYTA, Bratton initiated an edict. Starting with himself, his officials were to travel to and from work and to other official functions on the transit system. Subsequent discussions became more grounded in practical realities.

'Meet the public' events were introduced (a plan he had found successful during his time in Boston). Such meetings helped to confirm the view that the police were pre-occupied with dealing with serious crimes, ignoring 'petty' crimes of all kinds, whereas the public were far more concerned with day-to-day encounters with 'vandals and vagabonds'. It was from such confirmation that the policy of zero-tolerance became internally accepted. Another approach involved communicating his messages internally. Aware of the low priority of circulated paperwork, he recruited a journalist to support internal communications, which became more immediate and involving, including video messaging at roll calls.

Effective, quick-moving leaders find ways to use existing resources in the short term, while lobbying for more for the future. Bratton tended to win more resources for his people; he also worked at targeting 'hot-spots' in using what he had. For this sort of change he used hard facts to back his arguments. He was able to show, for example, that the policing of drug activities was inadequate and misdirected (it had been a Monday-to-Friday operation by custom and practice, and contrary to the evidence that drug dealing was a seven-days-a-week business).

Under conditions of crisis (the tipping-point condition), motivation is enhanced through a process of focusing on key groups of middle-range leaders. Bratton's particularly effective plan involved the 67 district commanders, each with two to four hundred staff. The commanders were mandated to be present at twice-weekly strategy review meetings where they were quizzed by a panel including senior officers and significant outsiders.

Participants were informed at short notice that they were to present the work of their precinct. The format ensured that there was little possibility for excuses or blame-laying. The process encouraged acceptance of responsibilities for strategy formation and execution. Each presenter was expected to speak about the summary information culled from their computer databases and explain the significance of the revealed crime statistics on operational decisions for dealing with the hot-spots. In this way, the commanders were visibly accountable for their actions. This tended to be a motivational bonus for those showing leadership abilities, although a less pleasant experience for the weaker leaders. A further consequence of the plan was a trickle-down effect, as the precinct commanders began organizing their own mini-strategic reviews at precinct level. Bratton worked at communicating a message that spoke to his officers at all levels, block by block, precinct by precinct, and borough by borough.

Bratton had learned the hard way that political intrigues could block strategies and people. He had been briefly side-lined, earlier in his career, paying the price for ignoring or crudely confronting political opponents. Over time, he developed his plan for dealing with opponents of his strategies. Internally, he moved swiftly to isolate the implacable opponents, if necessary removing them from positions of (negative) influence. Externally, he concentrated on building coalitions (his relationship with Mayor Guiliani has already been mentioned). The coalition was necessary to overcome resistance from the courts, who feared that the zero-tolerance strategy would multiply their workloads and make the justice system unworkable.

CM 7.3: An Information-based Leadership Strategy

This case illustrates the issues of strategic leadership within a not-for-profit organization and the interrelationship between strategy formulation and its implementation.[55]

John sets strategies that have life-or-death consequences for everyone living and working in a large metropolitan region of England. He is charged with setting and implementing the strategy for the region's emergency health services. His approach is strongly influenced by his background as a London School of Economics graduate. Taken on as a National Health Service 'fast-track' leadership candidate, he was conscious of the opportunities for better service that could be achieved through new technology.

Senior health service executives in the UK have to exercise leadership while discharging their responsibilities within government policy and operational and financial guidelines. They are also responsible as 'service providers' to the people within their geographical region.

At the time when John was introducing his change programme for the ambulance service (2002–3), the health service was facing wider government pressures for change. Later, Tony Blair, who was prime minister at the time, wrote about the difficulties of challenging 'givens within which the system operates . . . Changing them can be even harder. A whole web of custom, practice, and interest has been created around them; yet for the organization to make progress, they must be changed.'[56]

Other public services were also opposing change. Regional police forces were resisting efforts to bring about greater integration. More spectacularly, the fire service had entered into a bitter industrial dispute that had led to prolonged actions including 'limited cover' and withdrawal of labour on 'days of action' (strikes). At the heart of the confused claims and counter-claims was the issue of 'modernization' being sought by the government and requiring acceptance of changed working practices and the introduction of new technology.

John's strategic approach was to find ways of filling a performance gap – the time taken for ambulances to respond to emergency calls. He could see clearly how this could be achieved by introducing new technology that could build up a database of incidents and pin-point the location of all vehicles at all times. The 'custom, practice, and interest' described by Tony Blair meant that the crews would resist the idea of their locations being monitored in what they regarded as unacceptably intrusive ways.

Advanced tracking systems and logistic programmes had demonstrably improved times for response to emergency calls, and onward to hospital accident and emergency reception areas. The technology also provided comprehensive data that could be analysed for more strategic decisions. For example, it pin-pointed the peaks and troughs of demand. This demonstrated the need for changes in shift patterns, involving more unsocial hours.

The vision was of a technical system that would minimize call-out and delivery times. The strategic dilemma was to find improvements that would not be held up by intolerable negotiations that were miring change efforts in the other emergency services. However, in the negotiations the evidence was presented in formats that were clear and undisputed, and as being directed primarily towards necessary improvements in reaction times, and thus aligned with shared values.

John was aware of the 'Big Brother' aspect of the implementation of such a strategy. The tracking devices could have been used to examine the locations of specific ambulance crews at all times, as a means of monitoring and controlling working practices. This is a well-known example of a technological change being seen as a managerial opportunity and as a threat to those affected. Some years earlier, the installation of tachometers in commercial vehicles, identifying speed profiles, was widely attacked by drivers as 'the spy in the cab'. Through John's consistent emphasis that the technology changes would be directed only towards implementing the agreed strategy of improving emergency response times, the anxieties of union members were managed without disruption of work. Improvements were also measured so as to permit open discussion of productivity rewards.

Over time, the technology was used to influence other stakeholders, as more and more sophisticated evidence emerged of hot-spots requiring special attention; these included identification of localities, and even time-peaks for specific kinds of medical emergency, such as coronary emergency call-outs. Ambulance fleets were redeployed to take account of such data. Importantly, the data could be presented and discussed in order to evaluate the evidence of improvements in call-out times.

The 'pure' planned strategy became actualized in a form influenced by 'emergent' changes. The rational technical optimization was tempered by reframing of the change in line with the ethos of the service (saving lives) while respecting the informal practices of the ambulance crew members.

CM 7.4: Sun Tzu and Business Strategy

Mark McNeilly was a successful business strategist for IBM Corporation. He became increasingly impressed by an unusual source of inspiration, namely, the wisdom of the great Chinese general Sun Tzu, whose ideas are still influential after more than two millennia.[57] Since McNeilly's book was published it has gained international attention and been followed by other successful books, including one 'updating' the ancient military wisdom of Sun Tzu for modern military leaders.

Working from a scholarly English translation of Sun Tzu's work, and drawing on an interest in military history, McNeilly concluded that the principles were (with appropriate updating) still valid today for military strategists. He further concluded that they offered rich insights for business strategists. He then offered six strategic principles:

- win all without [all-out] fighting
- avoid [competitor's] strength; attack weakness

- deception and foreknowledge
- speed and preparation
- shape your opponent
- character-based leadership.

The principles are not totally self-explanatory. *Winning all without [all-out] fighting* suggests that victory is better if the former enemy is not destroyed, but is dealt with so as to become a future ally. *Deception and foreknowledge* argues for preparing for strategic initiatives, keeping in mind the dangers of a directly signalled attack on the competition's strong points. *Shaping your opponent* involves all sorts of interactions with competitors, including negotiations and alliances, taking into account a psychological appraisal of leadership characteristics. Where possible, taking advantage of emotions of competitors is an advised approach. *Character-based leadership* is a form of trait-based leadership style, with ethical principles, involving leading by example and with integrity. The style is presented as one that can be developed though study and practice.

McNeilly first argues that business strategy has evolved from military strategy. He suggests that the six principles encourage a more creative approach to strategy that might have avoided some of the corporate down-sizing caused by one-dimensional strategic thinking.

In illustration of ignoring the principle of win all without fighting, he gives chilling examples from industries that have entered price wars, such as airlines and cigarette companies. His conclusion is that strategists seem to forget that a 'battle' for market share should be seen as a means to corporate survival and prosperity, not an end in itself. The Sun Tzu principle supports the increased interest in the last few decades in strategic alliances, even among firms in a competitive marketplace.

He illustrates the principles at work in high-technology companies such as computers, where great efforts are made to retain customers for new generations of products. Competitive firms attack each other's products and the veracity of claims, in trade press releases and in any other media channels available.

He expands with a commercial example that has become a well-known classroom illustration: Sir Gordon White of Hanson plc achieved a hostile takeover of Smith Corona, during which there were various smokescreens involving bid offers. The deception is considered to have reduced the vigilance within Smith Corona, and helped Hanson to acquire additional shares at a reasonable price on the open market.

McNeilly also describes what happened to IBM when it attempted to change a culture of secrecy, aiming towards more openness. This resulted in employees sending out mixed messages, often criticizing the products of other IBM divisions. The company decided that such displays of openness had gone too far. The new head of IBM, Louis Gerstner, set about discouraging such public displays of infighting, as a matter of corporate policy.

INTEGRATION

We began the chapter by asking whether strategic leaders actually made a difference. Nahavandi and Malekzadeh reported that the evidence is far from conclusive.

Two factors were suggested as most likely to differentiate strategic preferences, namely a challenge-seeking orientation and a need for control. The two challenge-seeking styles are more associated with innovation. High challenge/low control leads to participative and open cultures of change; high challenge/high control leads to a more autocratic or directive style of change. Of the two challenge-averse styles, low challenge/high control leaders are best considered for roles within cost-differentiating strategies, and low challenge/low control leaders in benign climates where decisions and responsibilities are widely distributed.

Kimberly Boal and Robert Hooijberg reported that the literature shows that leaders make a difference through their cognitive styles and belief systems (values). The leader influences an organization's absorptive capacity, adaptive capacity, and managerial wisdom. The issue of strategic choice was further refined through the concept of *leader discretion* as a bridge between two kinds of theory, one claiming priority for leadership creativity, the other claiming priority for environmental forces.

Our contextual reports gave examples of leaders who made a difference, either as *implementers of policy* or as *formulators of strategy.* Their leadership discretion covered the manner in which they set out the strategy through which they would achieve their policy guidelines.

The principles of Sun Tzu's *Art of War* were used to suggest strategic ways of making a difference. Several of these principles (like many folk maxims), when examined collectively, are contradictory. For example, some cut across the principle of character-based leadership, which is also considered important (demonstrating integrity and trustworthiness).

The author distinguishes between deception that involves making false statements, and deception that arises from calculated withholding of information for corporate self-interest. These limits seem more about what is legally permissible than about what might be ethically dubious. These dilemmas will be addressed again in the next two chapters.

GETTING PERSONAL

A fundamental challenge is raised in this chapter for practising leaders. Do you, or don't you, 'make a difference' in your strategic efforts?

Have you scope to make a difference in contributing to the formulation of strategy, or are you at present mainly restricted to implementation work? In either case, the difference is likely to be as part of a collaborative effort in which leadership roles and practices are distributed.

Older maps present strategic leaders in heroic terms. Yet, unease at the super-hero leader is found in maps challenging the virtues of a charismatic leadership style and the New Leadership concepts of transforming leaders. This may be encouraging to readers who consider themselves to be more reflective in style. There is evidence of the value of the 'modest leader of fierce resolve' identified in the studies of level-five leaders.

Nahavandi and Malekzadeh suggest that the strategic leader may not have to provide a 'main effect', but rather is able to operate so as to moderate the effects of various factors between intended strategy and implemented outcomes.

Box 7.3: What Sort of Strategic Leader Am I?

We posed this question slightly differently at the start of the chapter. Do you have what it takes to become a strategic leader? Experienced leaders will have had the opportunity to relate the strategic maps to personal experience. In this way, it may become possible to approach afresh the question 'What sort of leader am I?' Perhaps the integrative model of Nahavandi and Malekzadeh suggests clues. You should have a sense of your own concern for challenge, and therefore of your likelihood of flourishing in an environment requiring innovation and entrepreneurial leadership. A sense of your need for control as contrasting to willingness to encourage (empower?) followers will indicate the style with which you would approach your leadership tasks.

'Wannabe' leaders have to take a view less based on direct leadership experiences. As an alternative self-reflection exercise, you may find it valuable to ask yourself about your ideal leadership role. What would you be doing? How would you be doing it? Do any of the leadership maps help you in this? The more convinced you are of the future you have pictured, the more likely that the exercise is tapping into your values and self-beliefs.

Whether experienced or 'wannabe' leader, treat this reflective exercise as a starting-point for further reflection and discussion with someone who knows you well, and whose opinion and feedback you will respect.

SUMMARY

At the start of the chapter we presented a dilemma posed by Hambrick: Does leadership matter, or is it a matter of finding the right answer by applying analytical techniques correctly? This dilemma is glossed over by those who reflectively accept the dominant model behind much of what is found in strategy texts. It contributes to a further dilemma of whether strategic leaders make a difference.

If strategies are largely deterministic, the significance of the strategic leader is minimal. Strategy can be safely left to a team of strategic planners. Hambrick and co-workers resolve this potential dilemma through the concept of leader discretion, which places leadership creativity as a component, but also shaped by constraints identifiable through strategic planning.

Another persistent assumption is that strategy can be understood through two sequential stages of formulation followed by implementation. Most textbooks give priority to formulation, seen as the domain of the strategically thinking leader. Implementation is treated as a more operational matter, with emphasis on the issues of project management covered in Chapter 3. The two-stage map is rarely challenged and has considerable face validity for executives as well as for strategy consultants and theorists. It leaves unanswered the question of effectiveness. If a strategy has been judged a failure, how might the lack of success be attributed to faulty formulation, and how might it be caused by faulty implementation?

Trends in mapping organizational strategy have swung towards interest in resource-based theories that emphasize knowledge management, intellectual property, and the innovative potential of knowledge workers. These approaches give more consideration to behavioural factors and processes. Nevertheless, the DRM remains more in evidence than do alternative formulations.

Over several decades, ideas from alternative maps are beginning to influence strategic theories. The more deterministic approaches place priority on identifying the appropriate strategy. The less deterministic ones treat strategy as being emergent as efforts are made to define and achieve organizational goals. This offers a way of addressing the dilemmas of the two-stage formulation, then implementation. A further shift is towards the distribution of responsibilities for strategy leadership. One move is captured in awareness of a small group of strategic leaders (top echelon maps). More radical ideas are to be found in maps that assume wider distributions of strategic influence (distributed leadership).

Into the future, strategy seems likely to remain important in mapping the challenges of business leadership. The subject has changed substantially with attempts to address increasingly complex and unclear environments. There is need for analytical competences of the kind 'they teach at business school'. Yet, implementation results in the emergence of unexpected ideas. This is an area in which learning, imagination, map-testing, and map-making become particularly important.

NOTES

1 Hambrick, D.C. (1989) 'Guest editor's introduction: Putting top managers back in the strategy picture', *Strategic Management Journal*, 10, 5–15.
2 John Kay, writing in the *Financial Times*, 15 March 2008, www.johnkay.com/2009/03/15/history-vindicates-the-science-of-muddling-through/, downloaded 17 June 2010.
3 Presentation by Keith W. Rabin, President, KWR International, Inc., to Board of Directors Retreat, Republic Bank of Trinidad & Tobago, 25 May 2002, http://kwrintl.com/PDF/repbank.pdf, downloaded 17 June 2010.

4 Leavy, B., & McKiernan, P. (2008) *Strategic leadership, governance and renewal*, London: Palgrave Macmillan, p. 8.

5 Adair, J. (1989) *Great leaders*, Guildford, UK: Talbot Adair; Heuser, B. (2010) *The evolution of strategy: Thinking war from antiquity to the present*, Cambridge, England: Cambridge University Press.

6 Leavy, B., & McKiernan, P. (2008) *Strategic leadership, governance and renewal*, London: Palgrave Macmillan, p. 2.

7 http://institutionalmemory.hbs.edu/person/christensen,_carl_roland.html.

8 Leavy, B., & McKiernan, P. (2008) *Strategic leadership, governance and renewal*, London: Palgrave Macmillan, p. 6.

9 Huey, J. (1993) 'How McKinsey does it', *Fortune*, 1 November, http://money.cnn.com/magazines/fortune/fortune_archive/1993/11/01/78550/index.htm, downloaded 4 May 2011.

10 www.insidehbs.com/top-employers-of-hbs-mbas/, downloaded 14 December 2010.

11 Grant, R.M. (2007) *Contemporary strategy analysis*, 6th edn, London: Blackwell; Johnson, D., Scholes, K., & Whittingham, R. (2008) *Exploring corporate strategy*, 8th edn, Harlow, Essex: FT Prentice Hall; Doyle, P., & Stern, P. (2006) *Marketing management and strategy*, 4th edn, Hemel Hempstead: Prentice Hall.

12 Kim, W.C., & Mauborgne, R. (2004) 'Blue ocean strategy', *Harvard Business Review*, 82, 10, 80. See also http://www.blueoceanstrategy.com/abo/what_is_bos.html, downloaded 6 June 2011.

13 Taleb, N.N. (2007) *The black swan: The impact of the highly improbable*, London: Penguin; Mintzberg, H. (1994) *The rise and fall of strategic planning*, Englewood Cliffs, N.J.: Prentice Hall; Eisenhardt, K.M. (1989) 'Making fast strategic decisions, *Academy of Management Journal*, 32, 3, 543–576.

14 McCormack, M.H. (1984) *What they don't teach you at Harvard Business School*, London: Collins.

15 Ibid., quotation from inside cover of book.

16 Ansoff, H.I. (1965) *Corporate strategy*, New York: McGraw-Hill.

17 Porter, M.E. (1985) *Competitive advantage: Creating and sustaining superior performance*, New York: Free Press.

18 Johnson, G., Scholes, K., & Whittington, R. (2010) *Exploring corporate strategy*, 8th edn, London: FT Prentice Hall; Thompson, Jr. A.A., Strickland III, A.J., & Gamble J.E. (2007/2010) *Crafting and executing strategy: The quest for competitive advantage*, 17th/18th edns, Boston: McGraw-Hill Irwin.

19 Drucker, P.F. (1955) *The practice of management*, London: Heinemann.

20 Ansoff, H.I. (1965) *Corporate strategy*, New York: McGraw-Hill.

21 Thomas, H. (2004) 'Strategic management: Its development and future directions', in Ghobadian, A., O'Regan, N., Gallear, D., & Viney, H. (2008) *Strategy and performance: Achieving competitive advantage in the global marketplace*, London: Palgrave Macmillan, pp. 289–307.

22 Hoskisson, R.E., Hitt, M.A., Wan, W.P., & Yiu, D. (1999) 'Theory and research in strategic management: Swings of a pendulum', *Journal of Management*, 25, 417–56.

23 Grant, R.M. (2007) *Contemporary strategy analysis*, 6th edn, London: Blackwell.

24 Harvard's claims of pioneering the introduction of the Case Method are widely accepted, and repeated in various texts: Ireland, R.D., & Hitt, M.A. (2005) 'Achieving and maintaining strategic competitiveness in the 21st century: The role of strategic leadership', *Academy of Management Executive*, 19, 4, 65–77 (reprinted from *AME* 1999, 13, 1). Harvard had been using the approach for several decades before the emergence of strategy as a discipline: McNair, M.P. (1954) *The case method at the Harvard Business School: Papers by present and past members of the faculty*, New York: McGraw-Hill.

25 Chandler, A.D. (1966) *Strategy and structure*, Cambridge, MA: MIT Press.

26 Prahalad, C.K., & Hamel, G. (1990) 'The core competence of the corporation', *Harvard Business Review*, 68, 79–91.

27 Thomas, H. (2004) 'Strategic management: Its development and future directions', in Ghobadian, A., O'Regan, N., Gallear, D., & Viney, H. (eds), *Strategy and performance: Achieving competitive advantage in the global marketplace*, London: Palgrave Macmillan, pp. 289–307.

28 Nahavandi, A., & Malekzadeh, A.R. (1993) 'Leadership style in strategy and organizational performance: An integrative framework', *Journal of Management Studies*, 30, 3, 405–425.

29 See chapter 4, and also particularly Bryman, A. (1996) 'Leadership in organizations', in Clegg, S.R., Hardy, C., & Nord, W.R., *Handbook of organization studies*, London: Sage, pp. 276–292.

30 Boal, K.B., & Hooijberg, R. (2000) 'Strategic leadership research: moving on', *Leadership Quarterly*, 11, 4, 515–550.

31 Nahavandi, A., & Malekzadeh, A.R. (1993) 'Leadership style in strategy and organizational performance: An integrative framework', *Journal of Management Studies*, 30, 3, 405–425.

32 www.bmj.com/cgi/content/extract/315/7121/1533.

33 Boal, K.B., & Hooijberg, R. (2000) 'Strategic leadership research: moving on', *Leadership Quarterly*, 11, 4, 515–550. Grint reaches a similar conclusion.

34 Hunt, J.G. (1991) *Leadership: A new synthesis*, Newbury Park, CA: Sage.

35 See Grant, R.M. (2007) *Contemporary strategy analysis*, 6th edn, London: Blackwell, pp. 21–23, for a brief summary of Mintzberg's contributions.

36 Hambrick, D.C., & Finkelstein, S. (1987) 'Managerial discretion: A bridge between polar views of organizations', in Cummings, L.L., & Straw, B.M. (eds), *Research in organizational behaviour*, Vol. 9, pp. 396–406, Greenwich, CT: JAI.

37 Eisenhardt, K. (1989) 'Making fast strategic decisions in high-velocity environments', *Academy of Management Journal*, 32, 3, 543–576.

38 Hitt, M.A., Keats, B.W., & DeMarie, S.M. (1998) 'Navigating in the new competitive landscape: Building strategic flexibility and competitive advantage in the 21st century', *Academy of Management Executive*, 12, 22–41.

39 E.g. Osborn, R.N., Hunt, J.G., & Jauch, L.R. (1980) *Organization theory: An integrated approach*, New York: Wiley.

40 E.g. Johnson, G., Scholes, K., & Whittington, R. (2010) *Exploring corporate strategy*, 8th edn, London: FT Prentice Hall. Their core model has three components of Strategic Position, Strategic Choices, and Strategy in Action. The text suggests that strategic leadership is embedded in the last of the three as a management function.

41 Ireland, R.D., & Hitt, M.A. (2005) 'Achieving and maintaining strategic competitiveness in the 21st century: The role of strategic leadership', *Academy of Management Executive*, 19, 4, 63–77 (reprinted from *AME* 1999, 13, 1).

42 Ibid., p. 63. Additional definitional information about strategic leadership can be found in: Christensen, C.M. (1997) 'Making strategy: Learning by doing', *Harvard Business Review*, 75, 6, 141–156; Hitt, M.A., Ireland, R.D., & Hoskisson, R.E. (1999) *Strategic management: Competitiveness and globalization*, 3rd edn, Cincinnati: South-Western College Publishing.

43 Ibid., pp. 63–64.

44 Bennis, W. (1997) 'Cultivating creative genius', *Industry Week*, 18 August.

45 For more on Great Groups see Finkelstein, S., & Hambrick, D.C. (1996) *Strategic leadership: Top executives and their effects on organizations*, St. Paul: West Publishing.

46 Ireland, R.D., & Hitt, M.A. (2005) 'Achieving and maintaining strategic competitiveness in the 21st century: The role of strategic leadership', *Academy of Management Executive*, 19, 4, 65–77 (reprinted from *AME* 1999, 13, 1), p. 66.

47 Wenger, E. (2006) 'Communities of practice: A brief introduction', www.ewenger.com/theory/, downloaded 5 April 2011.

48 Senge, P.M. (1997) 'Communities of leaders and learners', *Harvard Business Review*, 75, 5, 30–32.

49 Ireland, R.D., & Hitt, M.A. (2005) 'Achieving and maintaining strategic competitiveness in the 21st century: The role of strategic leadership', *Academy of Management Executive*, 19, 4, 65–77 (reprinted from *AME* 1999, 13, 1), p. 70.

50 Ibid., p. 72.

51 http://leaderswedeserve.wordpress.com/2010/05/28/strategic-competitiveness-in-the-21st%C2%A0century/.

52 Kim, W.C., & Mauborgne, R. (2003) 'Tipping point leadership', *Harvard Business Review*, April, 60–69.

53 www.gladwell.com/tippingpoint/index.html, downloaded 18 June 2010. See also Gladwell, M. (2000) *The tipping point: How little things can make a big difference*, New York: Little Brown.

54 Kim, W.C., & Mauborgne, R. (2003) 'Tipping point leadership', *Harvard Business Review*, April, 60–69.

55 Case prepared for *Dilemmas of Leadership*, 1st edn and updated to illustrate challenges for public sector leaders in the UK as policy changes disrupt strategic plans after a change of government (May 2010).

56 Blair, T. (2010) *A journey*, London: Hutchinson, p. 271.

57 McNeilly, M. (1966) *Sun Tzu and the art of business*, Oxford: OUP. He claims that the work influenced modern Chinese and Japanese military thinking, and that its principles can be found in the strategies of successful Western firms.

CHAPTER LEARNING OBJECTIVES

Learning focus
- Understanding power relationships

Key issues
- Critical theory and identity theory
- Gender issues and diversity studies
- Social identity

Dilemmas
- Dilemmas of inequality and exclusion
- Dilemmas of stereotyping

Platforms of understanding
- POU 8.1 Leadership and Gender Analysis: Veccio's Meta-analysis
- POU 8.2 Mapping Diversity: Nkomo and Cox

Contextual materials
- CM 8.1 An Evaluation of the Female Leadership Advantage Theory: Eagly and Carli
- CM 8.2 The Hidden Barack Obama
- CM 8.3 Carly Fiorina: Perfect Enough?
- CM 8.4 Roberto Goizueta

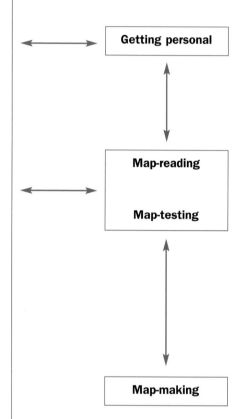

Getting personal

Map-reading

Map-testing

Map-making

8 DILEMMAS OF POWER, DISCRIMINATION, AND DIVERSITY

In the summer of 1999 . . . Carleton Fiorina was named new CEO of Hewlett-Packard . . . She claimed that women face 'no limits whatsoever . . . there is not a glass ceiling'.[1]

Management gurus now know how to boost the odds of getting a great executive: Hire a female.[2]

The term 'political correctness gone mad' is over-used to the point of absurdity by the right. The only way to kill it would be for the progressive left to also over-use it to the point of absurdity.[3]

Language is an important aspect of understanding gender because language defines the reality that we experience and because we cannot experience reality without using language.[4]

When you have studied Chapter 8 you will have been introduced to critical theory as a powerful means of exploring inequalities in social life, with particular attention to power relationships. Gender issues and other forms of discrimination are explored from the perspectives of critical theory, including the role of social identity in the formation of beliefs about leadership. You will have seen how critical theory and postmodernism are sophisticated approaches to map-reading, map-testing, and map-making.

As in earlier chapters, you are invited to explore these concepts as a benchmarking exercise, using your working definitions (Exercise 8.1).

Exercise 8.1: Your Personal Maps of Leadership Power, Discrimination, and Diversity

1 Without further study, note the most important ways in which you have encountered issues of discrimination at work and in your social life.
2 How do you believe discrimination might be connected to issues of power and influence?

ORIENTATION

In the previous chapter, business strategy was shown to have retained assumptions drawing on the DRM. In this chapter dilemmas of power and diversity are examined. These concepts and their dilemmas have not been easily addressed through approaches based on the DRM. Here we draw on alternative approaches. We concentrate on critical theory, and show its relationship to approaches developed within the related map of postmodernism.

The ideas will be familiar to students of the social sciences. Readers unfamiliar with the approaches may find it useful to take them as very sophisticated methods of map-testing and map-making. The maps challenge the fundamental principles of the DRM as a means of understanding the social world.

We will see how these approaches can reveal the repressive nature of power relationships in organizational practices. A working definition of power is provided by the critical theory scholars Cynthia Hardy and Stewart Clegg:[5]

> Power has typically been seen as the ability to get others to do what you want them to do.[6]

The definition provides a starting-point for understanding critical theory. A major concern is to explore the power relationships of social life, with the intention of doing something about them. Alvesson and Deetz comment that:

[S]ometimes, critical theory [is presumed to mean] all work taking a critical or radical stance on contemporary society [oriented] toward investigating exploitation, repression, unfairness, asymmetrical power relations . . . from class, gender, race or position, distorted communication and false consciousness.[7]

The vocabulary of exploitation and false consciousness illustrates how critical theorists have drawn on and extended work in the Marxist tradition.

Weber, writing shortly after Marx had died, considered that the power of absolute monarchs or tyrants had been transferred to leaders of modern institutions. For critical theorists, Weber's work was taken as acceptance of the legitimacy of managers to exercise

---

Box 8.1: Critical Theory and Postmodern Maps

Critical theory and postmodern approaches are related ways of understanding social realities. They challenge the fundamental principles of knowledge management associated with scientific investigations of the natural world.

The DRM of scientific investigation is grounded in a belief that a theory can be rationally tested for its objective truth. Knowledge represents a reality, the essential nature of the empirical world.

Critical theory and postmodern approaches share a belief that reality is a contested set of assumptions that have been socially constructed.

Postmodernism has provided powerful ways of exploring the nature of social   structed reality, including the deconstruction of texts (a sophisticated approach to   sting).

Critical theory draws on such map-testing to explore realities as socially constructed. In addition, it has the intention of revealing injustices in the social world.
support to emancipation or liberation actions.

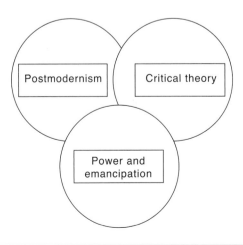

power and control within the emerging rational/legal ('bureaucratic') structures. Critical theorists seek to open a discussion on how employee power is suppressed within modern organizations, and how it might be liberated.

A more recent important influence on critical theorizing has been the work of Goffman. His studies of prisons, religious retreats, military organizations, boarding schools, and secure hospitals draw attention to 'institutionalization' processes through ritualized sets of actions or routines. 'Top-down' control is absolute and the power is 'one-way'. In these various ways, critical theorizing addresses significant dilemmas of leadership through its revision of maps of individual identity, control, and discrimination.

Critical theory and postmodernism are extremely complex, and rich bodies of work have become central to much theorizing within the social sciences. Readers may detect in the outline presented here some aspects of ways of map-reading, map-testing, and map-making. While this should be considered no more than a simplifying metaphor, it will have some explanatory power for readers unfamiliar with the concepts. In particular, the important postmodern approach to deconstructing texts may be seen as a powerful method of map-testing.

Most leaders face dilemmas of diversity at work. The issues may involve a combination of features such as gender, ethnicity, or nepotism (favouring a family member or friend). Discussion of such issues can be highly charged, with accusations of bias and prejudice. Here we pay particular attention to gender and ethnicity. This does not reduce the significance of other diversity issues such as ethnicity, social class, religious beliefs, age, or physical or mental characteristics.

As an orienting challenge we invite you to examine your beliefs and assumptions about diversity and its consequences for leadership (Exercise 8.2). Experienced leaders will be able to draw on their previous experiences. Less experienced leaders will none the less have some experiences of groups of various kinds to draw upon. These experiences may involve groups whose members were of similar educational background, gender, or ethnicity. Spend a few minutes considering the differences between highly diverse groups and more homogeneous groups. You will find that several of the leadership maps you have studied will suggest ideas for this challenge.

The exercise will have indicated how discrimination reveals itself in a range of forms. Gender discrimination is amongst the forms of widest significance. Women have moved into more and more powerful leadership positions in politics and the professions. However, gender discrimination remains, so that advances are less noticeable in business, where the infamous glass ceiling still exists and bars entry to most senior organizational positions of influence and power.[8]

In the first POU to be studied, Veccio examines claims for a 'women's advantage' for leadership roles (POU 8.1). In POU 8.2 Stella Nkomo and Taylor Cox Jr. outline the main territories of diversity studies. Their work explores the importance of social identity in the formation of beliefs about leadership.

The first of the contextual materials (CM 8.1) continues the debate introduced by Veccio with research by Eagly and Carli on the female leadership advantage. The following three

Exercise 8.2: Dealing with Diversity

You have been invited to be a leader of a working group made up of individuals of differing cultural and professional backgrounds.

Exercise 8.2 Questions

1 What differences do you expect these factors to make to the way the group members work together?
2 What might you, as leader, do to take account of the diversity within the group?
3 Can you think of possibilities based on the leadership maps you have studied?

- Contingency theories and situational leadership (Chapter 2)
- Team processes (Chapter 3)
- Transformational leadership (Chapter 4)
- Management of meaning (Chapter 5)
- Trust-based leadership (Chapter 6)
- Emergent and distributed leadership (Chapter 7)

[Exercise for personal reflection, or tutorial or classroom discussion.]

Box 8.2: The Vocabulary of Gender Studies

One of the most powerful tools for studying diversity, and specifically inequalities and prejudice, is that of interpretation and deconstruction of the meaning of texts. Feminist studies have applied a richer and more formalized means of map-testing and map-remaking to reveal previously hidden assumptions in society regarding the role of women. Feminism began a project to liberate women from male dominance (the emancipatory project). Its methodologies have drawn on critical theory and postmodernism, with considerable attention to the power relations concealed in culture and language.[9] Vocabulary became an important element in challenging or deconstructing gender issues. For example, researchers differentiate between the terms 'sex' and 'gender', preferring to use the former only to refer to biological categories, and the latter to refer to socially constructed differences. Sexuality is a matter of biological classification. Gender is defined by the manner in which sexuality is perceived culturally.

texts examine leaders for the perspectives they offer on diversity, power, and discrimination. The first is Barack Obama (CM 8.2), with particular attention paid to the way that his mother's values influenced his own. This is followed by the case of Carly Fiorina (CM 8.3), one of the few females to have achieved high office in corporate America, and by that of Roberto Goizueta (CM 8.4), a Cuban refugee who shattered the glass ceiling at Coca-Cola to become America's first billionaire corporate manager.

PLATFORMS OF UNDERSTANDING

POU 8.1: Leadership and Gender Analysis: Veccio's Meta-analysis

Veccio's meta-analysis was prompted by claims made in the 1990s that women were perceived as having advantages over men in many organizational roles. This had become known as the female leadership advantage theory.

The research is set against the history of leadership and, over a long period of time, the dearth of women leaders who had achieved the highest positions in business. All the evidence pointed to a historically widely held assumption that leadership was a masculine occupation. Culturally, the view was almost universal. Even 200 years after the Enlightenment, women had failed to achieve equality of opportunity. Empirical evidence that women could perform as well as men in business was hindered by the slow advance of women managers through the organizational glass ceiling.[10]

An opportunity arose through studies of leadership style in the 1970s that included leaders at operational and supervisory levels. A considerable wealth of data emerged that permitted comparison of the styles and effectiveness of men and women as leaders.

Results emerged that were perhaps less surprising to women in management than to men. On many measures, the female leaders were consistently reported as being more effective. The results supported legislation against discrimination in the workplace.[11] The dilemma for the majority of male leaders was clear: their careers were under threat through what became known as the feminine advantage in leadership studies.

Robert Veccio conducted a meta-analysis of studies of gender and leadership styles in the 1980s and 1990s in order to evaluate the evidence for the emerging theories of gender advantage. His analysis suggested that the evidence for a female advantage was being grossly misinterpreted. His view was that the studies showed statistical differences between male and female leaders. The female samples showed more aspects associated with a transformational style. However, Veccio reported that the gender differences accounted for only a small proportion of the total variance.

His conclusion was that a major error was being made in extrapolating from the results. He argued that there had been wide acceptance of a false belief in the 'natural' superiority of male leaders. However, he was concerned that a switch to a view of a feminine advantage was repeating the error based on stereotypic reasoning.

Furthermore, according to Veccio, early gender work was premised on an either/or dichotomy. Leaders were *either* feminine *or* masculine, with distinct biologically determined characteristics. The styles were further simplified into either/or features, among which a concern for tasks or people was particularly significant. Later, gender became regarded as more socially determined. This offered the possibility that an individual might be high *or* low on *either* of two dimensions of task and relationships.

This led researchers to the view that a 'both/and' approach was superior (more effective) over the uni-dimensional either/or styles. Direct evidence from the workplace provides evidence that leadership behaviours cannot be predicted by a simple attribution of a feminine- or masculine-style dimension. Each leader displays a range of behaviours, some more associated with male leaders, some with female leaders. Veccio concluded that more careful empirical studies are required to establish where and under what conditions superiority claims might be made on the basis of gender differences. An alternative perspective will be found in CM 8.1.

POU 8.2: Mapping Diversity: Nkomo and Cox

We take as our map a review of diversity by Stella Nkomo and Taylor Cox Jr.[12] These authors suggest that diversity is a construct that poses considerable theoretical and practical dilemmas. Characterizations of diversity can be specific or very broad, and focused at the level of the individual, social group, or society.

Diversity definitions of narrower scope tend to emphasize discrimination processes as consequences of diversity. Definitions of wider scope include both positive and negative consequences of individual and cultural differences.

Nkomo and Cox offer a narrow-scope definition of diversity as 'focusing on issues of racism, sexism, heterosexism, classism, ableism, and other forms of discrimination at the individual, identity group, and system levels'.[13] Race, ethnicity, and gender are the 'big three' areas most widely mentioned in the narrower definitions of diversity.

For a broader definition, they point to the view that regards diversity as referring to 'situations in which the actors of interest are not alike with respect to some attribute'.

Diversity is essentially concerned with diversity of *identity* as it is revealed for an individual or social group. The authors show how most theories of diversity directly address the consequences of identity:

■ *Social identity theory*, as its name implies, considers how an individual's identity relates to perceptions of self, and perceptions of others about one's self-identity.

■ *Organizational demography theorizing* has developed following a much-cited article by Jeffrey Pfeiffer, which gave the field its descriptive label.[14] The field explores the consequences of factors such as age, organizational tenure, education, and functional background, and gives priority to those aspects of organizational life that can be accurately observed and codified. Organizational demographic studies also incorporate gender and racial factors.

■ *Ethnology or ethnographic studies* This work offers explanations of identity in terms of cultural diversity. It includes the widely known studies of Hofstede, with the diversity discriminators of power-distance, uncertainty avoidance, individualism–collectivism, and masculinity–femininity. A fifth factor of Confucian values was added later.

■ *Race/gender studies* This work developed a broadly emancipative agenda, drawing on earlier theoretical perspectives of oppression and of the processes of assimilation of under-privileged groups and values by the dominant social groups. Thanks to this work, the evidence of discrimination (most widely illustrated for women and non-white employees of either sex) is now overwhelming. Issues of identity tend to deal with psychological trauma, and with damage to self-identity from discriminatory practices.

Race/gender studies are grounded in ethical or moral grounds for equality of opportunities. They consider the various ways in which diversity has failed to lead to equality in many walks of life, not least in the workplace. This expresses respect for diversity, and the ethical imperative for granting equal opportunities to individuals of all kinds. Of the other perspectives, the *organizational demographic* approach takes a more pragmatic approach, explaining why diversity may be a necessary feature for dealing with complex work problems. As noted in Chapter 3, diversity is necessary for enhanced innovation, and for other effective organizational responses to complexity.

The authors suggest that much that is restricting and damaging in stereotyping arises from dichotomous ('either/or') thinking. For example, this thinking opposes the binary categorization of maleness or femaleness.

CONTEXTUAL MATERIALS

CM 8.1: An Evaluation of the Female Leadership Advantage Theory: Eagly and Carli

Eagly and Carli responded to Veccio's analysis covered in POU 8.1, and to his rejection of the evidence for a female leadership advantage. They cast doubt on the reliability of his methodology, including the retention of earlier work on gender, which they described as belonging to the Goldberg paradigm.[15] Over 30 years earlier, Goldberg had demonstrated methodological problems unless biases are accounted for in comparative studies of males and females. Veccio's meta-analysis appeared to have disregarded these problems.

Eagly and Carli concentrated on the full range of leadership styles, well known from the work of Bass and co-workers, and measured by their full-range (multi-factor) Leadership Questionnaire. Results were included from leaders, peers, followers, or more senior peers. Eagly and co-workers found 45 studies of male/female leadership styles, each of which they considered had met their criteria for inclusion.

The striking feature of the meta-analysis is evidence of consistent and significant differences between the leadership scores of women and men for the transformational measures, in 44 studies. All transformational sub-scales gave higher means for female than male samples, with the most significant being those of charisma (as idealized influence measures), inspirational motivation, and intellectual stimulation.

In contrast, the male–female differences for the transactional factors were not statistically significant, with the exception of a weakly significant effect from the small number of studies (11) that examined management by exception. This means that transactional contingent reward, management by exception (passive), and laissez-faire styles were not found to provide significant gender-based differences.

The researchers point out that the results are of considerable importance in evaluating the female advantage issue. Female leader styles were found in this study to be consistently and positively correlated with transformational leadership. They connect this finding with the major finding from an earlier meta-analysis, in which transformational leadership had been found to have a significant and consistent positive correlation with effectiveness.[16] Thus the two findings point to the association between performance and female leadership as being stronger than the association between performance and male leadership.

The results were presented in the context of wide-ranging prejudice towards female leaders across cultures and working environments, which contributes to what other workers refer to as glass ceiling effects and which leads to continuing prejudice against the appointment of women to top positions. They suggest that, under such circumstances, women who do succeed are likely to be particularly effective.

Eagly and Carli concluded that there is a potential advantage in selecting women as leaders with a transformational leadership style, which is particularly effective in supporting organizational change. They respond to Veccio's criticism of the empirical findings, that the statistical differences between male and female leaders account only for a rather small proportion of the total variance. They argue that addressing such differences may have considerable practical consequences. They back up their argument with the metaphorical example of the aspirin effect. A medical trial of aspirin demonstrated a small but significant effect in managing heart conditions. Yet the medical experts considered the practical consequences to be so great that the trial was stopped so that the beneficial results could be shared as widely and quickly as possible. Eagly and Carli argue, by analogy, that the minor improvement statistically should be enough to permit the results to be shared as widely as possible (see Box 8.3).

Box 8.3: The Aspirin Effect – The Significance of Small Effect Sizes

Eagly and Carli produced statistical evidence widely used to back up the view that female leaders show more transformational qualities than male leaders. The evidence derives from a meta-analysis of contemporary studies that have applied Bass and Avolio's inventory of their full-scale leadership measure. The samples are mostly for middle-level organizational leaders, and the statistical evidence is clear. The female leaders sampled show significantly higher mean scores than male managers on the transformational scales. There were no significant differences on the transactional scales of contingent reward, management by exception (passive), and laissez-faire.

The results are accepted as an accurate finding from the available data. However, the relevance of the findings has been contested on the grounds that the mean differences reported are relatively small. In statistical terms they can be said to account for only a small proportion of the overall variance.

The critique offered is that the result is statistically significant but of little practical importance. Eagly and Carli argue, on the contrary, that the result is of considerable practical importance, drawing on what they call 'the aspirin effect'.

The aspirin effect is a term associated with a very influential medical trial to test the effectiveness of aspirin on patients with heart problems. Even before the trial was completed, the data showed that there was a small but significant reduction in heart problems in the sample treated with aspirin, compared with the samples not receiving aspirin.

Approximately 3 per cent fewer people experienced heart attacks when taking the aspirin treatment. The result was considered important enough for the trial to be ended prematurely, so that all the patients could benefit from the discovery.

If we return to the leadership finding, an aspirin effect implies that organizations that identify the best female leaders they can find and appoint them to more influential positions would increase transformational practices, with significant statistical and practical effects.

The argument has to be examined against the wider organizational map within which capable women are systematically overlooked for top jobs. The case is clear cut on social equity grounds. Other factors may dampen the predicted effectiveness of such a change (just as other factors continue to contribute to the majority of heart conditions, with or without the aspirin effect).

There are clearly revolutionary implications in such a claim. Readers may wish to reflect on the implications for selection of female and male leaders.

CM 8.2: The Hidden Barack Obama

Barack Obama, in the space of a few years, has become one of the most studied individuals on the planet. Numerous books and articles have been written about his origins, career, personal life, beliefs, education, and upbringing. Nevertheless there is a hidden Obama that requires a refocusing of attention. Some insights can be gleaned from his early life experiences and their impact on his adult beliefs and values. In particular, the influence of his mother deserves more attention than it has received.

Two 'facts' are perhaps the most shared and significant in the widely shared platform of understanding about Barack Obama. He is a black American who became the first black president of the United States of America. His ethnicity is well documented. Barack Obama Sr. was a Kenyan senior governmental economist who, like his son, was educated in Hawaii and at Harvard. His mother was a white American from the Midwest. President Obama is as much from Kansas as he is from Kenya.

Even these facts are challenged by some Americans. His origins became part of a belief which became known as the 'Obama birthing conspiracy'. This centres around the credibility of the evidence of his birthright as an American in Hawaii. Without his having evidence of citizenship through birth, his presidency would be declared illegal.

The controversial Darwinist Richard Dawkins observed the trap of seeing things as black or white. This occurs not just metaphorically, but as a matter of perceptual over-simplification. In his book *The Ancestor's Tale*, he used the example of another African American, former secretary of state Colin Powell. Dawkins uses photographs to illustrate that someone unaware of Mr Powell's background would probably conclude that he was white rather than black.[17] His point was that the photograph is neither of a black nor of a white person. Dawkins describes this as 'the tyranny of the discontinuous mind . . . which has been attributed to a racist "contamination metaphor" within white culture'.[18]

Culturally, there is a complexity to the heritage of Barack Obama (and of Colin Powell). For Dawkins, humans all carry genetic evidence of a common ancestry that is overlooked in unreflective attitudes toward one another.

The popular view of Barack Obama has tended to ignore the influence of his mother on the development of his beliefs and motivations in adulthood. Yet, various disciplines from ethology, anthropology, and post-Freudian psychology contribute insights into the nature of attachment theory.[19]

As one journalist has put it:

> Ironically, the person who mattered most in Obama's life is the one we know
> the least about [his mother] maybe because being partly African in America is
> still seen as being simply black and color is still a preoccupation above almost
> all else. There is not enough room in the conversation for the rest of a man's
> story.[20]

The view was supported by the president's wife, Michelle Obama. When asked by a schoolgirl whether she had always thought her husband would become president, she said no, but her early view of him was positive because of the way he talked of the formative influence that his mother had had on his beliefs and values.[21]

His own biographical accounts suggest that his mother has indeed been a formative influence on him. His parents' marriage was annulled when he was two years of age, and he hardly knew his father. Obama's mother, Ann Durham, appears to have been an independent-spirited individual who travelled widely from her home base in Wichita, Kansas before her family settled in Hawaii, where she met and married Barack Obama Sr. She became an academic with research interests in economic anthropology and rural poverty.

President Obama has written autobiographically about his mother's attitude to religion:

> My mother viewed religion through the eyes of the anthropologist that she would become; it was a phenomenon to be treated with a suitable respect, but with a suitable detachment as well. Moreover, as a child I rarely came in contact with those who might offer a substantially different view of faith. My father was almost entirely absent from my childhood, having been divorced from my mother when I was 2 years old.[22]

It is possible that President Obama, like his mother, takes an anthropological view of the world. Even his view of religion is one in which faith is admitted at the point at which reason can go no further. He noted:

> It was in search of confirmation of her values that I studied political philosophy, looking for both a language and systems of action that could help build community and make justice real . . . It was because of these newfound understandings . . . that religious commitment did not require me to suspend critical thinking, disengage from the battle for economic and social justice, or otherwise retreat from the world that I knew and loved that I was finally able to walk down the aisle of Trinity United Church of Christ one day and be baptized.

The first part of this analysis suggests that President Obama projects an image which becomes simplified in the eyes of many Americans as that of a person of colour. The second part suggests how his presidential style shares that of an anthropologist journeying to territories where he is a stranger, committed, perhaps empathic, but primarily as an objective observer. It also hints at his approach to dealing with deep personal dilemmas of faith and rationality.

CM 8.3: Carly Fiorina: Perfect Enough?

Carly Fiorina became a symbol of women's success in breaking through the discriminatory effects of the organizational 'glass ceiling'. Later, her belief that there were no longer any barriers to success for women in the American boardroom were severely challenged.

> In the summer of 1999 . . . Carleton Fiorina was named new CEO of Hewlett-
> Packard . . . She claimed that women face 'no limits whatsoever, there is not a
> glass ceiling'.

Carleton (Carly) S. Fiorina attracted attention as a business winner and a feminist role
model. Her success in leading a major corporate spin-off (of Lucent Technologies, in the
1990s) triggered international publicity. Her appointment as CEO of the Hewlett-Packard
organization, and her leading role in a controversial merger with Compaq, propelled her to
iconic status as a business leader. American business heroes of the recent past have tended
to be lauded as exceptional figures. The business press tends to offer portrayals of them as
the ultimate leaders and role models. Yet, for someone whose potential as a role model is
particularly potent, Carly has also been described as one of the most vilified women in
corporate America.

The Hewlett-Packard story has been a business school favourite for many years. Its high-
tech origins and development into a mega-star growth company in Silicon Valley at first
captured the imagination of Tom Peters (although he subsequently felt that the company
lacked the revolutionary zeal necessary to compete into the future). Collins and Porras cited
Hewlett-Packard as one of 16 visionary companies 'built to last' through their founding
principles.[23]

The company was founded in 1939 by two engineers who (it is alleged) 'stood in a garage
in 1939 and flipped a coin to see whose name would go first in the company logo'.[24] Their
goal was to create a great, innovative company driven by engineering excellence.

At the heart of the Hewlett-Packard success was the HP way, an articulated statement of
values and respect for employees and customers. Since the 1940s, care for employees has
meant an unusual policy of protection of employees from lay-offs. The culture was inspired
by the informal style of founders Bill Hewlett and Dave Packard in the 1940s. Their social
and organizational innovations have been as acclaimed as their company's technical
products. For example, they pioneered succession planning and management development
schemes in the 1950s while the firm still had only some 500 employees. Their original
scientific electronic calculator, the HP-35, was hailed in the 1970s as an invention that
changed the world, selling 300,000 within three years, against market estimates of 5,000.[25]
Its success helped to charge up the Silicon Valley phenomenon, feeding the market need
for more, faster, smaller, cheaper electronic products, and their electronic components.
Users of calculators saw prices fall to increasingly accessible values. Hewlett-Packard
continued on its highly innovative way, with a steady flow of imaginative electronic
products.

In the 1980s, the approach had been hailed as a proven commercial and human success.
By the late 1980s, however, the great growth days seemed to be at an end. Moss Kanter
mentions the firm twice, each time negatively, in her book on how giant corporations were
attempting to become more flexible. She cites a failed attempt to buy into a new market
sector, and the firm's rejection of approaches from Apple's founders, Steve Jobs and Steve
Wosniak.[26] Hewlett-Packard's stock price in 1990 had dropped below book value. By the

time Carly Fiorina was appointed CEO, the company was increasingly seen as losing out to competitive threats.

The original vision of Hewlett and Packard was the creation of a company that would generate high-value, highly innovative products. The story goes, that Bill Hewlett championed the hand-held calculator product because he had a dream of an electronic slide rule. The growth in its core printer market in the 1990s, fuelled by the internet boom, was for low-price, value-for-money personal and office products. The company had struggled to accept the need for change. Even its own successful product in that market was initially introduced against considerable opposition from within the organization.

On her appointment, Fiorina accepted the need for change and directed her efforts to achieving what was needed. Those efforts met with considerable resistance. During the merger that was to be the centre of her strategy, opposition became intense. Resistance was led by Walter Hewlett, the son of one of the founders, who had come to believe (rightly) that the merger would threaten the very core of the corporate philosophy.

The story of the Compaq merger had all the ingredients of a Hollywood film. A high-profile (and female) chief executive faces a culture deeply rooted in its founders' vision and the HP way. George Anders chronicles the rise of an outstanding communicator and business leader.[27] Somewhat contrastingly, *Business Week*'s Peter Burrows argued that Carly Fiorina had been engaged in attacking the essence of the company's success.[28] Business commentators suggested that the personality-dominated decision-making process at HP had overcome the firm's traditional beliefs and rational strategic considerations.

In 2005, Fiorina resigned as CEO and chairman of Hewlett-Packard. Critiques of her leadership weaknesses were laced with accounts of her private life. Biographies of business leaders are commonplace. It is worth reflecting on the nature of such works. The convention is to place an emphasis on the achievements of the leader. Typically, the book offers us an unambiguous account of the great leader.

A colourful private life or unusual personal characteristics tend to be downplayed or omitted completely in business biographies. In some contrast, the business press seemed rather interested in Fiorina's private life. Why might that have been the case? Might it help understanding of her business performance? In which case, should a similar treatment be applied more widely in biographies? Or might the judgement on Carly have something to do with widely held assumptions and beliefs about the suitability of women for top executive positions?

CM 8.4: Roberto Goizueta

Roberto Goizueta deserves study as a leader from a different cultural and ethnic background who reached the highest office in corporate America and helped in the establishment of Coca-Cola as a powerful global brand.

Roberto C. Goizueta was a Cuban immigrant who worked his way through the ranks of the Coca-Cola organization, becoming president and chairman. He was born into a prominent Cuban family that in pre-Castro times owned a Cuban sugar refinery. Goizueta was born in Havana on 18 November 1931. He was educated in a Jesuit school in Havana, and later sent to a private academy in Connecticut. There he polished his limited English by watching the same movies over and over. He subsequently earned a degree in chemical engineering at Yale University, before returning to Cuba in 1953 to join the family enterprise.

A year after returning to Cuba he joined the Coca-Cola bottling operation in Cuba, rapidly earning promotion as a bilingual technical manager. However, the political conditions in Cuba triggered his immigration to the United States, where, like so many political refugees, he arrived with no more than a suitcase of possessions and minimal financial resources. He would later reflect that such an experience prepares you to take risks in order to achieve your goals.

His initial work was for the company's Latin American interests, but his energy and competence brought him to the attention of the company's senior executives. He was promoted to corporate headquarters in Atlanta and he became a vice-president at 35, and subsequently chairman. He was widely regarded as a detail-and-facts executive, although he was credited with leadership of Coca-Cola's global expansion activities in the 1980s. The corporate stock rose by over 7,000 per cent during his tenure and, by retaining his stock options, he was eventually to hold 16 million shares, making him America's first billionaire corporate manager.

INTEGRATION

Diversity is an increasingly studied subject, with its specialist journals, databases, conventions, books, and thousands of articles. The establishment of global organizations gives impetus to the subject. Each global organization faces the dilemmas of diversity, starting with diversity at the level of the top-echelon team, almost always headed by a leader from the territory of the firm's national and legal origins. Where local headquarters are established, the issues of local and 'expatriate' leaders remain important.[29]

Today, a greater acceptance of diversity on ethical and economic grounds can be found in many institutions and sectors internationally. Barack Obama's rise to become president of the United States in 2008 has been widely hailed as evidence of the reality in that country of equality of opportunity. The examples in this chapter could be multiplied around the world. Women have taken their place as heads of state and held other high offices. Ethnic minorities have advanced within more dominant regimes in governments, universities, legal institutions, and in a range of public service roles around the world. In Malaysia, Chinese leaders are accepted alongside the legally constituted majorities of ethnic Malays (Bumiputras).

The courageous experiment in South Africa of a 'rainbow nation', initiated by the charismatic Nelson Mandela, is an inspiration in diversity leadership, after that country's earlier regimes of, first, colonization and then segregation (apartheid). Global organizations have accepted the principle of diversity management, and increasingly the 'entry barriers' for previously restricted groupings are being relaxed. Progress has been claimed, as evidenced by data collection on targets or quotas. Yet, the evidence is of slow rather than spectacular progress. In the United States, where diversity affirmation programmes have been prominent, surveys suggest that progress remains restricted for non-whites, and for females in particular, at higher levels of leadership.

Various studies suggest that successful women leaders have chosen to make a lateral leap to overcome the glass ceiling of corporate life. This may involve a meandering path, away from corporates, to founding a business of their own, and then later moving in to head a larger and more traditional corporation.[30] Women and various minorities resolve the diversity dilemma by becoming entrepreneurial founders of businesses of various kinds.

The profile of successful black leaders suggests a similar meandering path. A database of great American black business leaders of the twentieth century illustrates the pathways.[31] Thirty-one black leaders were identified (four were female) who rose in the context of a segregated society within which corporations developed to serve the needs of the segregated black minority groups. Several were former slaves, or children of slaves. The most numerous business leaders by industry sector were financial entrepreneurs (11) who set up savings and loan schemes, and insurance services established where previously no poverty safety net had existed. Typically, the leaders overcame severe discriminatory barriers to success, and the corporations were founded where white leaders were unable to compete.

The other main groupings were in newspaper and magazine publishing (6) and in personal care products (4). Smaller numbers of leaders founded food and drink retailing firms, technical and construction organizations, and an advertising agency.

From our POUs we begin to see the core issues of gender and diversity. The first dilemma engages with the issue of women as leaders, expressed as the feminine advantage. This view is contested by Veccio, who sees it as having the same weakness as earlier models of male leadership supremacy, namely that it establishes a superior and an inferior group of leaders, according to gender. Furthermore, he considers that both models draw on a simplistic reduction of human behaviours into two categories, either male or female. The feminine advantage view is strongly supported by evidence that women tend to have more transformational leadership styles, and that transformational leadership is well suited to contemporary, turbulent business situations.

In the review by Stella Nkomo and Taylor Cox Jr., the overarching concept, according to the authors, is that of *social identity*. This is a construct that we have not come across in the earlier maps of leadership. It proposes a common social root to all discriminatory behaviours as individuals find ways of dealing with 'selfness' and 'otherness'. We thus have the idea that glass ceilings, written about originally in the context of gender concerns, can be applied to discriminatory practices in general. More positively, to understand and reflect on gender dilemmas is to begin to develop further skills in dealing with such dilemmas.

Using a social identity map, we may be better equipped to understand the challenges that helped some leaders to shatter glass ceilings; we may understand how discrimination may have multiplicative effects, so that ethnic women leaders have tougher challenges ascending corporate pyramids than do ethnic males or white women.

Eagly and Carli defend the proposition that the feminine advantage has important practical implications. They deal with the criticism that the differences in means are modest, referring to the aspirin effect. From this, we may choose to infer that the replacement of male with female leaders in organizational life will be justified. Some of the heat is taken out of such a proposal if we consider that the statistical evidence by itself directly supports only the proposition that a larger proportion of women than of men are reported as having transformational leadership styles. What does seem to be *disconfirmed* is the existence of any evidence that men are more transformational in style than females in leading change processes. Even discounting ethical considerations (e.g. equality of opportunity), the preponderance of male leaders cannot be justified by any evidence of male leadership's superior effectiveness.

GETTING PERSONAL

Each leader and would-be leader faces his or her own highly context-dependent journeys. In this chapter we introduce the complexities that are largely hidden in the maps studied in earlier chapters.

The leader who has identified a rare talent among his or her subordinates will be all too aware of the dilemma of promoting, if that talent is from outside the dominant culture, gender, or demographics of its traditional leaders. Are there lessons to be learned from a social identity perspective? What actions may help in dealing with assumptions and stereotypes of 'what's different is dangerous'? What are the predictable consequences of 'affirmative action' for the expectations of those in the dominant corporate grouping?

The female would-be leader still faces a business world in which success is hindered by prejudice. Much the same principle applies to disadvantaged minorities. This is an experience shared by ethnic leaders, condemned for 'selling out' their racial kind for corporate advancement, or working-class leaders, accused for being class traitors.

One strategy for success is to find ways of making difference count. The corporate success achieved by Roberto Goizueta was, in part, through the acknowledgement of his skills at technology leadership. However, it was the valued difference of working with the company's Hispanic interests that also worked to his advantage.

MBAs seeking corporate jobs are encouraged by their placement tutors to compile a compelling CV. The preference is to present a person with a considerable number of points of similarity to the majority of senior people within the organization. These points include educational path, professional training, and job experience. Those candidates with unusual CVs are advised to find unusual jobs (there will be fewer applicants with appropriate credentials).

Candidates with military credentials should have more chances in jobs where the company already has a leader with a military background. Candidates who have worked for a not-for-profit charity may find more encouragement in for-profit sectors in the 'creativity' and service industries, and in work requiring creativity and innovation.

SUMMARY

One of the most powerful tools for studying diversity, and specifically inequalities and prejudice, is that of interpretation and deconstruction of meaning. This chapter introduces critical theory as better able to do so than methods based on the rational approach of the DRM. Power and its abuse are central to feminism and other studies within a project to bring about emancipating change. The approach applies the postmodern methodology of deconstruction of texts – feminism may be seen as a liberating or emancipatory response to male dominance. The approaches often draw on postmodernism to look deeply at the cultural narrative, revealing power relations that are concealed in language (Box 8.2).

For such reasons, vocabulary became an important element in challenging or deconstructing gender issues. For example, researchers differentiate between the terms 'sex' and 'gender', preferring to use the former only to refer to biological categories, and the latter to refer to socially constructed differences. Sexuality is a matter of biological classification. Gender is defined by the manner in which sexuality is perceived in society.

Box 8.4: 'What's Different is Dangerous': Diversity as a Contribution to Social Discomforts and Dysfunctions

Social integration remains a challenge to cultures around the world. Distrust of outsiders can merge into conflicts around ethnic and religious differences. The study of 'otherness' has become an important focus for critical analysis.

A general theory of the dynamics of diversity is known as homosocial reproduction. Evidence from a wide range of sources suggests that many individuals have deeply held and negative beliefs about outsiders. Explanations include stereotyping, as suggested by the materials in this chapter. In general, the evidence also suggests that the tendency to rejection of diversity reduces the capability of the group to display innovative and creative behaviours.[32]

The cognitive psychologist Michael Kirton provides a theory of diversity leadership that focuses on cognitive style.[33] According to Kirton, any social group will establish a shared culture based on understanding of individual cognitive styles, which discriminates primarily on a preference for incremental or radical change. The theory proposes that preferred style is a stable personality trait, although an individual may adjust behaviours according to environmental pressures.

People seek environments and leaders consistent with their preferred styles. Conflicts arise as people of differing styles interact and seek to solve problems at work. Individuals will leave those environments that are too distant from their preferred style. A stable environment attracts and retains people of incremental style (adaptors); a turbulent environment attracts and retains people favouring radical change (innovators). Adaptive groups seek adaptive-style leaders; innovative groups seek innovative leaders. However, the leaders most preferred by their in-group followers are those who are moderate adaptors in the adaptive groups, and moderate innovators in innovative groups.

Other researchers, such as McGill's Nancy Adler, have arrived at similar conclusions (homosocial preferences within multi-cultural groups, at the expense of improved creativity through diversity). Dr Adler places her emphasis on non-cognitive influences, resulting in subconsciously framed assumptions and beliefs, again including *stereotyping*. According to Adler, we are all prone to stereotyping, but we may be able to minimize self-fulfilling expectations and treat our stereotypic beliefs as working propositions that are open to revision through direct experience.[34] Understanding cultural differences involves emotional intelligence: empathy, awareness of the effects that individuals have on one another, and the non-verbal components of communications.

The case examples in the chapter are not in themselves examples written from the critical theory perspective. Rather, they provide texts that can be 'read' and tested. They have been selected as particularly appropriate for readers to apply map-testing as a means of deconstructing them.

NOTES

1 Mayer, M. (1999) 'In a league of her own', *Newsweek*, 2, 56, www.bsos.umd.edu/socy/vanneman/papers/CotterHOV01.pdf, downloaded 24 May 2011.
2 Eagly, A.H., & Carly, L.L. (2003) 'The female leadership advantage: A review of the evidence', *Leadership Quarterly*, 14, 807–834, at p. 808, citing Sharp, R. (2000) *Business Week*, 20 November, p. 74.
3 www.pickledpolitics.com/archives/1177, downloaded 22 June 2010.
4 Reeser, T.W. (2010) *Masculinities in theory*, New York: Wiley-Blackwell.
5 Hardy, C., & Clegg, S.R. (2006) 'Some dare call it power', in Clegg, S.R., Hardy, C., Lawrence, T.B., & Nord, W.R. (eds) *Handbook of organization studies*, 2nd edn, London: Sage, pp. 622–641.
6 Clegg, S.R., Hardy, C., Lawrence, T.B., & Nord, W.R. (eds) *Handbook of organization studies*, 2nd edn, London: Sage, p. 754.

7 Alversson, M., & Deetz., S.A. (2006) 'Critical theory and postmodernism approaches to organizational studies', in Clegg, S.R., Hardy, C., Lawrence, T.B., & Nord, W.R. (eds) *Handbook of organization studies*, 2nd edn, London: Sage, pp. 255–283, at p. 256.

8 Smith, R.A. (2002) 'Race, gender and authority in the workplace: Theory and research', *Annual Review of Sociology*, 28, 509–542.

9 Calás, M.B., & Smircich, L. (2006) 'From the "Woman's point of view" ten years later: Towards a feminist organization studies', in Clegg, S.R., Hardy, C., Lawrence, T.B., & Nord, W.R. (eds) *Handbook of organization studies*, 2nd edn, London: Sage, pp. 284–346.

10 Ibid.

11 International Labour Organization (2004) *Global employment trends for women* (March), Geneva: ILO.

12 Nkomo, S.M., & Cox, T. Jr. (1996) 'Diverse identities in organizations', in Clegg, S.R., Hardy, C., & Nord, W.R. (eds), *Handbook of organization studies*, London: Sage, pp. 338–356.

13 Cross, W.E. (1991) *Shades of black: Diversity in Afro-American identity*, Philadelphia: Temple University Press.

14 Pfeffer, J. (1983) 'Organizational demography', in Cummings, L.L., & Staw, B.M. (eds), *Research in organizational behavior*, Vol. 12, pp. 295–336, Greenwich, CT: JAI.

15 Goldberg, P. (1968) 'Are women prejudiced against women?', *Transactions*, 5, 316–322.

16 Lowe, K.B., Kroeck, K.G., & Sivasubramaniam, N. (1996) 'Effectiveness correlates of transformational and transactional leadership: A meta-analytic review of the MLQ literature', *Leadership Quarterly*, 7, 385–425.

17 Dawkins, R. (2005) *The ancestor's tale*, London: Orion.

18 Ibid., pp. 412–413.

19 Van der Horst, F.C.P. (2011) *John Bowlby – from psychoanalysis to ethology: Unravelling the roots of attachment theory*, Oxford: Wiley-Blackwell.

20 Ripley, A. (2008) 'The story of Barack Obama's mother', *Time*, www.time.com/time/nation/article/0,8599,1729524,00.html, downloaded 22 May 2011.

21 Michelle Obama speaking to school children on the theme of aspirations, during US president's state visit to England, 26 May 2011.

22 www.time.com/time/magazine/article/0,9171,1546298,00.html, downloaded 22 May 2011.

23 Collins, J.C., & Porras, J.I. (1994) *Built to last: Successful habits of visionary companies*, New York: Random House.

24 Leonard D. (1995: 52) *Wellsprings of knowledge: Building and sustaining the sources of innovation*, Cambridge, MA: Harvard Business School Press.

25 Vogel, C. (1992) 'Thirty products that changed our lives', *R&D Management*, 34, 11, 42.

26 Kanter, R.M. (1989) *When giants learn to dance: Mastering the challenges of strategy, management, and careers in the 1990s*, Englewood Cliffs, NJ: Simon & Schuster.

27 Anders, G. (2003) *Perfect enough: Carly Fiorina and the reinvention of Hewlett-Packard*, New York: Portfolio.

28 Burrows, P. (2006) 'What Carly doesn't say', www.businessweek.com/technology/content/oct2006/tc20061011_008506.htm?chan=technology_technology+index+page_today%27s+top+stories, downloaded 23 May 2011.

29 Adler, N.J. (1991) *International dimensions of organizational behavior*, 2nd edn, Boston, MA: PWS Kent (4th edn, 2002, Cincinnati, OH: South Western, Thompson Learning).

30 Moore, D.P., & Butter, E.H. (1997) *Women entrepreneurs: Moving beyond the glass ceiling*, London: Sage.

31 20th Century American Leaders Database (2004), Harvard Business School, www.hbs.edu/leadership/ethnicity.

32 Boone, C., Van Olffen, W., Van Witteloostuijn, A., & De Brabander, B. (2004) 'The genesis of top management team diversity: Selective turnover among top management teams in Dutch newspaper publishing, 1970–1994', *Academy of Management Journal*, 5, 633–656.

33 Kirton, M.J. (2003) *Adaption–innovation in the context of diversity and change*, London: Routledge.

34 Adler, N.J. (2002) *International dimensions of organizational behavior*, 4th edn, Cincinnati, OH: South Western, Thompson Learning, p. 99.

CHAPTER LEARNING OBJECTIVES

Learning focus
- Understanding power relationships

Key issues
- Critical theory and identity theory
- Gender issues and diversity studies
- Social identity

Dilemmas
- Dilemmas of inequality and exclusion
- Dilemmas of stereotyping

Platforms of understanding
- POU 9.1 Ciulla's Map of Ethical Leadership
- POU 9.2 Moral Leadership: Sandra Sucher's Work

Contextual materials
- CM 9.1 Jean-Pierre Garnier: The Price of Leadership
- CM 9.2 Roland: The Ethical but Manipulative Leader
- CM 9.3 The Dilemmas of Authentic Leadership
- CM 9.4 Wikileaks: Dilemmas in the Age of Social Media

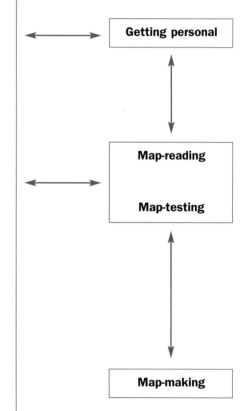

Getting personal

Map-reading

Map-testing

Map-making

9 ETHICAL DILEMMAS

There are few social sanctions for bad behavior. Executives who have served jail time are back on TV and are still celebrities. More to the point, they aren't shunned by their colleagues.[1]

[All] leaders have two responsibilities. They are responsible and accountable for the performance of their institutions . . ., they are responsible also, however, for the community as a whole.[2]

The social responsibility of business is to increase its profits.[3]

Is there any ethical dilemma in business? Is there a value judgment behind the oil business strategies, or is it all about money? Does the CEO of Exxon have a heart?[4]

If we look at what makes or breaks companies and careers, ethical misconduct tends to unravel things more quickly and more permanently than other kinds of business mistakes.[5]

Before studying the content of Chapter 9 you have an opportunity to reflect on your current understanding of ethics and leadership. You may be able to apply skills you have acquired in map-testing to examine what sense you make of two statements about the topics of the chapter.

Exercise 9.1: Evaluating Two Conflicting Leadership Maps

The following statements suggest two different leadership perspectives.

■ 'Leaders have two responsibilities. They are responsible and accountable for the performance of their institutions and also, however, for the community as a whole.'
■ 'The social responsibility of business is to increase its profits.'

Exercise 9.1 Question

1 **Without carrying out further research for information, how do you assess the POUs of the two statements?**

[Exercise for personal reflection, or tutorial or classroom discussion.]

The statements you examined in Exercise 9.1 reflect maps that reveal a dilemma about the nature of business leadership. Statement 1 clearly poses a dilemma of two possibly conflicting responsibilities for a leader. You may have contrasted the statement with the widespread belief that business is only about 'the bottom line'.

Statement 2 is rather subtle. You may have noticed that it is a sophisticated defence of the 'one bottom line' belief. In addition, it explicitly rejects the idea of corporate responsibility as an additional bottom line. This statement suggests awareness of ethical issues, but considers that the ethical side of business leadership can be left to look after itself. These issues are important aspects of this chapter.

ORIENTATION

Ethical dilemmas confront leaders in all walks of life. They become particularly acute in businesses facing crises associated with ethical mismanagement. In what follows it should be noted that some authors treat morality as a sub-set of ethics, while others examine ethics as a sub-set of morality.[6] More formal clarification of the terms will be provided as necessary.

Commercial businesses exist as agencies of economic exchange. From this perspective, leaders are primarily concerned with achieving the economic goals of those businesses of which they are part. Business leaders are judged on commercial grounds, and ethics come into the picture only if the business is economically disadvantaged by charges of unethical practice.

This time-honoured view is widely held in the world of business, and noted tolerantly by Adam Smith, writing with the authority of a moral philosopher. It implies that the practice of business is, of itself, morally neutral, although Smith was wise enough to indicate that such freedom required legislation to prevent the freedom from turning into collusion and monopolistic distortion of a free market. On these grounds we may well consider that business and ethics should be kept apart.

In the decades leading to the end of the twentieth century, the most widely read leadership textbooks tended to place ethics as a kind of add-on. In the first decade of the new millennium two significant sets of events made it difficult to ignore the ethical dilemmas confronting leaders.

At the start of the decade, the Enron organization collapsed,[7] revealing corrupt practices that derived from the actions and intentions of its leaders. To some commentators, the rise and fall of Enron seemed to be a real-life illustration of the social commentary of the 1986 film *Wall Street*, that the world of big business finance was intrinsically amoral.[8]

The Enron story was no more than the rumblings prior to an even greater set of financial crises and malpractices throughout the decade. As the economic crisis of 2007–8 developed, public anger became directed toward the perceived unfairness of the reward systems of international banking executives. Business, and particularly financial, executives were identified as having played a part in the economic tremors that were felt around the world.

Governments, led by the USA and the UK, addressed the financial crisis by refinancing the banks. Yet the economic logic was to reveal the dilemma of institutions that were 'too big to fail'. In March 2010 Federal Reserve Chairman Ben Bernanke told a conference of bankers: 'As the crisis has shown, one of the greatest threats to the diversity and efficiency of our financial system is the pernicious problem of financial institutions that are deemed "too big to fail".'[9]

The economists had identified moral hazard in social processes that put temptation in the way of business executives who faced no risk of losing their livelihoods through their financial decisions.

Post-Enron, the importance of wider corporate responsibilities became more widely accepted by business leaders, with encouragement from legislation at national and international levels.[10] This resulted in the appointment globally of corporate directors with responsibilities for ethics, diversity, and the environment.

The turbulent events of the new millennium's first decade accompanied social and technological changes which, in shorthand, were referred to as the social media revolution.[11] As we will see in this chapter, there were considerable ethical consequences for the behaviours of leaders of all kinds.

For some leaders, matters of ethics arise as an unwelcome intrusion into the pursuit of economic success. Nevertheless, such leaders have to find ways of assessing the risks facing companies that fall foul of regulatory guidelines (or, worse, of transgressing against legal restrictions). Crudely speaking, the dilemmas are whether the costs of being ethical will damage profitability. Leaders who wish to set high ethical standards in the practices of their organizations face various dilemmas. As they consider their business on a day-to-day basis, they become aware that ethical values do not come with a simple formula. Often there are conflicting values to be weighed up.

In the next part of the chapter we examine the key points of the orientation section.

In POU 9.1, Joanne Ciulla argues that ethical behaviour is not an optional extra, but a vital dimension for understanding leadership processes. However, the evidence is that the leadership literature ignores ethical dilemmas, or pays lip-service to high ethical conduct of good leaders. She invites us to consider what we mean when we refer to 'good leadership'. Does 'good' refer only to effectiveness in achieving economic goals? She argues that we then have trouble if such leadership is 'not good' for the moral well-being of followers.

POU 9.2 summarizes a textbook on moral leadership that is used as part of a Harvard Business School elective. Its approach of describing, analysing, and judging for ethical decision-making has similarities to that of map-reading, testing, and making.

The four contextual examples explore a range of ethical dilemmas. The case study of Jean-Pierre Garnier (CM 9.1) reveals the clash of values amongst stakeholders in assessing the value added by a leader, as reflected in his remuneration package. In CM 9.2 we study a leader who believed in what might be called ethical manipulation, comparing his beliefs with those of people who would see him engaged in a form of disempowering leadership. CM 9.3 introduces the concept of authentic leadership and indicates how the concept brings dilemmas with it when an authentic style lacks self-confidence and fails to reassure followers. Finally, in CM 9.4 we explore the dilemmas of freedom and security raised by the activities of the Wikileaks organization.

PLATFORMS OF UNDERSTANDING

POU 9.1: Ciulla's Map of Ethical Leadership

Joanne Ciulla conducted a deep exploration of leadership studies in order to understand the status of ethics. We can be in no doubt of her intention to provide a map: her review is entitled 'Leadership ethics: Mapping the territory'.[12]

She suggests that the pressing issue for practising leaders, as well as researchers, is to understand how to confront the moral or ethical dilemmas associated with leadership. In everyday terms, the fundamental dilemma is between beliefs about morality (conduct) and beliefs about achievement (effectiveness or performance). Debates about whether Hitler was a good leader demonstrate how slippery a concept is the term 'good'.

Ciulla's study suggests that ethical leadership is treated in token fashion in most overview studies of leadership. Tokenism is a term more commonly applied to the process of discrimination, in which an individual is accepted into a group as a token representative of a marginalized sub-group (e.g. by ethnicity or gender). The pressure for accepting the token individual comes through a morally strong case. Through tokenism, the group avoids criticism of unethical behaviour, while not having to embrace the ethic thoroughly. Leadership ethics is treated in a text in a tokenistic fashion if little effort is made to integrate it with the main concerns of the text.

In a study of 1,800 article abstracts, Ciulla found very few offering in-depth discussion and critique. Yet, many researchers and practising leaders directly or indirectly find a need to mention ethics as a 'good thing' for leaders to display. So much so, that the textbooks tend to make an unequivocally positive reference to ethical behaviour, while at the same limiting the references to a few paragraphs, or possibly to a self-contained chapter, mostly without serious critique of the concept.

Ciulla concludes that leaders and researchers consider that ethics is largely a matter of practical knowledge, not requiring theoretical exploration. Unfortunately, a general lack of awareness of the accumulated body of knowledge often leads authors to simplistic rehashes of sophisticated ethical ideas. She considers that such treatments are further hindered by what might be described as a reductionist approach. Reductionism fails to help us to understand broader issues, such as the personal ethics of leadership.

The literature of leadership is widely concerned with differentiating superior leaders from others. This can be seen in the emphasis placed on leader characteristics. Trait theories searched for the 'right stuff' of leaders and leadership. They could be said to be seeking an explanation of what is good leadership. The dilemmas arise because the reductionist methods are weaker in addressing the issue of what leadership should be doing in an ethical sense. Ciulla illustrates this with evidence that, under some circumstances, effective results are achieved without placing a priority on treating people well. This approach to leadership

---

Box 9.1: Tokenism in Leadership Studies

Joanne Ciulla suggests that leadership studies mostly treat ethics in a tokenistic way. Tokenism results from accepting a morally strong case for inclusion of an individual in a group, even if the dominant members of that group would prefer not to. Tokenism implies lip-service to the moral case, and the individual remains marginalized, although apparently accepted into the group.

The group appoints a limited number of 'token' women, or members of a different ethnic background, and superficially treats them as equal to others in the group as a matter of principle. In practice, equality in terms of salary, preferment, and social integration is unlikely to occur.

is too concerned with describing what leaders do, rather than with understanding the moral consequences of what is being done.

Ciulla identifies two influential contributions to a deeper understanding of the performance/ethics dilemma. These are the ideas of James MacGregor Burns and of Robert Greenleaf. We have come across Burns in Chapter 4 as a founding figure in transformational leadership. His treatment emphasized the transformation and moral development of followers.[13] Burns proposed that a leader is able to progress followers to 'higher' levels of ethical development. For example, preoccupations with survival of self may be transcended by commitment to broader ethical considerations in their ways of relating to others. Immediate gratification of needs (likely to be through transactional processes) is less pervasive as consciousness grows of longer-term and wider considerations.

Burns has a model of leadership in which the leader is differentiated from followers as having a higher or more developed sense of ethical values. This view is uncomfortable for those who prefer a more egalitarian perspective. Burns is suspicious of efforts of consensus as possibly reducing the possibility of moral progress. His process of transforming people requires in a leader a willingness to engage with the different values and permit constructive conflict between them (on the grounds that the moral values will eventually outdistance more selfish and transactional perspectives). In the process, the followers are increasingly prepared for leadership roles themselves. The process thus addresses the weakness of more coercive leadership styles, which essentially reinforce transactional follower behaviours.

The second of Ciulla's examples is the work of Robert Greenleaf, outlined in his book *Servant Leadership: A Journey into the Nature of Legitimate Power and Greatness*.[14] Greenleaf was initially influenced by the mystical tale *The Journey to the East* by Hermann Hesse. The main character (implicitly Hesse) and other travellers were accompanied by a servant, Leo, who attended to their chores and who sustained and uplifted them when they were struggling. When Leo mysteriously disappears, the group loses its way. Later, it emerges that Leo was the leader of the group.

The powerful central idea in Greenleaf's book is that leadership is essentially about attending to the moral needs of followers. The consequence, as with Burns' transforming leader, is the development of followers into morally responsible and autonomous leaders. Here, autonomy implies the freedom and willingness to undertake the duties of servant leadership. The idea of servant leadership appeals to those with humanist value systems, as well as to those with religious value systems.

Ciulla considers that Burns and Greenleaf help us to understand the moral dilemmas facing business leaders. Both place moral issues at the heart of leadership and deny the possibility of treating ethics as a desirable but optional extra. While ethical leadership may make sound commercial sense, they do not consider that ethical leadership should be justified on pragmatic analysis.

For Burns and Greenleaf, good leadership is characterized as a categorical imperative, the term found in Kant's philosophy which may be understood as a universally accepted principle of moral actions.[15]

POU 9.2: Moral Leadership: Sandra Sucher's Work

In her book *The Moral Leader*,[16] Sandra Sucher outlines Harvard Business School's course on moral leadership, one of the longest-running and most influential programmes on the subject. It is part of the Harvard tradition of commitment to learning through critical questioning as a means of personal development. This is described as study through 'describing, analysing, and judging'.[17] These processes may be seen as having much in common with the map-reading, map-testing, and map-making framework found in *Dilemmas of Leadership*.

The Moral Leadership course at Harvard was initiated in the 1980s by Robert Coles, a psychiatrist, Pulitzer-Prize winning novelist, and educator with interests spanning the sciences and humanities as well as business. Coles applied the ancient educational principle of personal learning through engaging students with the great works of literature.[18] Coles defines moral leadership as 'intellect calling upon the energies of conscience, with the loyalty of others a signal that a call has been contagiously successful'.[19]

From its inception, the course adhered to the principle that philosophical or critical questioning can lead to recognition of practical issues and that 'our ability to grapple with [moral issues] alone and with others, is a step on the road to moral action'.[20]

Students study selected texts, both ancient and modern, to explore the questions: 'What is the nature of a moral challenge? How do people "reason morally"? How is moral leadership different from any other kind?'[21] The course texts include works by Sophocles, Machiavelli, Joseph Conrad, and contemporary writers such as Kazuo Ishiguro and Chinua Achebe. These works are studied to explore the nature of moral challenges and the skills of studying the challenges (moral reasoning), and direct the learning towards developing personal beliefs and actions for moral leadership.

Sucher's work opens with chapters dealing with what she terms moral challenges. These are often indistinguishable from the dilemmas of leadership in which the context has a particular emphasis of a moral rather than technical or professional nature.

Moral dilemmas are introduced by an example related by Jean-Paul Sartre, who relates the story of a young Frenchman in the 1940s who feels compelled to oppose the occupation of France. The decision would require him to abandon his ageing and unwell mother, who is utterly dependent on his support. Sucher writes about the heart-wrenching nature of such a moral challenge. The illustration captures one of the most complex of dilemmas. The challenge is not to establish what is the right thing to do, but to decide what to do when each choice can be justified through a different set of moral implications.[22]

Sucher suggests that Sartre is introducing an example of a particularly important type of moral challenge. She notes: '[L]eading ethicists have argued that true ethical dilemmas only exist in right versus right scenarios.' She cites the ethicist Rushworth Kidder, who argues that these are 'genuine dilemmas precisely because each side is firmly rooted in one of our basic, core values'.

Kidder identified four basic 'right versus right' challenges, describing these as 'dilemma paradigms in which competing values exist on both sides of a moral challenge. [These are]:

- telling the truth versus maintaining loyalty
- short-term versus long-term considerations
- individual versus community
- justice against mercy.[23]

Sucher argues that leaders 'routinely face *right versus right* challenges . . . having to determine for example how an organization's actions will affect constituencies with different needs. Appreciating [such challenges] is thus a practical consideration and one which might prove vital to you and your own exercise of leadership.'

Business leaders spend less time concerned about moral questions than do philosophers. Insensitivity to moral considerations is a form of moral blindness that results in decision outcomes that might have been predicted and avoided. There may be a kind of a painful awakening from such a condition as moral blindness turns to moral awareness.[24]

Three approaches are suggested that might assist a leader in developing skills in dealing with moral challenges or dilemmas:

- reasoning through moral challenges
- reasoning through moral codes
- reasoning through moral theories.

Reasoning through moral challenges Awareness of the different kinds of moral challenge helps. For example, the leader is able to escape from the helplessness of not knowing the 'right' thing to do ethically if she realizes that there is no unique 'right' thing, but rather a need to act in awareness of more than one 'right thing' or set of moral considerations. The types of moral challenge include family versus patriotic duties, in Sartre's example; and the challenges posed by conflicting traditional and modernizing forces.[25]

Reasoning through moral codes Sociologists have tended to regard society as establishing the acceptable conventions and practices of society. Among the forms of conditioning is the propagation of norms of morality replicated in conditions such as legal codes, rituals, and the practices of organized religion. Professional groups develop their own codes of ethics, as do smaller communities, families, and even individuals.

Reasoning through moral theories A range of philosophical maps suggest ways of thinking more deeply about, and negotiating moral dilemmas:

- *Utilitarianism* The greatest good or least harm from actions to society.
- *Kantianism* Act according to obligations believed to be morally required. An action is morally just if the actor would be willing to see that action made a universal law.
- *Liberal Individualism* Rights or obligations that can justifiably be imposed by individuals or groups on others.
- *Communitarianism* Ethical decisions are those focusing primarily on nurturing and strengthening the common good.

Sucher notes the evidence of leaders who are operationally effective and yet who are 'widely held to have been pursuing immoral goals or utilizing morally repugnant means to achieve their ends'.[26]

To distinguish the concept from the behaviours of other forms of leader, she offers a 'straightforward definition of moral leadership' as: 'Directing a morally acceptable or laudable cause, sustained by means that are also widely accepted to be moral.'[27]

She also quotes the definition by Robert Coles, the pioneer of the Harvard course on Moral Leadership: 'intellect calling upon the energies of conscience, with the loyalty of others a signal that a call has been contagiously successful'.[28]

Sucher suggests that moral authority should also be considered. 'Authority is, in essence, based on a social contract between the leader and the led . . . leaders are judged in the moral domain [through] the decisions they make while building and exercising their authority.'[29]

CONTEXTUAL MATERIALS

CM 9.1: Jean-Pierre Garnier: The Price of Leadership

London, England, Monday 19 May 2003. The customary calm of GlaxoSmithKline's (GSK) Annual General Meeting was shattered by a vote against the remuneration package proposed for its CEO, Dr Jean-Pierre Garnier. The package was reported as providing a 'golden parachute' for the CEO of the second-largest pharmaceutical company in the world, in the event of his dismissal before the 2007 termination date of his prevailing contract. The details were widely reported as amounting to $28 million.[30] The figures quoted were estimated by the Pensions Investment and Research Consultancy at $35.7 million (£22 million), disputed by GSK, since it included some $12 million of already vested share options.

The story can be traced to the restructuring and merger activities of the world's pharmaceutical companies in the 1990s. Beechams merged with Smith Kline, which then merged with Glaxo to form GlaxoSmithKline. The incumbent CEO, Dr J.-P. Garnier, was hailed at the time as one of Europe's rising business stars.

The vote (marginally over 50 per cent against) was symbolic. It had no legally binding power over the board's decision and was brought about by opposition from small shareholders (predictably opposed to the perceived generosity of such awards) and institutional investors, particularly the representatives of the pensions funds through the Association of British Insurers. Institutional shareholders in the United Kingdom are traditionally hands-off, preferring to work discreetly towards protecting their interests (primarily, the contribution of the company to the value of their portfolios). It was believed to be the first time that such a vote had carried the day. Standard Life, a major shareholder (holding 110 million shares), had already publicly stated its intention of opposing the proposal.

Since the completion of the $195 billion merger between the British drug companies Glaxo Wellcome and SmithKline Beecham in December 2000, the company had maintained its market leadership in the $300 billion global drug business. First-quarter results reported that pharmaceutical profits had grown 11 per cent, to $2 billion, on sales of around $7 billion from 'megabrands' such as the diabetes treatment Avandia and a recently launched asthma medication.

Shortly before the vote, Sir Christopher Hogg, chairman of GSK, had announced that the company had commissioned an independent inquiry into the remuneration packages of its executives. He also indicated that the opposition to the proposals would be taken very seriously by the company, regardless of the outcome of the vote. The vote followed new investor protection legislation passed in the UK earlier in the year and which represented one aspect among several that contributed to the incident, which was regarded at the time as potentially significant for future pay deals for business leaders.

> Garnier, who is known as JP, has already wrung $580 million in cost savings from overlapping businesses. And the stock? Up 12% since New Year. Garnier is determined to make the new GSK 'king of science'. So he has reshaped the company's massive research and development effort into competing teams to boost productivity. The payoff could be big: the company should launch 15 new drugs [in the next two years]. For JP, it's just the start.[31]

The merged company retains European (British) legal status, with many operations being located in the United States, as well as plants and research dotted around the world. As such, there are sometimes cultural ambiguities to be managed. For example, the company appeared, on the one hand, to hold the more robust American corporate view on CEO remuneration. Its public statement on the proposed package had originally been based on the argument that top people had to receive top rewards in order for a world-class company to recruit the best leaders and retain their services in a competitive world. Yet, the company also retained its European cultural heritage, together with its notions of inequality and collective contributions to achievement or failure, which contributed to beliefs about the distribution of rewards. In Europe, debate regarding corporate 'fat cats' had been around for several years, fuelled by the payments received by senior executives of newly privatized organizations who had in general failed to demonstrate their contributions to added shareholder value. The 'top people should receive top pay' argument had been considerably weakened as a consequence. The previous week, at the annual meeting of investors at the Royal & Sun Alliance, 28 per cent of votes had been cast against that company's remuneration proposals.

That is not to suggest that the culture was particularly swayed by non-economic arguments. Opposition to the basic principle that top people deserved top salaries came only from the distant voices of the outlying groups opposed to the more general structures of capitalism, and those seeking more social and environmentally sensitive institutions. These voices were less directly significant in this specific corporate incident (although they should not be discounted as contributing to the wider debate on corporate governance). The weight of opposition came from institutional stakeholders who had already supported the even more important symbolic vote to reinstate the executive board of the company. They had no ethical quarrel with the principle of top pay for top people. Rather, they pointed out that the

Box 9.2: Big Pharma's Ethical Dilemmas

Case examples drawn from one pharmaceutical company are likely to bear comparison with practices found in the others. Dilemmas of leadership are shared in a similar way.

Their global operations have developed a common business model. Their practices are similar enough for them to be referred to collectively as 'Big Pharma'. Their medical discoveries have saved countless lives. They need to charge high prices for their products in order to continue the expensive business of discovering and commercially exploiting new drugs and assorted medical supplies.

The business model relies on intellectual property rights granted to patented drugs available by prescription. Unpatented drugs or generics are substantially cheaper than prescription drugs. They may also be less effective and the newer ones will have more variable quality control. Big Pharma lobbies energetically against the dangers of doctors prescribing the cheaper generics.

Pressure has been placed on drug companies to be more transparent about their funding of doctors who advocate a particular non-generic drug.[32]

The issues that faced Jean-Pierre Garnier (CM 9.1) have continued to present dilemmas for Big Pharma, which receives criticism for its excessive focus on political lobbying. Critics remain unconvinced that Big Pharma has been committed enough to implement policies that would address the medical needs of the most needy around the world.[33]

Leaders within Big Pharma argue that their business model offers the best prospects for medical advances that will benefit everyone, with support from non-financial institutions.

---

substantive vote was over what a failed executive should expect on the termination of his contract. If Dr Garnier (as leader) was to receive a commission for the financial success of the merger, that was one thing. But corporate performance since the merger was not as strong as had been predicted. They believed that the leader should also take the hit under these circumstances.

Nor were the prospects for the short-term seen to be bright. Key profit streams from GSK's best-selling drugs were coming under challenge from cheaper, generic drugs as patents expired (as had happened to the antibiotic Augmentin the previous year). The company had played down the prospect of replacements for its declining drug lines.

The corporate reputation of the drug giants had also been under threat from alleged lack of social responsibility towards suffering in third-world countries. This made them a target for criticisms.[34] Only a few months earlier, the State of New York had sued GSK, together with the American major drug company Pharmacia, alleging that they inflated their drug prices.[35]

In an article for the *Guardian* newspaper a few months before the meeting of GSK shareholders, journalist Sarah Bosely wrote the following:

> It takes a big man to run the second largest pharmaceutical company in the world . . . Jean Pierre Garnier, who years ago lost some of his French identity, if not his accent, to the ubiquitous American initialising and became universally known in the pharmaceutical world as JP, doesn't wear a tie. Why would he? . . . Within his own parameters . . . JP is not only a big man but a good man. Some call him a humanitarian. He has been awarded the Legion d'Honneur by the French government. He has indisputably taken GSK several rungs higher on the ladder of altruism than any other drug company. But at the end of the day, he says, he runs a for-profit company. And if people are still dying of AIDS in Africa, it is because their governments are ineffective, or do not care. It is not to do with the greed or indifference of the pharmaceutical companies. . . . JP's vision is clear. He is willing to supply not just antiretrovirals but other medicines poor countries need for epidemics, such as malaria, at cost, he says. Combivir [a dual combination AIDS drug] . . . sells at $1.70 a day. For a Malawian woman . . . it might as well be the price of a flight on Concorde. His answer is twofold: order from GSK in bulk, perhaps for the whole of sub-Saharan Africa, and the price will drop and, secondly, persuade the rich countries to support the Global Fund so that poor countries will have the money to buy GSK's drugs. It's win-win for Glaxo. It need do nothing that is incompatible with the capitalist ideology of the marketplace or would upset the shareholders, even if it may seem ironic – to those who were baying for JP's blood over the recent offer from the GSK board to boost his pay to £20m – that he should be asking effectively for government subsidies.[36]

Opposition was further sharpened by pressures on the institutional investors. Pension funds, those sleeping giants, had been awakened by the 'pensions gap' facing ageing contributors and recipients. Corporate pension schemes were becoming difficult to manage and therefore coming under closer scrutiny. The corporate investors found themselves searching for economies and ways of cutting out any fat. The somewhat collusive relationship with corporations was changing. Glaxo had already indicated a scheme along similar lines, and somewhat more modest in scale, in 1992. At that time, there had been more muted objections. When the new scheme came along, the timing, lack of corporate progress, the difficulties facing the institutional stakeholders, and the new legislation were all factors that may have contributed to the dramatic vote.

The vote was hailed at the time as having historic significance. It made sense in different ways to different groups of people. The institutional investors believed they had sent out a warning against reward packages that were not linked to 'added value' promised by the leaders involved. The social-responsibility lobby took heart at future opportunities for drawing attention to other forms of corporate abuse of power. Small shareholders felt that they had at last had some influence over decisions that affected their savings. Glaxo accepted the need to revisit its remunerations policies and procedures, with greater input from disinterested outside experts.

CM 9.2: Roland: The Ethical but Manipulative Leader

Manipulation is a term generally used with negative connotations. Focus on the desired ends overcomes concerns for potential dilemmas suggested by dubious means. In this case study, we see a leader arguing that manipulation may be 'in the best interests' of his subordinates, or even, more broadly, a necessary and effective way of achieving goals as compared with more open (less manipulative) approaches.

Roland had a successful career within an international organization.[37] He was thoughtful and self-aware, willing to take responsibility for others often of lesser self-awareness and social skills. Roland considered it important for him to achieve results. His view was that 'the company' (i.e. its decision-makers) arrived at high-order goals and objectives. The company, while demanding, was also ultimately aware of what were reasonable targets. The professionals for whom Roland was responsible were mostly cooperative, with some more difficult than others ('bloody-minded' according to Roland).

In work and outside, Roland had an easy charm about him. He rarely lost his temper, was adept in deflecting anger, and generally liked to find 'win-win' outcomes to potential conflicts at work. He tried to treat everyone with respect and courtesy (secretarial and support staff warmed to his approach). As his career advanced, he set himself a personal development programme and was able to bring many ideas into his work practices from his training in interpersonal skills, and even creativity management. He later became a successful independent consultant with briefs in reconciliation and change management. One of his favourite approaches was that of reverse negotiation. 'Let me work out what I think is best for you and how we might be able to achieve it together. You work out what you think I want and how we can both achieve it. I find we get better results than from the old ways of doing this.' He often did.

One of Roland's principles was that he would try at all times to be as open and honest as he could. This would always have limits. He would relate the dangers of being told something 'in confidence' about a third party. For Roland, openness and honesty were not so much moral absolutes as potentially conflicting moral guidelines that had to be repeatedly 'managed'.

Roland had also realized that at times his wants did not coincide with those of others in the organization. 'If I have to, I go in for manipulation,' he was known to remark. 'But I have some ground rules. I will never do anything I believe will be against someone's interests. So I might have to withhold some information, for example. Sometimes it all works out the better because of what someone did not know in the short term. But if I get asked "Is there something you are keeping back from me", then I will admit I have been holding back, and I can't say any more until whenever I think I can be more open.'

Roland had worked out an approach, within his self-determined ethical framework, that he believed could be called manipulative ('scheming, calculating, controlling'). 'You may think it's manipulative, but I don't see there's anything wrong with the way I do it.'

He became a role model for many in his organization. His leadership skills were highly effective; and he was widely regarded as someone of great integrity. Roland defined his own boundaries for what he considered to be acceptable influencing methods. In his own eyes, he is sometimes 'forced' to be manipulative. At such times he attempts to do it in a way that has benign consequences for others.

CM 9.3: The Dilemmas of Authentic Leadership

At the start of the twenty-first century interest grew in the concept of authentic leadership. In part, this may be traced to a search for an ethical kind of leadership contrasting with the morally bankrupt behaviours associated with many leaders in the Enron scandal of 2000–1,[38] and subsequently in the global credit crisis of 2007–8.

Authentic leadership conceals dilemmas that confront leaders struggling with issues of corporate and moral responsibility. For example, should a leader demonstrate authentic feelings of uncertainty or inadequacy? Or should reassurance be offered through the 'mask of command'?

The concept of authenticity can be traced back to early Greek civilization. Its roots derive from philosophical considerations of the universals of human moral behaviours.[39] A special issue of *Leadership Quarterly* in 2005 examined the emerging concept of developing authentic leadership capabilities.[40] One of the editors was Bruce Avolio, already recognized for his contributions to the New Leadership paradigm and its transformational form. The editorial overview clearly indicated that authentic leadership involved a moral component, and also took a developmental and 'positive' stance. Walumbwa, writing a few years later with co-authors again including Avolio, provided a definition:[41]

> We define authentic leadership as a pattern of leader behavior that draws upon and promotes both positive psychological capacities and a positive ethical climate, to foster greater self-awareness, an internalized moral perspective, balanced processing of information, and relational transparency on the part of leaders working with followers, fostering positive self-development.

The urgency of identifying authenticity in leadership had been recognized following a wave of corporate scandals in the early 1990s.[42] The moral dimension in the definition was echoed by advocates such as Professor Bill George, former chairman and CEO of Medtronic Inc.[43]

Interest in authentic leadership grew along with concern about the lack of authenticity of leaders following the high-profile scandals that had emerged in 1990s corporate America. Its proponents set about characterizing and measuring authenticity, as a step towards enhancing its impact and reversing what was considered a decline in moral leadership in business.

May, Chan, and Avolio[44] proposed a moral component as essential to authentic leadership: The rationale was presented as 'a method for fostering sustainable authentic moral behaviors in leaders . . . committed to transparently evaluating alternatives so that decisions are both functionally sound and morally justifiable, [showing] commitment to one's personal growth and that of others.'[45]

Bernard Bass is associated with the development of new leadership ideas, and particularly with transformational leadership. The original concept drew attention to the uplifting and transforming impact that the leader had on followers. Yet such leaders shared characteristics with dictatorial and corrupt leaders. To resolve the dilemma he, 'defines the problem away' by introducing the category of the pseudo-charismatic leader.

> Truly transformational leadership . . . must be grounded in moral foundations. [Its] four components of authentic transformational leadership (idealized influence, inspirational motivation, intellectual stimulation, and individualized consideration) are contrasted with their counterfeits in the dissembling pseudotransformational leadership.[46]

This suggests concern for the so-called Hitler dilemma (the evil transformational leader), 'defining it away' through the notion of the counterfeit or inauthentic.

Dilemmas of authentic leadership have been pointed out by Chang and Diddams.[47] Authenticity, they argue, is a construct that focuses on alignment between self-awareness and actions. They argue that authenticity is more easily associated with humility than with leadership. Neither self-knowledge nor leadership is necessarily associated with authenticity. Their title expresses this as a dilemma of 'hubris or humility'.

Charismatic leadership was shown in Chapter 4 as being prone to hubris, the ancient fate that befalls the arrogant human. The dark side of charisma arises from characteristics of narcissism and even of megalomania.[48] Chang and Diddams suggest that a widely shared admiration for charismatic leaders ignores the virtues of modesty. Maybe, they suggest, leadership development should attend to that underestimated virtue in order to promote the 'right' sort of authenticity. Jim Collins has also noted the virtue of modesty in his Level 5 leaders, with their characteristic of 'quiet but firm resolve'.[49]

CM 9.4: Wikileaks: Dilemmas in the Age of Social Media

One of the first dilemmas of the age of social media was the tension between security and freedom of information, arising from the capacity of the web to transmit uncensored information rapidly and globally. The Wikileaks controversy illustrates the dilemma powerfully.[50]

Wikileaks states its mission as:

> the defence of freedom of speech and media publishing, the improvement of our common historical record and the support of the rights of all people to create new history. We derive these principles from the Universal Declaration of Human Rights. In particular, Article 19 inspires the work of our journalists and other volunteers. It states that everyone has the right to freedom of opinion and expression; this right includes freedom to hold opinions without interference and to seek, receive and impart information and ideas through any media and regardless of frontiers. We agree, and we seek to uphold this and the other Articles of the

Declaration. . . . The great American president Thomas Jefferson once observed that the price of freedom is eternal vigilance. We believe the journalistic media plays a key role in this vigilance.[51]

The right to freedom of opinion and expression becomes a dilemma when those rights impact on the rights of freedom from oppression of other people. From its origins as a freedom of information site in 2004, Wikileaks became a globally significant source of news with its publicizing of an enormous number of documents originally communicated as highly confidential diplomatic intelligence.

In 2010 it released what it described as *The Afghan War Diary*:

> [A]n extraordinary compendium of over 91,000 reports covering the war in Afghanistan from 2004 to 2010. The reports cover most units from the US Army with the exception of most US Special Forces' activities. The reports do not generally cover top secret operations or European and other ISAF Forces operations. We have delayed the release of some 15,000 reports from the total archive as part of a harm minimization process demanded by our source. After further review, these reports will be released, with occasional redactions, and eventually in full, as the security situation in Afghanistan permits.

The company also chose to release information from its sources via three traditional news sources, the *New York Times*, Germany's *Der Speigel*, and the UK's *Guardian*.[52] The journalist Jay Rosen quickly noticed the dilemma facing the editors chosen by Wikileaks:

> The WikiLeaks report presented a unique dilemma to the three papers given advance copies of the 92,000 reports . . . The editors couldn't verify the source of the reports – as they would have done if their own [journalists] had obtained them – and they couldn't stop WikiLeaks from posting it, whether they wrote about it or not. So they were basically left with proving veracity through official sources and picking through the pile for the bits that seemed to be the most truthful.

The *Afghan War Diary* secured Wikileaks' position as an influential social media site. It became the centre of its own story. It attracted powerful defenders as well as powerful opponents seeking to curb what they regarded as dangerous and politically destabilizing content as in an open letter sent to Wikileaks founder Julian Assange:

> Reporters Without Borders, an international press freedom organisation, regrets the incredible irresponsibility you showed when posting your article 'Afghan War Diary 2004–2010' on the Wikileaks website on 25 July together with 92,000 leaked documents disclosing the names of Afghans who have provided information to the international military coalition that has been in Afghanistan since 2001.[53]

The story of Wikileaks is intimately connected with the actions of its founder, as indicated in a BBC profile:[54]

To his fans, Julian Assange is a valiant campaigner for truth. To his critics, though, he is a publicity-seeker who has endangered lives by putting a mass of sensitive information into the public domain. In another twist in a controversial career, he is the subject of an international arrest warrant issued by Swedish prosecutors . . . The claims surfaced after he visited Sweden in August [2010] and relate to separate sexual encounters which his lawyer says were entirely consensual. Mr Assange says the allegations are part of a smear campaign against him and his whistle-blowing website.

The enthusiasm of supporters of Wikileaks, and the strength of opposition from others, demonstrates a fundamental dilemma. Assange and his organization believe in the importance of making information freely available while taking precautions to protect any dangerous consequences to individuals, including their own informants. Opponents believe that no such precautions can protect individuals from unintended consequences of the process. The dilemma of freedom of information or damaging consequences of making 'sensitive' information freely available is one facing leaders in a wide range of circumstances.

INTEGRATION

The two POUs address the question of whether leaders can ignore ethics at work. For both authors, the answer is a clear negative. Ciulla argues that leaders have tended to ignore ethics, concentrating on a search for the secrets of leadership through what leaders are observed to do, while implicitly being concerned with what good leaders do. Ciulla calls for more recognition that good leadership refers to productive behaviour that is also grounded in moral or ethical principles.

Ciulla has revisited the old question of whether ends justify means, this time in the context of leadership effectiveness and morality. For her, the answer is an unequivocal 'no'. She has demonstrated why 'good' leadership cannot be decoupled from ethical considerations and why leadership research needs to pay more attention to ethical issues. However, we would also consider that arriving at 'good' decisions remains problematic, and that ethical dilemmas remain to be confronted.

Drug companies argue that medical advances have saved countless lives and that sustained profitability within the industry creates jobs. To provide drugs at lower cost appears to be ethical, but in the long run damages people's health by reducing the level of investment in research, and the wealth of economies, through destroying profits. As part of the same argument, the corporations require the best leaders, who can be attracted and motivated by being offered a share in the additional surpluses generated through their leadership.

As was seen in CM 9.1, ethical leadership presents dilemmas to leaders of drug companies, whose mission is so often presented as saving human lives through their medical advances. Yet their leaders may have to defend both the high costs of drugs and the remuneration packages within the industry (see Box 9.2).

The drug companies argue that it is the responsibility of governments, not corporations, to arrange for subsidies to permit low-cost drugs. Should business leaders attend only to their legal and corporate obligations, leaving ethical considerations to others? Or should they operate such that ethical concerns are essential aspects of their corporate planning and actions?

These ethical concerns may also be applied to other forms of 'bottom line', such as corporate social responsibility and environmental impact assessments (Box 9.3).

According to Ciulla, ethical thinking becomes second nature to a leader for whom ethics lies at the heart of leadership, not on the periphery. The organization is also more attuned to ethical possibilities, rather than having to react to ethical pressure from outside. Sucher offers suggestions for testing a leadership story for its ethical basis.

From such considerations it is possible to test evidence to see whether the cases studied are consistent with ethics being at the heart of the organization, or whether the organizations are following a more pragmatic course of responding to pressures from outside forces.

GETTING PERSONAL

When you came to this chapter, you may have felt a sense of unease about its subject matter. You may well have approached business and business leadership expecting to learn about influencing, and been surprised to find ethics as a subject of concern.

Box 9.3: Environment, Ethics, and Leadership

An area of ethical dilemmas for corporations arises in matters of environmental concern. The ethical imperative is broadly that of preserving the environment for future generations. Organizations, as consumers and converters of natural resources, are increasingly confronted with such ethical issues.

One widely accepted principle is respect for the survival of species facing extinction through changes to habitats. The rights of humans to fish for food supplies are protected by organized culls of seals, a competitive predator for fish stocks. One corporate response has been the doctrine of sustainability. This accepts the ethical obligations of avoiding damage to the environment while holding to a belief in the social virtues accruing from technological innovation and progress through the economic freedom to trade.

It becomes a dilemma for leaders who concern themselves with operating in an ethical fashion under conditions where they have also committed themselves to corporate well-being through their leadership actions. This implies exerting leadership influence with the primary consideration of achieving corporate goals. Corporate acceptance of good environmental practices has sometimes been seen as a moral development process.[55]

You may now be in a better position to review your map of ethical leadership and to consider new ways of dealing with leadership dilemmas. Ciulla suggested that such thinking becomes second nature to a leader for whom ethics lies at the heart of leadership, not on the periphery. The organization is also more attuned to ethical possibilities, rather than having to react to ethical pressure from outside.

Before you started reading this book, you will have developed personal ethical beliefs. Some of those beliefs will have come as 'moral instruction' in your earliest years at home, at school, and perhaps from religious instructors. Later there may have been intense discussions late into the night with friends. Ethical beliefs develop through our social experiences, and through indirectly acquired principles. Studying your personal leadership maps provides opportunities for developing what has been called a moral compass, described in CM 9.3 as acquiring an internalized moral perspective.

SUMMARY

In this chapter, the fundamental dilemma between beliefs about morality and beliefs about effectiveness of performance are explored. We have seen that a widespread dilemma for business leaders lies in the tension between commercial well-being and ethical probity. The contextual issue comes from the structure or form of organizations as legally constituted primarily for the economic considerations of their stakeholders. Statements about the importance of good leadership or strong leadership conceal dilemmas, including ethical dilemmas. These dilemmas become critical when leaders considered to be good and or strong are judged as unethical and criminally responsible because of their leadership behaviours.

The fate of ethically flawed leaders at the turn of the twentieth century highlighted the need for leaders and other organizational stakeholders to develop greater awareness of the taken-for-granted issues of good leadership or strong leadership. We follow the map of ethics in leadership developed by Ciulla. She points to the absence of interest in ethics on the part of the map-makers we have encountered in our earlier chapters.

In her mapping of the territory, Ciulla suggests that the subject of ethical leadership is often dealt with in a tokenistic fashion in most leadership texts. Tokenism involves the apparent acceptance of a set of values or beliefs by a group who would prefer to exclude the individual. The actions are a means of protecting the group from accusations of prejudice against the individual and the individual's identified social characteristic.

Tokenism in relation to ethical issues in leadership maps may reflect the way ethics is approached in practice. Espousing ethical policies for the business and then displaying contradictory moral conduct might make a business open to an accusation of 'tokenism', just as in the case of diversity management. Ciulla suggests that ethics is a matter of common sense and does not require any formal education in ethical theories. Within such common-sense mapping, she argues that the fundamental dilemmas for business leaders arise from attempts to deal with the tensions between conduct (morality) and performance.

One approach is for leaders to find a pragmatic justification for actions – morality in the service of corporate economic responsibilities. Their organizational obligations require that leaders are effective (if they are not, then their ethics are not usually an issue; their position as leader will be challenged on their lack of achievement). A different approach is to argue that morality is good for business. This is the pragmatic view that attention to ethics is aligned with business success. Sometimes this is seen as a justification for manipulative behaviours 'in the interests of others'. Similar arguments are made about the application of Machiavellian principles for the social good (Box 9.4).

Box 9.4: Machiavellianism

One of history's most famous (or infamous) leadership consultants was Niccolò Machiavelli, adviser to the powerful in sixteenth-century Italy. His advice was intended primarily to support and preserve the power of his 'clients'. The basis of his writings is pragmatism, whereby the ends (preservation of power) justify any means to achieve them.

Today, there is interest in the Machiavellian orientation in public life. It has been studied in connection with business leadership, although as a topic it tends to be omitted from many leadership texts. Nevertheless, it permits us to address one of the dilemmas of business leaders. In practical terms, it supports the popular belief that nice guys come last; that winning (the goal) is all that matters (i.e. the way you win is irrelevant, as long as you are not disqualified from the game for breaching the rules).

A famous business game (the red-blue game) permits individuals (representing groups) to negotiate and break the rules in order to win the game. One outcome is clear: intentions to deal ethically are fragile and the game typically deteriorates into breaches of agreements and widespread Machiavellian behaviours. One of the learning points is that the process often results in 'lose-lose' outcomes, in comparison to the potential gains if each side had behaved more ethically. Yet game theory (developed in experiments such as this one) remains an accepted discipline for understanding human decision-making behaviour.

In an Indian study of managerial ethics the authors tell of an ancient text, the Arthashâstra or the science of material gain.[56] The Arthashâstra is written in the same mode as Machiavelli's much quoted *The Prince*. The focus is on the rights of the leader to impose his right to rule. The rulers have no moral sanctions restricting their treatment of their subjects, who have either to accept the rules imposed on them or to accept equally unrestricted and severe penalties. The end (preservation of the leader's right to rule) justifies the means to achieve that end, including an early proposal for the use of spies and the science of deception in order to gain useful intelligence. Unlike Machiavelli, the Brahmin author of the Arthashâstra, Kautilya, considered the end to be an ordered regime with protection under the law, to the benefit of all.

Other studies have explored the Machiavellian orientation in samples of business leaders and others. One study compared managers, MBA students, and MBA faculty. The managers showed a significantly lower Machiavellian orientation than did the students and faculty.[57]

Ciulla points to the dilemmas for those holding such pragmatic views (what to do when ethics appear to be damaging your business?). She points to the ethical imperative of leadership developed by Burns in his theory of transformational leadership and by Greenleaf in his model of servant leadership. Burns and Greenleaf place deeper moral issues at the heart of leadership dilemmas. These maps offer some moral certainty for leaders in terms of ethical values.

Burns introduced the concept of transformational leadership as a leadership in which the leader raises the moral horizons of followers. Any denial of this ignores that which was essentially different about new leadership maps. Similarly, Greenleaf holds that good leadership results when employees find meaning in and take on the morality of their leaders.

In conclusion, this chapter has repeatedly raised the question of whether leadership is ultimately a moral process. The challenge is for leaders to work towards influencing for the moral good. If so, leaders as role models have an *obligation* to align the values of their organization's members with the leadership direction, and to accept that the morality of leaders and those being led can have a strong influence on mapping the leadership process.

However, the pragmatic leader will find comfort in the observation that '[l]eadership is, in part, a struggle of flawed human beings'.[58]

NOTES

1 Jeffery Pfeffer, interviewed in http://blog.guykawasaki.com/2007/07/ten-questions-w.html# ixzz0xaoRJFHX, downloaded 25 August 2010.
2 Quoted in Hesselbein, F. (2010) 'How did Peter Drucker see corporate responsibility?', *Harvard Business Review*, http://blogs.hbr.org/what-business-owes-the-world/2010/06/how-did-peter-drucker-see-corp.html, downloaded 27 June 2010.
3 Freedman, M. (1970) 'The social responsibility of business is to increase its profits', *New York Times Magazine*, 13 September, downloaded from www.ethicsinbusiness.net/case-studies/the-social-responsibility-of-business-is-to-increase-its-profits/, 27 June 2010.
4 Vandenhove, S. (2005) 'Business ethical dilemmas: The oil industry and climate change', downloaded from www.pik-potsdam.de/avec/peyresq2005/talks/0928/van_den_hove/students_ Vandenhove. Summarized by Maxim, L., & Vandewalle, M. for the AVEC summer course on business ethics, Powerpoint: www.pik-potsdam.de/avec/peyresq2005/talks/0928/van_den_ hove/presentation_vandenhove.pdf.
5 www.marketwire.com/press-release/New-England-College-of-Business-and-Finance-Celebrates-101st-Commencement-1282020.htm, downloaded 27 June 2010.
6 Ibid., p. 23.
7 Petrick, J.A., & Scherer, R.F. 'The Enron scandal and the neglect of management integrity capacity', *Mid-American Journal of Business*, 18, 1, 37–49.
8 McLean, B., & Elkind, P. (2003) *The smartest guys in the room*, New York: Portfolio Trade; Salter, M.S. (2008) *Innovation corrupted: The origins and legacy of Enron's collapse*, Boston, MA: Harvard University Press.
9 www.reuters.com/article/idUSTRE62J0SM20100320 downloaded 15 Jan 2011; www.telegraph. co.uk/finance/newsbysector/banksandfinance/7072935/Banks-considered-too-big-to-fail-are-too-important-to-ignore-says-John-McFall.html, downloaded 15 January 2011.
10 See ISO26000 Guidance on Social Responsibility, www.sis.se/upload/632755963519968005.pdf; for the European position see: http://europa.eu/legislation_summaries/employment_and_social_

policy/employment_rights_and_work_organisation/n26039_en.htm, both downloaded 28 January 2011.

11 www.attitudedesign.co.uk/the-social-media-revolution/, downloaded 28 January 2011.

12 Ciulla, J.B. (1995) 'Leadership ethics: Mapping the territory', *Business Ethics Quarterly*, 5, 1, 6–28.

13 Burns, J.M. (1978) *Leadership*, New York: Harper & Row.

14 Greenleaf, R.K. (1977) *Servant leadership: A journey into the nature of legitimate power and greatness*, New York: Paulist.

15 This does not eliminate the moral dilemmas facing leaders, but rather offers a starting-point for critical reflection, which was Ciulla's original intention. An excellent introduction to Kant's philosophy can be found at http://plato.stanford.edu/entries/kant/, downloaded, 30 May 2011.

16 Sucher, S.J. (2008) *The moral leader: Challenges, insights and tools*, Oxford: Routledge.

17 Ibid., pp. 12–13.

18 Coles, R. (1989) *The call of stories, teaching and the moral imagination*, Boston MA: Houghton Mifflin. See also, Coles, R. (2000) *Lives of moral leadership: Men and women who have made a difference*, New York: Random House.

19 Coles, R. (2001) *Lives of moral leadership: Men and women who have made a difference*, New York: Random House, quoted in Sucher, S.J. (2008) *The moral leader: Challenges, insights and tools*, Oxford: Routledge, p. 124.

20 Sucher, S.J., ibid., p. 3.

21 Ibid., p. 3.

22 Ibid., p. 21.

23 Summarized from ibid., pp. 25–26, citing Kidder, R. (1995) *How good people make tough choices: Resolving the dilemmas of ethical living*, New York: Fireside.

24 Discussed elsewhere in *Dilemmas of Leadership* as the revelation and conversion of St Paul, and more generally as the insight phenomenon associated with discovery processes.

25 Achebe, C. (1994) *Things fall apart*, New York: Anchor.

26 Sucher, S.J. (2008) *The moral leader: Challenges, insights and tools*, Oxford: Routledge, p. 124.

27 Ibid.

28 Coles, R. (2001) *Lives of moral leadership: Men and women who have made a difference*, New York: Random House, quoted in Sucher, S.J. (2008) *The moral leader: Challenges, insights and tools*, Oxford: Routledge, p. 124.

29 Sucher, ibid., pp. 125–126.

30 Herald Tribune and BBC websites, 20 May 2003.

31 Business Week Online, 11 May 2001.

32 www.cbsnews.com/stories/2011/05/29/eveningnews/main20067228.shtml, downloaded 30 May 2011.

33 http://projects.publicintegrity.org/rx//report.aspx?aid=823, downloaded 31 May 2011.

34 The current Glaxo official website at the time indicated social responsibility initiatives ('investments') that could be presented as not too different in scale from the remuneration package proposed for their CEO.

35 BBC website, 14 February 2003, citing press release from New York Attorney General, Eliot Spitzer.

36 Bosely, S. (2003) 'Jean-Pierre Garnier', *Guardian*, 18 February.

37 The case draws on unpublished notes prepared for *Dilemmas of Leadership*. Roland is an alias for a British business executive who worked closely with the author over a period of years.

38 Petrick, J.A., & Scherer, R.F. 'The Enron scandal and the neglect of management integrity capacity', *Mid-American Journal of Business*, 18, 1, 37–49.

39 Walumbwa, F.O., Avolio, B.J., Gardner, W.L., Wernsing, T.S., & Peterson, S.J. (2008) 'Authentic leadership: Development and validation of a theory-based measure', *Journal of Management*, 34, 1, 89–126.

40 Bruce, J., Avolio, J.B., & Gardner, W.L. (2005) 'Authentic leadership development: Getting to the root of positive forms of leadership', *Leadership Quarterly*, 16, 3, 315–338, downloaded from

www.sciencedirect.com/science/article/B6W5N-4G1GFCC-1/2/1920c271670a7e50f7c9b42 eca231b8d. The text advocates efforts directed towards the development of desired leadership forms.

41 Walumbwa, F.O., Avolio, B.J., Gardner, W.L., Wernsing, T.S., & Peterson, S.J. (2008) 'Authentic leadership: Development and validation of a theory-based measure', *Journal of Management*, 34, 1, 89–126.

42 Cooper, C.D., Scandura, T.A., & Schriesheim, C.A. (2005) 'Looking forward but learning from our past: Potential challenges to developing authentic leadership theory and authentic leaders', *Leadership Quarterly*, special edition, 475–493.

43 George, B., & Sims, P. (2007) *True north: Discover your authentic leadership*, San Francisco: Jossey-Bass, www.billgeorge.org/, downloaded 3 November 2010; George, B., Sims, P., McLean, A.N., & Mayer, D. (2007) 'Discovering your authentic leadership', *Harvard Business Review*, 85, 2, 129–138; George, B. (2003) *Authentic leadership: Rediscovering the secrets to creating lasting value*, San Francisco: Jossey-Bass.

44 May, D.R., Chan, A.Y.L., & Avolio, B.J. (2003) 'Developing the moral component of authentic leadership', *Organizational Dynamics*, 32, 3, 247–260, http://linkinghub.elsevier.com/retrieve/pii/S0090261603000329.

45 Ibid., p. 247.

46 Ibid., p. 1.

47 Chang, G., & Diddams, M. (2009) 'Hubris or humility: Cautions surrounding the construct and self-definition of authentic leadership', American Academy of Management Conference, Green Management Matters, *The Academy of Management Proceedings*, 2009.

48 Although this dilemma may be 'defined away' through introduction of the pseudo-charismatic form (May, D.R., Chan, A.Y.L., & Avolio, B.J. (2003) 'Developing the moral component of authentic leadership', *Organizational Dynamics*, 32, 3, 247–260, http://linkinghub.elsevier.com/retrieve/pii/S0090261603000329).

49 http://hbr.org/hb-main/resources/pdfs/comm/microsoft/level-five.pdf, downloaded 20 May 2011.

50 A BBC summary of the history of Wikileaks can be found at www.bbc.co.uk/news/technology-10757263, downloaded 25 January 2011.

51 http://wikileaks.ch/About.html.

52 http://mirror.wikileaks.info/wiki/Afghan_War_Diary,_2004–2010/, downloaded 25 January 2011.

53 http://en.rsf.org/united-states-open-letter-to-wikileaks-founder-12–08–2010,38130.html, downloaded 25 January 2011.

54 www.bbc.co.uk/news/world-11047811.

55 Roome, N. (1992) 'Developing environmental management strategies', *Business Strategy and the Environment*, 1, 1, 11–24; (1994) 'Business strategy, R&D management and environmental imperatives', *R&D Management*, 24, 1, 65–82.

56 Sharma, P., & Bhal, K.T. (2004) *Managerial ethics: Dilemmas and decision making*, New Delhi: Sage.

57 Siegel, J.P. (1973) 'Machiavellianism, MBAs and managers: Leadership correlates and socialization effects', *Academy of Management Journal*, 16, 3, 404–412.

58 Joseph L. Badaracco, Jr., quoted in Lagace, M. (2001) 'Why leaders need great books', http://hbswk.hbs.edu/item/2327.html, downloaded 28 June 2010.

CHAPTER LEARNING OBJECTIVES

Learning focus
- The relationship between creativity and leadership

Key issues
- Putting creativity in context
- Change-centred leadership
- Benign structures for releasing creativity
- Creative organizations and cultures

Dilemmas
- Creativity as an enemy of rational thinking
- Destructive nature of creative change
- Creativity as mysterious and mythical

Platforms of understanding
- POU 10.1 Creativity Past, Present, and Future
- POU 10.2 Creativity and Leadership: The Contributions of Teresa Amabile

Contextual materials
- CM 10.1 Sternberg's Propulsion Model of Creative Leadership
- CM 10.2 Change-centred Leadership: A Third Leadership Style
- CM 10.3 'Creativity Is a Leader's Secret Weapon'
- CM 10.4 Richard Florida's Theory of Creative Cultures and Creative Leadership

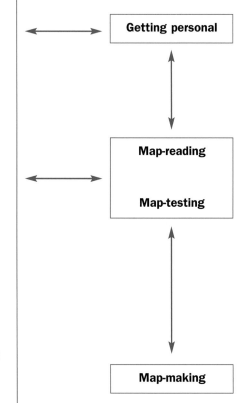

Getting personal

Map-reading

Map-testing

Map-making

10 CREATIVITY AND LEADERSHIP
DILEMMAS OF DREAMS, DENIAL, AND CHANGE MANAGEMENT

The concept of creativity may trail clouds of glory, but it brings along also a host of controversial questions. The first of these is: What is it?[1]

Creative leadership can be of three general kinds: leadership that extends existing ways of doing things, leadership that challenges existing ways of doing things, and leadership that synthesizes different existing ways of doing things.[2]

Leaders will need to be creative to stay abreast of rapid change. They will need to identify and develop creativity in individuals, nurture creativity in teams and align processes to spread creativity throughout the organisation.[3]

ORIENTATION

In this chapter, you will see how an effective leader engages creatively with many of the practical challenges faced in business and in social groups. There are several dilemmas facing the creative leader, which also take us into the related territories of change management and innovation.

In keeping with the orientation exercises of earlier chapters, you are invited to reflect on your working definition of creativity by tackling Exercise 10.1.

How did you approach the exercise? You will probably have made sense of creativity as having something to do with the production of new ideas. This happens to be an important part of a widely shared POU of creativity, when the concept is referred to without further formal clarification.

From it we can make a connection to the processes of map-reading, map-testing, and map-making. These also result in the discovery of new ideas. These ideas may be solutions to problems, or they may be the personal insights that help us to revise and remake our knowledge structures. In other words, creativity may be seen as being connected with our personal learning processes.

A good starting-point for more formal maps of creativity is afforded by an influential map drawn up by the American researcher Melvin Rhodes in the 1960s. Just as Stogdill catalogued and evaluated the multiple definitions of the process of leadership, Rhodes carried out a similar exercise for creativity. He concluded that the large numbers of definitions he found could be simplified into four overlapping factors.[4] This became known as the 4P model of creativity, and is shown in Box 10.1.

From Rhodes it can be seen that creativity is 'something to do with' a creative *person* engaged in the *process* of discovering ideas which are new and useful. The process results in creative outputs or *products* (these are sometimes referred to as innovations). The context may be regarded as *press* (a psychological term referring to the environmental field of forces).[5]

Exercise 10.1: Making Sense of the Processes of Creativity and Mapping

1 The term 'creativity' is often used in informal discussion as if there were a shared POU about the process. In your own words, what do you mean when you use the term 'creativity'?
2 Can you see connections between the process of creativity and the processes of map-reading, map-testing, and map-making?

Box 10.1: The 4P Model of Creativity

In the 1960s, the American researcher Mel Rhodes surveyed definitions of creativity and proposed a four-factor mapping, which has been accepted ever since.

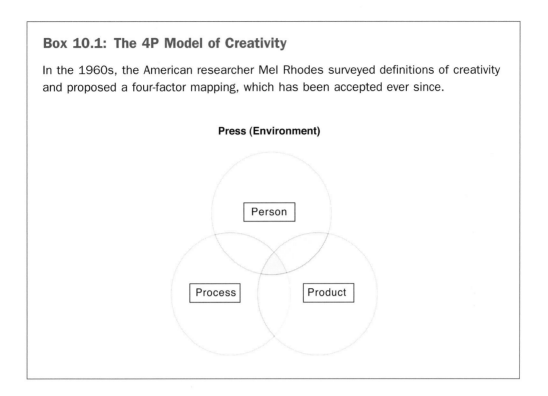

Press (Environment)

Person

Process

Product

PLATFORMS OF UNDERSTANDING

POU 10.1 takes a historical perspective of creativity that can be compared with the historical accounts of leadership covered in earlier chapters. POU 10.2 introduces the contributions made to the contemporary creativity literature by Professor Teresa Amabile of Harvard Business School and her co-researchers. The work has had a substantial impact on our understanding of creativity, leadership, motivation, and the interrelationships between these three vast fields of knowledge and interest.

POU 10.1: Creativity Past, Present, and Future

This material is based on a keynote speech by the present author, reviewing creativity, at the start of an international conference on creativity in Buffalo, New York, in May 2008.[6]

My talk tonight is entitled 'Creativity Past, Present, and Future'. This echoes the title of an article by J.P. Guilford, one of the pioneers of Creativity Research, 'Creativity: Yesterday, Today and Tomorrow', written over forty years earlier.[7] By one of those quirks of multiple invention, the title is unintentionally too close for comfort to an excellent contemporary review, 'Creative Problem-solving: Past, Present and Future', which was written by two distinguished creativity researchers, Gerard Puccio and John Cabra, who have been instrumental in inviting me here tonight.

Following Guilford's example, I shall briefly examine historical achievements and contemporary perspectives before offering a few speculative thoughts on the future for creativity research and practice. Our journey will take us from earlier to current times, with pauses at some of the most interesting vantage points in between, although at times the route does not follow a rigid time line.

We can find evidence of very early accounts of what today we would call the creativity myths of ancient cultures. In these ancient mythological constructions, creativity was identified with its essentially feminine essence. It may be worth noting that the early creation myths do not square up with the way in which creativity has in more modern times been linked with iconic figures of genius – with a disproportionate level attention paid to males. To redress this bias is one of the challenges for the future.

Strictly speaking, creativity has a different conceptualization, which we have introduced retrospectively into our interpretations of artefacts from earlier cultures. The Greeks, for example, considered that an artist was an *imitator* of the perfection that was everywhere around us. Art (*techne*) involved strict subjection to laws and rules. Artists were instrumental in the production of work according to rules.

In its earliest representations, creativity was associated with mythology, mystery, madness, and even magic.[8] This is now described as the traditional, romantic (or even primitive) perspective. However, these beliefs coexist with more modern treatments, much as charismatic leadership coexists with modern 'post-charismatic' notions. The early creativity myths trace what Arthur Koestler called 'man's changing vision of the universe'. Creativity was both individualistic and fatalistic. The creative individual was at the same time 'the chosen one' and also the instrument of a higher power. Koestler subsequently drew on his cosmological studies in writing his most influential contribution to the literature of creativity. That was *The Act of Creation*.[9] Works of art were granted respect, but as evidence of the existence of a divine power. The artist was revered, but only as a means through which the divinity chose to reveal itself. The creativity of a work of art permitted reflection on the supernatural creator of the universe.

Creativity does not seem to have been problematic and worthy of deep study until about the time of the broad philosophical rupture in Western thought often described as the Enlightenment. Science, rationality, and modernity sought to eliminate the 'primitive' concepts associated with the earlier conceptualizations.[10] The Enlightenment is generally located as the frontier of mediaeval thought in the late seventeenth century. Universities began to discard their mediaeval traditions (although retaining others to this day), thus heralding a new age of reason. Empirical science began to replace natural philosophy as the means of acquiring valid knowledge.[11]

However, Enlightenment scholars faced a challenge (or a dilemma) in explaining the process that gave rise to the highest expressions of discovery and artistic creativity. In an age that prized rationality, creativity seemed to be something other than a rational process.

There was something mysterious about the facility of the greatest artists and, later, scientists. Later, in the 1980s, Charles Handy argued that we were moving beyond the age of reason, into a new age of unreason that called for new and 'unreasonable' thoughts and actions, i.e. for creativity.[12]

The productivity of the highest form of genius sometimes appeared to be effortless, an outpouring of talent and youthful precocity. To be sure, there were counter-examples, such as the monumental struggles of a Beethoven or an Einstein. But nevertheless, creativity remained a phenomenon with pre-modern overtones long after the Western Enlightenment.

By the start of the twentieth century, the flourishing of new methods of enquiry into human behaviours gave impetus to studies into the nature of human thought processes. Even then, creativity remained under-researched, in contrast to efforts to understand intelligence. It might be argued that intelligence was regarded as central to rationality, while creativity was having difficulty in escaping from its irrational if romantic grounding.

This was the point made so effectively by Guilford in the middle of the twentieth century. He is today recognized as influencing the course of education in the United States towards greater emphasis on encouraging and nurturing creative talent. In the 1960s, within a decade of Guilford's speech, Buffalo, in New York state, was to become a focal point for research and the application of techniques or ways of deliberately stimulating creativity. Alex Osborn developed his famous brainstorming technique here. He was joined by Sidney (Sid) Parnes in founding the Creative Education Foundation and, later, the *Journal of Creative Behavior*. Osborn's brainstorming technique was refined into a general model for creative problem-solving, known as the Parnes-Osborn approach.

Theoretical ideas were also being developed by leading psychologists such Paul Torrance, who introduced one of the most widespread general tests for stin creativity. The Torrance Tests of Creative Thinking assessed an individual's c ty for generating original ideas under controlled psychometric conditions.[13] A copy of the tests was even added to the payload of one of NASA's spacecraft, a symbolic sen f evidence of human achievements into space.[14]

By the 1960s, Buffalo was hosting influential gatherings of leading scholars as well as practitioners interested in creativity. Parnes helped to retain awareness of a stage model for creativity[15] introduced by Graham Wallas, born at the end of the nineteenth century. Wallas became Professor of Political Science at the London School of Economics, and a major political figure in British politics. His book *The Art of Thought* (1921) had proposed a stage model for the creative process. The four-stage model remains much cited to this day as:

1 Preparation
2 Incubation
3 Illumination (or insight)
4 Validation.

Parnes believed passionately that creativity could be deliberately enhanced. The Parnes-Osborn approach became an influential approach to stimulating creativity in problem-solving teams. The various stages have been modified and relabelled. The family tree (and its links to the earlier Wallas model) can easily be detected from one of the versions (OFPISA) published by the Creative Problem Solving Institute in the 1990s:

- objectives-finding
- fact-finding
- problem-finding
- idea-finding
- solution-finding
- acceptance-finding.

Subsequent generations of researchers and practitioners at Buffalo have extended and enriched the earlier approaches.[16] Across the Atlantic, supported by visits in each direction, further modifications to the Parnes-Osborn system were being tested in various practical environments. In the UK, one of the more recent modifications, whose shared origins with OFPISA can easily be seen,[17] is the MPIA version:

- mapping
- perspectives
- ideas
- action [ideas].

Also in Europe, other 'assists' to creativity were being developed in the last quarter of the twentieth century. Edward de Bono was perhaps the best-known of applied theorists, for his celebrated concept of 'lateral thinking'.[18] Another significant contribution came from Tony Buzan, through his work on mind-maps.[19] Students at Manchester Business School applying the MPIA version of the original Parnes-Osborn model are encouraged to begin their project work by making a collective Buzan diagram or mind-map. One student described the result as a spider-diagram, an endearing name that we have retained ever since.[20]

Another important technique for stimulating creativity is the TRIZ approach, attributed to the former Russian patents officer, Genich Altshuller. TRIZ draws on principles extracted from a comprehensive analysis of the inventive principles behind successful patents. These principles have now been codified in a way that helps to trigger invention processes by individuals and teams in search of innovative ideas. The concept reached the English-speaking world in a roundabout way, via the Vietnamese scholar Phan Dung.[21]

The creative individual had received a disproportionate degree of attention in pre-modern cultures. Rhodes, in the 1960s, showed that definitions of creativity were primarily concerned with the person as the unit of analysis. Parnes and Osborn were among those who extended interest in creativity to its applications within wider social groups. By the 1980s, there was a growing interest in creative teams, creative leaders, and creative organizations. Gareth Morgan was among the generation of organizational theorists searching for new 'images of organization' in this relatively under-explored field.[22] They proposed that ideas may be regarded as sociological constructions or interpretations.[23]

In this respect, we see a similar move to the non-essentialist treatments of leadership that accompanied the New Leadership studies of the 1980s.[24]

Confusion over creativity is made worse by lack of clarity about entrepreneurial flair and creative achievement. Some idea of the difficulties is revealed if we 'compare and contrast' the stories of such twenty-first-century leaders as Richard Branson, Kiichiro Toyoda, Steve Jobs, Anita Roddick, and Marjorie Scardino. We might agree that each has achieved great things. But they refuse to be pigeon-holed so as to provide a neat profile for the creative leader of a creative organization.

It can be argued that creative organizations can be found in any industry. Examples can be found, however stable the environment, where fresh ideas are embraced, tested, and assimilated into innovation. Mersey Care NHS Trust in the UK is one illustration from a highly regulated professional healthcare environment. This is an organization that has transformed itself by creating room to generate fresh ideas and then apply them in reflexive cycles of action and learning.[25]

One of my favourite current examples is the Chinese multinational giant Haier.[26] Another series of studies, conducted by the Saudi Arabian scholar Abdullah Al-Bereidi, has suggested that even in highly regulated financial services environments, creativity can still be present within activities relating to professional task requirements.[27]

There is an entire industry sector in the twenty-first century characterized by its creativity. The rise of the so-called creative industry deserves special mention. The organizations in it are the fastest-growing economically, around the world. The industry sector has been identified as being made up of the practices of:

- architecture
- arts and antiques
- design
- performing arts
- electronic games
- media.[28]

Today's creative and successful organizations cannot be expected to remain dominant as did those of earlier eras.[29] Mechanical typewriters persisted for a century before IBM arrived. IBM was superseded by Microsoft within a decade. Now [2004] we are seeing Microsoft under threat from its younger rival, Google.

Some experts argue that the term 'creativity' is now so widely and popularly used that it is nearly meaningless as a starting-point for serious scholarship. I don't agree, because there are several ways of dealing with the problem of definition. The simplest is to situate creativity or, as Teresa Amabile would say, to put it in context, rather than to seek a universalistic definition.[30] As with leadership, creativity theories have suffered from a surfeit of definitions. However, a working definition of creativity found acceptable by many researchers today would be:

Creativity is the ability to generate ideas which are novel, surprising and valuable.[31]

'. . . but does it work in theory?' An early magisterial work by Mo Stein in the 1970s called for more careful empirical studies linked to theoretical principles. Much the same can be said four decades later. Across a range of professions, there have been practitioners and enthusiastic advocates of techniques for stimulating creativity who have claimed direct and creative benefits through personal experience. But the challenge thrown down by Stein can hardly be said to have been adequately addressed, even today.[32]

Creativity, as is also the case in other domains, has been studied by distinguished theorists for many years. For a recent lecture I was able to list a range of theories that have developed with the rise of social science disciplines over the last century. These included theories of:

- insight
- self-actualization
- transcendence
- cognitive reframing
- Darwinism
- information-processing
- problem-solving
- experiential learning.

Fortunately we have a new generation of knowledge guides to help us explore the various theoretical territories. Teresa Amabile has rightly gained a leading position in the field. In Europe I would recognize in particular two figures whose work has influenced several generations of creativity researchers. These are Michael Kirton, whose Adaption/Innovation model helped profoundly in distinguishing between creativity style and creativity effectiveness;[33] and Edward de Bono, for his approaches to stimulating creativity, which go far beyond lateral thinking, the most celebrated technique with which he has been associated.[34]

I have indicated how modernity has gone a long way towards setting itself up as a replacement of earlier beliefs. But the Enlightenment dream of a fully rational world has not quite worked out. The brilliant and innovative artist Marcel Duchamp, allegedly declared at an exhibition of technology that '. . . painting is washed up. Who will ever do anything better than that propeller?' Fortunately, Duchamp and other creative pioneers found ways of 'doing something better'. They began locating their creativity in products that went somewhere different than the beautiful, functional lines of technological products. Other theorists have found postmodern treatments that challenge the primacy of novelty and the potential in nostalgia for creative work.

I was recently discussing the nature of creativity with a mathematical colleague. He was intrigued by the account of the stage model of creativity after Wallas. The next day he sent me a long e-mail which I only part understood. He related how he had realized that time and again he struggled with mathematical problems 'just like in the theory'. It seems he would be unable to sleep until some intuition and a hunch rescued him from insomnia. He was able to recall various examples from his recent work. His story is no more than affirmation that some of the old ideas about creativity retain their credibility, at least in the field of scientific discovery.

My second example could not be more different. Like many around the world, I despair over seeming endless conflicts and bloodshed. I take comfort from the story of how peace came to Northern Ireland after decades of bloodshed. It was anticipated by the great Irish poet Seamus Heaney. The real-world achievement came about by a process in which many showed great political judgement, and in my view, creative leadership. It was a triumph of hope over experience. As Heaney expressed it in *The Cure at Troy*:[35]

> So hope for a great sea-change
> On the far side of revenge.
> Believe that further shore
> Is reachable from here.

The story may well serve for other contexts for creating peace around the world. That would indeed be a worthwhile creative enterprise.

Over time, attention in creativity research has broadened from a focus on the individual to a focus on the nature of creativity within wider social groups. How might the creativity of a team be enhanced? How about an organization? To retain our metaphor of a journey of exploration, we are entering the early stages of the twenty-first century to glimpse exhibits still under construction. But there are some hints of what they might contain 'on the further shore'.

POU 10.2: Creativity and Leadership: The Contributions of Teresa Amabile

Since the publication of *The Social Psychology of Creativity* in 1983,[36] Teresa Amabile's research ideas have helped to change the way in which the subject has been understood. At the time of the book's writing, the dominant set of beliefs about creativity had been based on ideas concerning the psychological characteristics of the creative individual. It is instructive to note the similarity to research into leadership, in this respect. The book gained acceptance for the possibility that a social psychological perspective could be a promising approach for future research work into creativity.

With colleagues first at Brandeis and then Harvard, Amabile has made advances on a series of fronts which contribute to leadership studies. These have included:

- intrinsic motivation theory
- a componential theory of creativity
- the consensual assessment approach to assessing creative product
- an assessment methodology for leadership and creative climate.

1 *Intrinsic Motivation Theory*

From her earliest published studies, Amabile had developed a view that an intrinsically motivated state was conducive to creativity. The concept offered support for studying creativity by finding ways of removing constraints to its actualization. She cited the work of Carl Rogers, who had believed that there is an inner focus of self-actualization that becomes diminished by attention to external factors, including the attitudes and behaviours of others.

The initial evidence came from classroom observations in which children demonstrated greater willingness to engage with tasks that were not accompanied by external stimuli or rewards. The original statement of the hypothesis added that an externally motivated state was detrimental to creativity. Later versions modified the model to admit one type of extrinsic motivator that reinforced the impact of intrinsic motivation.

The original hypothesis was at odds with evidence from studies of rewarding employees in the workplace, and challenged theories of motivation by examining conditions under which extrinsic motivators (or 'levers', or 'assistors') introduced by a teacher or manager might support creativity. The newer version is more aligned with evidence beyond the classroom, where creative individuals in business, sport, politics, and social domains, appear to be influenced by external rewards as well as by intrinsic motivation.

While the theory remains open to further examination, it has been of considerable value. It stands as a warning to proposals for motivating people simply by offering external rewards. It suggests approaches by which leaders may release creativity among colleagues, and it indicates that such methods need to take intrinsic motivation into account.[37]

By 1999, writing with co-worker Regina Conti, Amabile suggested that:

> Some forms of extrinsic motivation may combine positively with intrinsic motivation . . . this is most likely when intrinsic motivation is initially high, and when the external motivators are perceived as supporting rather than limiting autonomy and skill development.[38]

Amabile considers that a capacity to resist inhibition of intrinsic motivation may derive from a stable personality trait such as independence from social influence (cf. OCEAN model of traits). However, much of her work also examines how interventions, particularly at the level of a team leader, might overcome external impediments to creative behaviours, and to intrinsic motivation.

2 *A Componential Framework for Creativity Theorizing*

Componential models of creativity attempt to specify component elements (abilities, skills, traits, etc.) that are involved in the production of creative behaviours.[39] Amabile's model was presented as 'a framework that can be used to develop a theory of creativity'.[40] The framework proposed three components: task motivation; domain-relevant skills; and creativity-relevant processes.

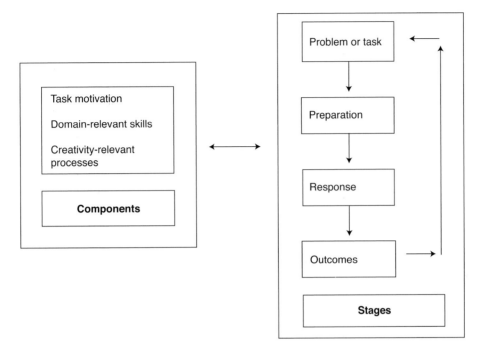

Figure 10.1 Amabile's Componential Model of Creativity[41]

Task motivation is modelled as primarily intrinsic, perhaps mediated for better or worse by extrinsic motivators. The three components are visualized as occurring in a stage-type sequence of processes familiar to those found in the stage processes of the creative process proposed by earlier workers. A problem or task is presented, followed by stages of preparation, response generation, and validation.

The three components are believed to be necessary and 'multiplicative. The levels of the three components for an individual's attempt at a given task determine that individual's overall level of creativity at that particular task.'[42]

Amabile presents these as a sequence which can be compared with other stage-models that have been proposed for the creative problem-solving process.[43]

3   *The Consensual Assessment Methodology for Creativity*

Amabile and co-workers have addressed technical difficulties in establishing a satisfactory assessment measure for creativity by the requirements of the DRM. Her approach takes as its fundamental premise that, within a domain, creative productivity can be assessed by a community of experts within that domain. The approach has been challenged for its departure from the DRM's concern for objectivity.[44]

According to Amabile 'It is extremely difficult, given our current state of knowledge, to describe the nature of creativity judgements in any general way. Thus it seems most appropriate to simply rely on the assumption that experts in a domain do share creativity criteria to a reasonable degree.'[45]

Hennessey and Amabile concluded that

> The Consensual Assessment Technique (CAT) for assessing creativity is based on the assumption that a group of independent expert raters, persons who have not had the opportunity to confer with one another, and who have been trained by the researcher are best able to make such judgements.[46]

Other researchers modified it to deal with criticisms of its deficiencies according to DRM criteria.[47]

4 *An Assessment Methodology for Leadership and Creative Climate*

Amabile and co-workers have developed a range of measures for assessing the climate for creativity. The most carefully evaluated is the KEYS instrument.[48] It is based on earlier work on creative climate.[49]

Extensive studies repeatedly show that the creativity of individuals in working teams and projects is mediated by the work environment. The KEYS inventory, which deploys Likert-style self-report inventory items, has identified the most important factors as:

- organizational encouragement
- recognition given for creative work
- mechanisms for developing new ideas and a shared vision
- supervisory encouragement
- supportive team leaders
- work group supports
- challenging work
- freedom and control over one's work and how to do it.

The four elements of Amabile's work provide a map of creativity within which creative actions are intrinsically motivated. The measures of creativity suggest an affinity with the social constructivist maps introduced in Chapter 5. Taken collectively, there is a coherence that goes some way to addressing dilemmas of creativity, such as its resistance to clarification and validation when studied through the perspective of the DRM.

CONTEXTUAL MATERIALS

CM 10.1: Sternberg's Propulsion Model of Creative Leadership

Robert Sternberg has made many important contributions to the understanding of creativity. Within these, he has explored the nature of creative leadership. His propulsion model suggests there are three general kinds of creative leadership.[50]

Box 10.2: Sternberg's Propulsion Model and Creative Leadership Styles

Sternberg's propulsion model suggests there are three situational contexts that produce eight creative leadership types. The contexts support incremental change, radical change, and synthetic or integrative style, respectively.

Incremental style 1 Replication	Leader seeks to maintain the status quo of the organization. While not obvious, the style requires considerable creative efforts, for example to retain market dominance of a brand.
Incremental style 2 Redefinition	Leaders redefine the rationale of the status quo. A football manager may claim to be the one playing in the spirit of the game; a politician loses an election 'but wins the moral argument'.
Incremental style 3 Forward incrementalism	Leadership supports the general strategic direction in which the organization is heading. Coke Lite; Special-K cornflakes; most new-season automobiles.
Incremental style 4 Advanced forward incrementalism	The fundamental leadership idea (or vision) is 'ahead of its time'. The Dutch company Philips was known for patenting advanced technologies that succeeded later in diluted form in competitive firms.
Transformational style 1 Redirection	Leadership redirects focus in an organization, perhaps by rethinking its markets or product designs while retaining core skills. Electronic typewriters; computers; electric cars.
Transformational style 2 Reconstruction/ redirection	'Retro-innovation' supported by nostalgia. 'Good old-fashioned values of our founder.' Mechanical versions of radios, watches.
Transformational style 3 Re-initiation	A leap in the dark from the familiar to meet a perceived opportunity or threat. Space flight; carbon-capture coal-fired power stations; micro-wave cookers; desalination plants.
Integrative style Synthesis	Existing paradigms are brought together to create a hybrid new paradigm. E-books; petrol/hydrogen automobiles.

Sternberg offers an investment metaphor for creativity which asserts that creative individuals are quick to see value in ideas while others assess their value as low or even worthless. The theory explains why so-called creative ideas are initially regarded with suspicion, and then as obvious.[51] However, the earlier theory lacked a sense that there might be different kinds of creative leader.

With co-researchers James Kaufman and Jean Pretz, Sternberg examined variations of creative leadership.[52] The leadership styles are ways to propel people metaphorically from where they are to 'wherever the leader wishes them to go'.[53]

The researchers suggest that their classification 'maps into Kuhn's in that we view the types of leadership that maintain current paradigms as analogous to normal science, and those paradigms that reject current paradigms as analogous to revolutionary science'.[54]

The propulsion model sets out its ground clearly and invites us to see creative leadership as highly context dependent. This, and its emphasis on 'what leaders do', places it among the contingency maps of Chapter 2.

> In sum, leadership is [neither] creative [nor is it] not-creative. Rather it can be more or less creative in different ways. What type of leadership will emerge in an organization depends in part on the leader, but also in part upon the organizational environment.[55]

CM 10.2: Change-centred Leadership: A Third Leadership Style

Numerous studies have differentiated leadership style into two dominant factors. These are often labelled as a concern for people and a concern for task. A newer theory, backed by empirical studies, proposes a third, change-oriented style.

The division of leadership styles into task-oriented and people-oriented can be traced to work that originally concerned itself with work practices at operational levels within large American organizations. Organizational behaviour texts offer a historical time line from the Ohio state studies of the 1930s to the celebrated management grid of Blake and Mouton. Most studies thereafter found no need to look much further than the two factors. However, a group of Scandinavian researchers has put forward an interesting possibility of a third, change-centred leadership style.

Blake and Mouton famously proposed that a combination of the two basic factors in a leadership style ('more of both') adds value to leadership efforts. Other researchers were later to take a more situational approach. But there has rarely been a challenge to the dominance of the basic two-factor model of leadership style.

The work of Goran Ekvall and his colleague and former student Jouko Arvonen was recently published in English, which will bring it to more international attention. Their theory is easy to understand. Their research first re-examined in detail the reported data from the items of the Ohio questionnaire (SPDQ, LBDQ versions). They found that change-centred leadership had been measurable through the inventories (in such items as 'tries out new ideas with the group'). But during the original studies, and since, the results gave no statistical support to a third leadership style favouring change-orientation beyond the two established styles/factors.

The Scandinavians have been able to replicate the work, applying the Ohio methodology with mainly Swedish, Finnish, and US organizational samples. Jouko Arvonen, summarizing the work recently, reports that over 6,000 responses have been collected in five separate studies.[56] Factor analysis revealed from all studies the appearance of an additional, change-centred leadership style, defined in terms of visionary qualities, creativity, action for implementation, and risk-taking.

Arvonen believes that management is increasingly being required to show skills in 'neo-charismatic' or transformational leadership. He suggests that the new style has emerged as a contingent consequence of new work challenges. This provides a fascinating hypothesis to explain the emergence of change-centred leadership. The implications are profound in challenging a two-factor model of managerial style that has persisted in maps of management behaviours since the early Ohio studies.[57]

Further studies will be required to test this idea. However, the concept offers an innovative proposal that goes beyond the more frequent two-factor maps of leadership style popular in the contingency era of the 1960s to 1980s (Chapter 2).

CM 10.3: 'Creativity Is a Leader's Secret Weapon'

Researchers at Manchester Business School have established a link between effective leaders and their skills in encouraging creative change. The importance of creativity to leaders has been widely underestimated.

Since its inception in the 1960s, Manchester Business School (MBS) has been engaged in applied studies into creativity and leadership. The work began within its teaching programmes. Across several decades, approximately 4,500 participants in 700 teams have been studied.

MBS provides an unusual approach for studying leadership behaviours, known as the Manchester Method. Teams of business students engage with real-life business projects for an organizational client. The general principle of 'learning while doing' is not unique to Manchester, although it is probably more fully integrated into the MBA syllabus there than at other schools.

A general principle of creative team leadership emerged from these studies. The tutors found three levels of project team performance, which they traced to a team's leadership. A small proportion of weak teams ('teams from hell') struggled to reach any effective result in their project. The majority of the teams ('standard teams') achieved the goals set them to the satisfaction of the client. Only a minority of teams performed beyond expectations ('dream teams').

A clear differentiating principle in the behaviours of high-performance teams is the establishment of conditions favouring creativity, which have been termed *benign structures* supporting creative results. In a 'dream team' the leader succeeds in reducing the impact of the negative behaviour patterns of team members by providing a more benign structuring of work patterns.

A minority of teams successfully go beyond their project briefs to achieve unexpected, imaginative, and yet relevant results. A typical example from the most recent projects involved a team working to a brief from a successful entrepreneur, Imran Hakim. The product was the fast-growing 'iTeddy', an innovative educational toy designed to help pre-school children learn as they play. The interactive teddy bear has a computer chip in its tummy. The students came up with a new business model for the company, based on a redesigned website, which is under construction.

Other projects have sometimes been substantial. Smaller teams work towards a collective goal by splitting up a large project into sub-projects. For example, in a project for UNIDO, each individual team explored sustainability in an industry sector. Collectively, the work produced a diagnostic tool across sectors, now in use by UNIDO to support the transfer of technology into its third-world sustainability projects.

The results were interpreted as an extension to the accepted team development model of stages labelled as forming, storming, norming, and performing.[58] The map identified two barriers to team effectiveness. The first barrier blocks the development of the poorest teams, probably at the storm stage of team development. Standard and dream teams progress beyond the first barrier, but then the second barrier arrests progress for the majority of the residual teams.

The second barrier is at the norm stage of team development. Only by breaking out of the accepted norms is a team able to establish new norms. Then we have the conditions in which a team is able to exceed the expectations of its corporate sponsor, and also its own assumptions about the project.

The studies offer ways of developing creative leaders and supporting the production of benign structures. Students are encouraged to experiment with an approach derived from the Parnes-Osborn creative problem-solving methodology, which encourages teams to structure the stages of mapping a problem, clarifying goals, generating ideas, and developing actions plans.

A further set of creativity triggers draw on Edward de Bono's celebrated lateral thinking methods. Other ways of structuring creativity include ways of dealing with unconscious rejection mechanisms towards new ideas in teams. The team leader is sensitized to the importance of developing a positive 'Yes And' approach, to replace a negative 'Yes But' approach.

In the past, creativity may have been considered as being distinct from the skills needed for success as a leader. This view is likely to be revised in the future, as leaders learn how to achieve added value through the introduction of those creativity-supporting approaches or benign structures which help to overcome assumptions that are restricting change. Our work suggests that creative leaders reconfigure the structures under which team members operate, reducing the impact of the negative behaviour patterns of team members by providing a more benign structuring of work patterns.

CM 10.4: Richard Florida's Theory of Creative Cultures and Creative Leadership

Richard Florida's best-selling books have drawn attention to the nature of creative leadership and the conditions for the development of a creative society. His ideas have also attracted attention and controversy.

The core of the argument developed in *The Rise of the Creative Class* is the existence of conditions that reinforce the development of creative environments at the levels of a city or region.[59] These creative centres, furthermore, attract creative thought leaders.

A benign circle of creativity and prosperity occurs within an environment that supports and therefore attracts creative talent.

This hypothesis is backed up by Florida's empirical studies, and more specific claims for the factors that attract and retain creative talent. At the broadest level, he has characterized the creative class as 'bohemians', a generic label for knowledge producers such as information technologists, artists, and musicians. He suggests that openness to diversity, including minorities such as lesbians and gay men, helps to promote the supportive environment that reinforces a creative community.

Florida argues that for creativity and economic development, a city or region has to attend to '3 Ts':

- technology
- talent
- tolerance.

The policy implications of Florida's work have been criticized, particularly because there appear to have been major investment decisions that have been partly justified by notions of attracting those high-productivity individuals of the creative class. Both his methodology and conclusions drawn from the empirical work fuelled controversy about his basic thesis.[60] Typical of the objections was one in an article in *The Wall Street Journal* in 2004:

> Looking for other ways to measure the distinguishing characteristics of the new-economy cities, Mr. Florida developed a so-called Bohemian Index, which counted the number of artists, writers and performers in a city. He added a Creative Class Index to measure a city's concentration of knowledge workers (scientists, engineers, professors, think-tank employees). Each index, Mr. Florida was stunned

to find, correlated highly with the other indexes. Cities with many gays were also places with lots of performers, creative workers and tech companies. At this point, Mr. Florida made two big and dubious leaps in logic . . . What enticed these workers, the professor concluded with very little evidence, was that the cities were 'tolerant, diverse and open to creativity.'[61]

Nevertheless, Richard Florida's work continues to attract attention internationally.[62]

INTEGRATION

The materials in this chapter address current understanding of creativity as presented in maps drawing on different platforms of understanding. Creativity is also examined in the context of leadership. How do the maps help explain the links between creativity and leadership, and why is creativity a leader's secret weapon?

There are certainly closer links between creativity and leadership than might be imagined from studying most maps of the two concepts. Yet the historical account in POU 10.1 shows how they draw on shared assumptions. Each field has a surfeit of definitions, in part due to applications across a wide range of professional domains. Each has a long historical heritage that eventually was replaced by studies grounded in the DRM. It might be argued that attempts to 'tame' ancient ideas of creativity and leadership concealed dilemmas. Creativity is a leader's secret weapon because its power remains hidden until exposed through map-testing of a kind that is sensitive to the creativity needed for effective leadership. Table 10.1 shows the concealed similarities in the mapping of creativity and leadership.

The maps summarized in Table 10.1 suggest the first steps towards constructing a working definition for creative leadership by combining those of creativity and of leadership.

A creative leader achieves (creative) goals through the exercise of (creative) processes and production of creative products and thereby influencing others. For Amabile, in POU 10.2, the context needs to support creativity, which is a primary role of the creative leader. For Moger and Rickards (CM 10.3), the creative leader succeeds by introducing a creative climate through the introduction of creative structures ('benign structures'). Similar themes can be found in the contextual materials. Sternberg (CM 10.1) and Arvonen (CM 10.2) offer alternative styles of creative leadership. Richard Florida focuses on creative entrepreneurs whose products set up a virtuous creative loop by attracting greater numbers of creative individuals into the positive cultural climate they have helped to create.

Table 10.1 Creativity and Leadership Compared

Creativity	Leadership
Many different definitions reflecting partial and individualistic treatments, and an extended history prior to formal, modern scholarly study.	Many different definitions reflecting partial and individualistic treatments, and an extended history prior to formal, modern scholarly study.
Definitions can be reduced to four overlapping factors of person, process, product, and press.	Definitions can be reduced to means of exercising influence or power over others.
Modern studies extended across discrete fields such as psychology, education, aesthetics, innovation, design.	Modern studies extended across discrete fields such as psychology, politics, performance arts, business, warfare.
Big C and Little C Creativity. The former of wide-ranging impact. The latter, found at an everyday level, associated with personal discovery processes.	Big L and Little L Leadership. The former achieved by a minority of outstanding individuals who changed the course of major events. The latter demonstrated by a wide range of people in social roles (parents, teachers, team leaders, etc.).
Concept has been extended to other species. Primates have demonstrated creative problem-solving (of the Little C type).	Concept has been extended to other species. Perhaps sometimes the concept has been borrowed from observed behaviours common to other species ('alpha-male' territorial disputes).
The great majority of texts about creativity have ignored the concept of leadership as a creative process.	The great majority of texts about leadership have ignored the concept of creativity as a leadership process.
A widely accepted working definition of creativity: the process leading to the generation of ideas meeting three criteria of novelty, relevance, and feasibility.	A widely accepted definition of leadership: the process of achieving goals through the exercise of influence on others.

GETTING PERSONAL

One of the barriers to creativity is the assumption that creativity is something special. This happens to be part of a particular map in which creativity is a trait of highly gifted individuals. Yet, as was shown in Chapter 2, and here, the 'nothing special' map holds to the view that everyone can develop their leadership performance. A similar argument applies to creativity and to creative leadership.

Many individuals acquire a map that is part of a self-image that is summed up as 'I'm not creative'. Entire professions are prone to taking this perspective. So are cultures. It was the great American researcher into creativity, Paul Torrance, who pointed out that different cultures have different ways of actualizing creativity at the levels of the individual or social group. He recognized, for example, a greater willingness to work collectively in some cultures.

Some readers may have had an unchallenged lack of belief in their capabilities as creative individuals, and therefore as creative leaders.

This may have been based on a 'something special' POU of creativity. Taking a different perspective, a leader operates creatively by encouraging the flourishing of self-motivated actions in others (Amabile). For Sternberg, creative leadership manifests itself in a variety of styles which propel a group towards designed visionary goals. For Moger and Rickards, it is a leadership form that pays attention to 'benign structures', including creativity-supporting techniques.

The reader may well find it worthwhile to consider these alternative ways of 'being creative' and 'becoming a creative leader'.

SUMMARY

This chapter attempts to integrate the fields of creativity and leadership. The maps of creativity and of leadership have tended to focus on the individual. Neither has been explained by a rational model approach. Issues of discovery and creative insight require less functional mappings.

When the two maps are considered together, creative leadership connects well with the map of transformational leadership.

For many individuals, in their professional lives creativity has been a leader's secret weapon. The weapon is unleashed whenever a difficult issue is confronted and a hard-to-resolve dilemma addressed.

Creativity at the level of the social group has been relatively under-studied. Advances are being made, and extend beyond the domain of cognitive psychology. The work promises much to help sense to be made of notions of the creative group, organization, and culture.

The strong claim made in this chapter is that effective leadership is utterly dependent on creativity directed towards desired change, in and through others.

NOTES

1 Boden, M.A. (ed.) (1994) *Dimensions of creativity*, Cambridge, MA: MIT Press.
2 Adapted from Sternberg, R.J., Kaufman, J.C., & Pretz, J.E. (2004) 'A propulsion model of creative leadership', *Creativity and Innovation Management*, 13, 3, 145–153. See also Sternberg, R.J., Kaufman, J.C., & Pretz, J.E. (2003) 'A propulsion model of creative leadership', *Leadership Quarterly*, 14, 455.
3 Summarized from Batey, M. (2011) 'Is creativity the no. 1 skill for the 21st century?', http://batey.tm.mbs.ac.uk/leadership/is-creativity-the-number-1-skill-for-the-21st-century,/ downloaded, 5 May 2011.
4 Rhodes, J.M. (1961) 'An analysis of creativity', *Phi Delta Kappan*, April, 305–311; (1987) 'An analysis of creativity', in Isaksen, S.G. (ed.), *Frontiers of creativity research: Beyond the basics*, Buffalo, NY: Bearly, pp. 216–222.

5 The term 'press' is to be found in organizational psychology studies of cognitive functioning and adaptation factors. See for example: http://gerontologist.oxfordjournals.org/content/40/5/549.short, downloaded 6 April 2011.

6 Developed from the keynote address presented at the 2nd Creativity and Innovation Management (CIM) International Conference, Integrating Enquiry and Action, Buffalo, NY (28–30 May 2008), www.jpb.com/creative/cim_meeting.php.

7 Guilford, J.P. (1967) 'Creativity: Yesterday, today and tomorrow', *Journal of Creative Behavior*, 1, 3–14.

8 Isaksen, S.G. (ed.) (1987) *Frontiers of creativity research: Beyond the basics*, Buffalo, NY: Bearly; Parnes, S.J. (ed.) (1992) *Sourcebook for creative problem-solving*, Buffalo, NY: Creative Education Foundation.

9 Koestler, A. (1959) *The sleepwalkers: A history of man's changing vision of the universe*, Harmondsworth: Penguin; (1964) *The act of creation*, London: Hutchinson; (1967) *The ghost in the machine*, 1990 reprint edn, Harmondsworth: Penguin.

10 Ryle, G. (1949) *The concept of mind*, New Univer edition, Chicago: University of Chicago.

11 Porter, R. (2000) *Enlightenment: Britain and the creation of the modern world*, London: Allen Lane.

12 Handy, C. (1988) *The age of unreason*, London: Hutchinson.

13 Torrance, P. (1962) *Guiding creative talent*, Englewood Cliffs, NJ: Prentice Hall.

14 Raina, M.K. (1996) 'The Torrance phenomenon: Extended creative search for Lord Vishvakarma', *Creativity and Innovation Management*, 5, 3, 149–150.

15 Parnes, S.J. (1992: 1) *Sourcebook for creative problem-solving*, Buffalo, NY: Creative Education Foundation.

16 Puccio, G., & Cabra, J. (2009) 'Creative problem-solving: Past, present and future', in Rickards, T., Runco, M.A., & Moger, S. (eds), *Routledge Companion to Creativity*, Oxford: Routledge, pp. 327–337.

17 Rickards T., & Moger, S.T. (1999) *Handbook for creative team leaders*, Aldershot, Hants: Gower.

18 de Bono, E. (1967) *The use of lateral thinking*, London: Jonathan Cape. For a recent review see Dingli, S. (2009) 'Thinking outside the box: Edward de Bono's lateral thinking', in Rickards, T., Runco, M.A., & Moger, S. (eds), *Routledge Companion to Creativity*, Oxford: Routledge, pp. 338–350.

19 Buzan, A. (1972) *Use your head*, London: BBC Publications.

20 Rickards T., & Moger, S.T. (1999) *Handbook for creative team leaders*, Aldershot, Hants: Gower.

21 For an early English-language paper see Dung, P. (1995) 'TRIZ: Inventive creativity based on the laws of systems development', *Creativity and Innovation Management*, 4, 1, 19–29.

22 Morgan, G. (1986) *Images of organization*, Newbury Park, CA: Sage.

23 Burrell, G., & Morgan, G. (1979) *Sociological paradigms and organisational analysis: Elements of the sociology of corporate life*, London: Heinemann.

24 *Dilemmas of Leadership*, 1st edn cites Grint, K. (1997) *Leadership: Classic, contemporary and critical approaches*, Oxford: OUP.

25 Chivers, M., & Yates, A. (2010) 'The narrative turn in action learning practices: From restitution to quest', *Journal of Action Learning Research and Practice*, 7, 3, 253–266.

26 Xu, F., & Rickards, T. (2007) 'Creative management: A predicted development from research into creativity and management', *Creativity and Innovation Management*, 16, 3, 216–228.

27 Al-Bereidi, A., & Rickards, T. (2010) 'Team creativity in highly regulated contexts: A quantitative investigation in accounting offices in Saudi Arabia', *Arab Journal of Administrative Sciences*, 17, 1, 137–167.

28 Department of Culture, Media and Sport (DCMS) (1998) *The creative industries mapping report*, London: HMSO. For a recent review see Jeffcutt, P. (2009) 'Creativity and knowledge

relationships', in Rickards, T., Runco, M.A., & Moger, S. (eds), *Routledge Companion to Creativity*, Oxford: Routledge, pp. 88–98.

29 Eisenhardt, K.M. (1989) 'Making fast strategic decisions', *Academy of Management Journal*, 32, 3, 543–576.

30 Amabile, T.M. (1996) *Creativity in context*, Boulder, CO: Westview.

31 Boden, R. (2009: 179), 'Computers and creativity: models and applications', in Rickards, T., Runco, M.A., & Moger, S. (eds), *Routledge Companion to Creativity*, Oxford: Routledge, pp. 179–188. See also Rickards, T. (1999: 22) *Creativity and the management of change*, Oxford: Blackwell; Isaksen, S.G. (ed.) (1987) *Frontiers of creativity research: Beyond the basics*, New York: Bearly.

32 Stein, M.I. (1974) *Stimulating creativity, Individual procedures*, Vol. 1, New York: Academic Press; (1975) *Stimulating creativity, Group procedures*, Vol. 2, New York: Academic Press.

33 Kirton, M.J. (1976) 'Adaptors and innovators: A description and a measure', *Journal of Applied Psychology*, 61, 622–629; (1994) *Adaptors and innovators: Styles of creativity and innovation*, 2nd edn, London: Routledge; (2003) *Adaption–innovation in the context of diversity and change*, London: Routledge.

34 de Bono, E. (1967) *The use of lateral thinking*, London: Jonathan Cape. For a recent review see Dingli, S. (2009) 'Thinking outside the box: Edward de Bono's lateral thinking', in Rickards, T., Runco, M.A., & Moger, S. (eds), *Routledge Companion to Creativity*, Oxford: Routledge, pp. 338–350.

35 'The Cure at Troy', http://csbookshelf.wordpress.com/2007/12/08/the-cure-at-troy-seamus-heaney/.

36 Amabile, T.M. (1983) *The social psychology of creativity*, New York: Springer-Verlag.

37 Amabile, T.M. (1996) *Creativity in context*, Boulder, CO: Westview.

38 Conti, R., & Amabile, T. (1999) 'Motivation/drive', in Runco, M.A., & Pritzker, S.R. (eds), *Encyclopedia of creativity*, San Diego, CA: Academic Press, Vol. 2, pp. 251–259.

39 Lubart, T.I. (1999) 'Componential models of creativity', in Runco, M.A., & Pritzker, S.R. (eds), *Encyclopedia of creativity*, San Diego, CA: Academic Press, Vol. 1, pp. 295–300.

40 Amabile, T.M. (1996) *Creativity in context*, Boulder, CO: Westview, p. 93.

41 Fig. 10.1 is based on the framework to be found in ibid., p. 94.

42 Ibid., p. 95.

43 These models are examined later in this chapter. See Parnes, S.F., Noller, R.B., & Biondi, A.M. (1977) *A guide to creative action (revised workbook)*, New York: Charles Scribner; Parnes, S.J. (ed.) (1992) *Sourcebook for creative problem-solving*, Buffalo, NY: Creative Education Foundation; Puccio, G., & Cabra, J. (2009) 'Creative problem-solving: Past, present and future', in Rickards, T., Runco, M.A., & Moger, S. (eds), *Routledge Companion to Creativity*, Oxford: Routledge, pp. 327–337; and materials Rickards, T., & Moger, S.T. (1999) *Handbook for creative team leaders*, Aldershot, Hants: Gower.

44 A debate developed between Amabile and the Hungarian theorist Magyari-Beck: Magyari-Beck, I. (1994) 'Creativity studies and their paradigmatic background', *Creativity and Innovation Management*, 3, 2, 104–109; Amabile T.M. (1994) 'Recognising creativity: A reply to Magyari-Beck', *Creativity and Innovation Management*, 3, 4, 244–245, regarding the justification for the subjective grounding of the assessment procedures advocated by Amabile.

45 Amabile, T.M. (1996) *Creativity in context*, Boulder, CO: Westview, p. 42.

46 Hennessey, B.A., & Amabile, T.M. (1999) 'Consensual assessment', in Runco, M.A., & Pritzker, S.R. (eds), *Encyclopedia of creativity*, San Diego, CA: Academic Press, Vol. 1, pp. 347–359.

47 O'Quin, K., & Besemer, S.P. (1989) 'The development, reliability, and validity of the revised creativity product semantic scale', *Creativity Research Journal*, 2, 267–278; Besemer, S.P. (2006) *Creating products in the age of design: How to improve your product ideas*, Stillwater, OK: New Forums.

48 Amabile, T.M., Conti, R., Coon, H., Lazenby, J., & Herron, M. (1996) 'Assessing the work environment for creativity', *Academy of Management Journal*, 39, 5, 1154–1184.

49 Ekvall, G., Arvonen, J., & Waldenstron-Lindblad, I. (1983) 'Creative organisational climate: Construction and validation of a measuring instrument', FaRadet, Report No 2, Stockholm, Sweden: The Swedish Council for Management and Work Issues.

50 Sternberg, R.J. (1999) 'A propulsion model of types of creative contributions', *Review of General Psychology*, 3, 83–100.

51 Sternberg R.J., & Lubart, T.I. (1995) *Defying the crowd: Cultivating creativity in a culture of conformity*, New York: Free Press.

52 Sternberg, R.J., Kaufman, J.C., & Pretz, J.E. (2004) 'A propulsion model of creative leadership', *Creativity and Innovation Management*, 13, 3, 145–153.

53 Ibid., p. 146.

54 Ibid., p. 151. The reference is to Thomas Kuhn's influential analysis of how science proceeds mostly in an incremental fashion punctuated by revolutionary periods; Kuhn, T. (1970) 'Reflections on my critics', in Lakatos, I., & Musgrove, A. (eds), *Criticism and the growth of knowledge*, Cambridge: Cambridge University Press, pp. 231–278.

55 Sternberg, R.J., Kaufman, J.C., & Pretz, J.E. (2004) 'A propulsion model of creative leadership', *Creativity and Innovation Management*, 13, 3, 145–153, p. 152.

56 Arvonen, J. (2009) 'Change-oriented leadership behaviour: a consequence of post-bureaucratic organizations?', in Rickards, T., Runco, M.A., & Moger, S.T., *Routledge Companion to Creativity*, Oxford: Routledge, pp. 302–311.

57 Judge, T.A., Piccolo, R.F., & Ilies, R. (2004) 'The forgotten ones? The validity of consideration and initiating structure in leadership research', *Journal of Applied Psychology*. 89, 1, 36–51.

58 Tuckman's team development model. See Mullins, L.J. (2010) *Management and organizational behaviour*, 9th edn, Prentice Hall for the original model and the MBS two-barrier version of it.

59 Branscomb, L., Kodama, F., & Florida, R. (1999) *The rise of the creative class: And how it's transforming work, leisure and everyday life*, New York: Basic Books.

60 Glaeser, E.L. (2005) 'Review of Richard Florida's *The rise of the creative class*', *Regional Science and Urban Economics*, 35, 5, 593–596.

61 Malanga, S. (2004) 'The curse of the creative class: A New Age theory of urban development amounts to economic snake oil', *Wall Street Journal*, www.opinionjournal.com/extra/?id=110004573.

62 Tinagli, I., Florida, R., Ström, P., & Wahlqvist, E. (2007) *Sweden in the creative age*, Göteborg, Sweden: Göteborg University; Moger, S., & Rickards, T. (2009) 'Uppsala Creativity Day, 2 March 2009', *Creativity and Innovation Management*, 18, 3, 242–243.

CHAPTER LEARNING OBJECTIVES

Learning focus
- ■ Your emerging personal development map

Key issues
- ■ Twenty-first-century leadership themes
- ■ The future of leadership
- ■ Coexistence of leadership maps

Dilemmas
- ■ Personal responsibilities and global issues
- ■ Is the twenty-second century worth worrying about?

Platforms of understanding
- ■ POU 11.1 Yukl's Map of the Future of Leadership
- ■ POU 11.2 Rost's Map of Twenty-First-Century Leadership

Contextual materials
- ■ CM 11.1 The Social Basis of Influence
- ■ CM 11.2 Emotional Intelligence and Leadership
- ■ CM 11.3 Positive Turbulence
- ■ CM 11.4 The End of Leadership?

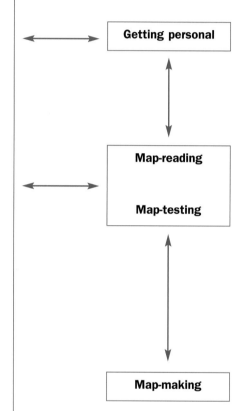

11 EMERGING ISSUES AND DILEMMAS

In an increasingly turbulent world, the idea that leaders must adapt their behaviour to changing conditions seems even more relevant today than it was decades ago when the theories were first proposed.[1]

The 'unrational' team leader looks at why teams don't work and covers the same bases as the rational leader. Then, the 'unrational' leader goes deeper trying to bring unconscious feelings out in the open so they can be dealt with.[2]

We are left with a dilemma: leadership is an indeterminate skill that masquerades as a determinate skill.[3]

It has been a recurrent theme throughout *Dilemmas of Leadership* that the contemporary business scene is one of unprecedented uncertainties and rapid change.[4] Events of global significance in the first decade of the twenty-first century included financial crises, political, technological, and social upheavals all of which saw most leaders unprepared.

When the general point is applied to leadership, we face the question of whether rapid change is making earlier leadership maps and practices unreliable, out of date, and irrelevant. Before addressing the question with fresh information, you may find it valuable to reflect on what you recall about the journeys and maps found in the earlier chapters of *Dilemmas of Leadership* (Exercise 11.1).

The exercise draws attention to the major maps of leadership that have been outlined in this book. You may have noted the pervasive influence of the DRM, and how the more recent maps have emerged out of the dilemmas of the DRM.

Attention is now turned to even more recent emerging trends in leadership as we attempt to assess potentially significant challenges into the future.

According to systems theorist Jeffery Goldstein,[5] emergence may be defined as 'the arising of novel and coherent structures, patterns and properties during the process of self-organization in complex systems'.

Exercise 11.1 will have refreshed your memory of the various maps and the dilemmas of earlier chapters. From them, it now becomes possible to see the rise and fall of dominant maps of leadership. The evidence from prehistoric cultures suggests a persisting belief in a predestined personal fate or destiny.[6] Even in these maps, there was evidence that leaders were special, albeit special instruments of fate, and had to be granted loyalty and respect. It was many millennia before the fatalistic assumption was challenged and associated dilemmas recognized.

Over time, a profound human dilemma became articulated through philosophical efforts and in dramatic works of art. This was the possibility that an individual could challenge fate. The dramatic representation of this idea was at the heart of Greek tragedy, emphasizing how acts of unjustifiable ambition (*hubris*) risked retribution from the gods (*nemesis*). The dramas served to remind audiences of the dangers of challenging fate and the dire punishments consequent upon such actions. The ancient ideas persisted into the twenty-first century and are still in use to describe the consequences of behaviours believed to be arrogant and unacceptable.[7]

The general and great radical break with the earlier fatalistic map is often associated with the eighteenth-century Enlightenment. Fatalism was rejected as a primitive and unenlightened belief system or cosmology. It was to be replaced by a great idea which became dominant globally and which retains much of its influence today. The mapping has often been described as the Dominant Rational Model (DRM). Its main feature is belief in the power of rational thought to permit the triumph of human beings over ordained fate imposed by nature or supernatural forces.

The DRM rejected early, unenlightened ideas, and provided its own descriptions of them as heroic and romantic treatments. It may be argued that terms such as 'heroic' and 'romantic'

Exercise 11.1: Reviewing the journey

Chapter and theme	Notes
1 Overview of principles of mapping/learning/ defining Outline of important leadership maps	
2 Born or made maps of leadership The nature/nurture dilemma	
3 Working in teams The dominant functionalist map coordinates/ controls but is weaker on boundary uncertainties and social processes through participative leadership	
4 Charismatic leadership an ancient concept 'modernized' as transformational leadership Dilemmas of narcissistic charismatics	
5 Symbolic leadership (management of meaning) challenges rational 'managerialist' maps Perception as reality	
6 Trust Is trust exploitative? Dilemmas of trust, authenticity and responsibility	
7 Strategic leadership Is strategy more than functionalism? Does strategic leadership matter?	
8 Discrimination, diversity and dominance Dilemmas of power and exploitation	
9 Ethical dilemmas How important are ethical considerations in business leadership?	
10 Creative leadership 'Creativity is a leader's secret weapon'	

leadership were labels provided within the era of the DRM to differentiate the new age of reason from earlier, unenlightened eras.

The influence of the DRM has been profound, and permeates much within educational systems, as well as in the belief systems of scientifically trained managers today. However, even the DRM was challenged. Some of these challenges for leaders were identified through mappings found in the later chapters of the book. Further challenges are provided in the POUs and CMs of this chapter.

By the 1980s, the emerging threats to the DRM came from groups of researchers who rejected its principles from different conceptual positions. Broadly, the DRM had revealed a lack of power in dealing with dilemmas of modernity. The new leadership maps seemed better equipped to deal with the possibility that leadership was a social construct (rather than an objective essence). In particular, the potential for transformational leadership was recognized.

Claims for the new leadership map were themselves seen to be insufficient to replace the DRM. Bryman's seminal paper on leadership in the first edition of the *Handbook of Organization Studies* drew attention to the emerging New Leadership movement.[8] In 2006, the revised paper in the second edition acknowledged dilemmas of New Leadership, noting that 'much if not most New Leadership writing is wedded to a rational model of organizational behaviour'.[9] In other words, New Leadership was arguably rather closer to the DRM map than might have been assumed.

In this final chapter we examine the most recent mappings of leadership for insights into emerging twenty-first-century leadership themes. Chapter 10 began the process with its claims for creative leadership. We now encounter additional POUs and contextual readings. They offer evidence of what has been described as 'the rich, diverse and creative state of contemporary leadership research'.[10]

Table 11.1 Rise and Decline of Dominant Leadership Beliefs (Maps)

Era	Mappings	Dilemmas
Early 'pre-history'	Fatalistic cosmology	Unknown (beliefs presumed to be largely uncontested)
Heroic	Special revolutionary leaders	Free will versus destiny
Modern	Dominant Rational Model	Reason versus faith; control versus emancipation
New Leadership	Constructivist	Certainty versus ambiguity; essentialism versus non-essentialism
Emerging twenty-first-century trends	Creative leadership; networks; followership; complexity theories; authentic leadership	Coexistence of beliefs; no clear dominant mapping of leadership among 'modernist' management scientists, critical theorists, systems theorists, postmodernists

Note that earlier ideas were never completely lost. Instead, there is a coexistence of ideas which can be inferred from the persistence of the dilemmas over time.[11] This is illustrated by the 'born or made' dilemma. For many people, the ancient conundrum remains both critical and contemporary. The DRM challenged but has not eliminated deeply held religious and cultural beliefs.

ORIENTATION

The DRM associates itself with the methods and achievements of science (hence, scientific management). For much of the industrial era *modern* (as opposed to *pre-modern*) business practices were considered a characteristic of successful management. Modern was good. Rationality was good. Its positive features can be found in the functionalist models of project management of Chapter 3 and the strategic leadership ideas of Chapter 7. It remains a widely taken-for-granted map for many professional managers, and its continued dominance is one reason why the book offers analytical schemes to expose its dilemmas and pave the way to considering alternative maps.

Researchers who challenged this model signalled their opposition by dealing with the concepts of rationality and irrationality in different ways. Charles Handy suggested in the 1980s that we were moving to an age of unreason. Fleetham in 2005 drew attention to the way the DRM had established negative associations of the term 'irrationality'. He deliberately introduced the clumsy-sounding term 'unrational' to stand for actions that add to and complement rational behaviours.[12]

The DRM has informed almost every page of this book. It remains a starting-point for a taken-for-granted view shared by business practitioners and the emerging associated professions of management consultants and business school scholars. Just as the earlier maps survived alongside the DRM, we should not expect newer maps to replace it. Instead, other perspectives are likely to become recognized and tested alongside rationalist maps that will owe much to the DRM as leaders make sense of their professional worlds.

Its history included an influence in the rise of the dominant maps of scientific management that have become known as Taylorism and Fordism after two of its pioneering figures.[13] According to the DRM, the business leader is someone who brings rational logic to the practices for designing and developing the industrial organization. The functionalism of Taylorism and Fordism provided many of the dilemmas of leadership encountered in previous chapters. The newer maps often developed from attempts to address these.

PLATFORMS OF UNDERSTANDING

POU 11.1 explores the future of leadership. It presents a perspective from the work of Gary Yukl, whose maps can also be found in earlier chapters. He provides a systems approach addressing possibilities of complex interactions, including feedback among interacting factors, and intermediate factors.

POU 11.2 is an interesting and thorough investigation of the leadership maps of the past, and a proposal for the leadership form of the future. The map was drawn up by Joseph Rost as a guide for leadership in the twenty-first century. His view is that the twentieth-century leadership paradigm was forced into ethical dilemmas through organizations assuming that the leader could define the collective purposes and needs of employees.

POU 11.1: Yukl's Map of the Future of Leadership

Gary Yukl reviewed the field of leadership at the start of the twenty-first century.[14]

He confirms the important changes occurring since the late 1980s, including theories of transformational and charismatic leadership. His later leadership maps differed from the earlier, thoroughly rationalistic ones, through attention to processes emphasizing values and emotions, influencing followers to 'higher' level aspirations. Yukl is concerned to address concerns regarding the conceptualization and measurement of leadership processes. In doing so he acknowledges the dilemmas within contemporary conceptualizations of leadership. He enumerates a range of major issues:

■ simplistic either/or thinking (or models) of leadership
■ omission of relevant behaviours
■ a focus on 'one-to-one' leader/follower processes
■ dubious methodologies for measuring leadership.

Yukl notes the dangers of ignoring earlier theories, which would itself be an example of either/or thinking. He argues that older theories become a bedrock on which new theories arise, and to which new theories sometimes return in a more contemporary form.

Either/or thinking is also a characteristic of two-factor models of leadership. Before the 1980s, there was the differentiation between task-oriented leaders and people-oriented leaders. In the 1980s, leaders were differentiated from managers. It was suggested that individuals were either managers who did things right or leaders who did the right things. New leadership studies offered either transformational leadership or transactional leadership. Charismatic leaders (in modern contexts) were contrasted with non-charismatic leaders.

Dyadic theories (such as Leader/Follower Exchange) also simplify leadership into the impact of one person on another, and minimize the significance of contextual factors and distributed leadership. More generally, the absence of multi-level theorizing (the leader, the core group, the organization in its environment) has inevitably led to omissions of relevant factors.

Yukl is also concerned about the validity of the methodologies favoured by leadership researchers. Data collected through structured surveys have tended to be biased towards the individual leaders. Furthermore, the information is more likely to report on the frequency of a specified behaviour, rather than the skilfulness of its enactment. Difficulties in gaining access to leaders 'in the field' has meant that few studies have been able to conduct follow-up studies, so that the stability of the data over time has to be assumed. The call for 'mixed' quantitative/qualitative designs has tended to fall on deaf ears. The new leadership campaign continued to be waged with antiquated methodological methods.

Enthusiasm for new leadership may have contributed to premature abandonment of earlier concepts (such as traits, and 'classical' concepts of charisma). Yet, the newer theories have then reintroduced the old ideas 'through the back door' (as in the case of charisma, 'tamed' to fit the proposed measures of transformational leaders).

Another emerging theme is awareness of ethical dilemmas. For Yukl, these arise when the multiple obligations on leaders are taken seriously, rather than obligations utterly directed to the needs of a dominant stakeholder (owners). The issue becomes one of resolving conflicting obligations to workers, owners, and customers.[15]

POU 11.2: Rost's Map of Twenty-First-Century Leadership

In the 1990s, a scholarly and comprehensive study, *Leadership for the twenty-first century*, by Joseph Rost attracted considerable attention among leadership researchers. The book was acknowledged by James McGregor Burns as the successor to his own seminal contribution, written three decades earlier. The book received praise for its scholarly approach and its thorough critique of the entire period of twentieth-century leadership. Its central message is that leadership in the twenty-first century should escape from an unhealthy dominance of thinking that was too close to the beliefs of a bygone era. This contention sat comfortably with emerging ideas about distributed leadership, the ethical integrity of leadership, and the processes of mutual sense- and meaning-making within change programmes.

Rost is critical of much of late twentieth-century leadership as grounded in faulty foundations. He further considers that there has been a lack of help for leaders (whatever the definition) in dealing with ethical dilemmas. He is therefore also critical of the formal ethical canon, whether based on religious or on other moral philosophical grounds. The knowledge, he suggests, has little relevance for a leader facing conflicting duties and obligations. He considers that legislation aimed at promoting ethically desired results tends to reinforce leaders in a leadership mind-set of 'staying legal' rather than 'staying ethical'. He considers that this has become increasingly germane to situations of moral ambiguity, where people hold sincere views on opposing sides of dilemmas such as AIDS, affirmative action, environmental sustainability, freedom of information, intrusion on the rights of others, and differing cultural views of gifts versus bribery.

Rost has two main targets for his critique of twentieth-century leadership, and two prescriptions for the future. The targets are the lack of definitional clarity of the subject, and what he calls the fallacy of the industrial paradigm. The prescriptions for the future are a new definition, securing a new theory of leadership, and a plea for a multi-disciplinary treatment.

He notes the confusions extending back to the 1940s, when Chester Barnard criticized the domain for its dogmatism and drivel. Rost's careful examination of over 200 definitions he found in the literature concluded that authors had failed to untangle leadership from other behavioural activities. From this analysis he arrives at a surprising and interesting conclusion, namely that there is a universal definition implicit in the apparent diversity. The core definition had never been revealed because it had been confused by a failure (by everyone) to grasp the possibility that leadership is a term used to indicate a special kind of management. As an epigram, Rost suggests that leadership has been broadly equated with good management. He also expands what good management is about. So the implicit shared definition in the industrial era has been:

> Leadership is great men and women with certain preferred traits influencing followers to do what the leaders wish in order to achieve group/organizational goals that reflect excellence defined as some kind of higher-level excellence.

> Management is an authority relationship (contractual power) between at least one manager and one subordinate who coordinate their activities to produce and sell particular goods and/or services.

The apparent diversity of ideas suggested to Rost that there was a collective theory around the beliefs within industrial society:

- a mechanistic view of organizations (the structural/functional view)
- management as the pre-eminent professional mode
- a focus on the person of the leader
- the primacy of organizational goals and goal achievement
- a self-interested and individualist outlook
- a utilitarian ethical perspective
- a technological and rational belief system or paradigm.

The universalistic assumptions were seen as:

- hierarchical control of followers by leaders
- unilateral top-down goal setting and communication flows
- leaders know best.

Rost then offers the following as a definition for leadership in a post-industrial society:

> Leadership is an influence relationship among leaders and followers who intend real changes that reflect their mutual purposes.

The definition seeks to remove the ethical dilemma of the more general definitions of leadership that cover the behaviours of a Hitler as well as a Mandela. Its most imaginative aspect is its emphasis on intentions of leaders to act so as to reflect mutual changes. From our maps of ethics we can see that Rost's arguments are essentially grounded in ethical considerations and beliefs. His recognition of the mutual involvement of others with leaders is why his theory has been described as a communitarian one.

Rost was later to recognize that the term 'follower' was too close to the vocabulary and thinking that he wanted to consign to a former era (the industrial era), and he replaced it in his work with the term 'collaborators'.[16] He argues that leadership studies have been swamped by the dominant influence exercised by the Industrial Age paradigm. Yet, he notes other disciplines, notably education, the public sector, and political leadership, each struggling to establish their unique silos of leadership know-how and theory. His proposal is that leadership studies should free itself from the dangers of being a single disciplinary approach, and reinvent itself in multi-disciplinary form.

Rost's work was received in the 1990s as a significant contribution to leadership thought. For Rost, moral principles in the industrial era are those of an even earlier classical liberal philosophy which paid more attention to the rights of individuals, and particularly material rights, at the expense of what might be called higher-level non-materialistic and altruistic considerations. He admits that he is no formal scholar of ethics, and calls for those who are to help provide models appropriate to the needs of the present time.

The general thrust of his argument might be taken in support of transformational leadership as pioneered by his mentor, Burns. Yet, leadership scholars have greeted his work warily. Critical evaluation has come principally from the field of ethics, where he has been particularly attacked for a misunderstanding of the ethical principles he considers to be inappropriate for leaders in their work practices.

His critics acknowledge that the principles of a more distributed and collaborative leadership concept have considerable appeal. His ideas are also seen as rich sources of debate. In essence, they help us to move away from the idea of a leader identified totally with an assigned role, and towards the idea of a more flexible function, occupied by multiple players in a more complex set of relationships.

Despite his rejection of the philosophic tradition, it is pointed out that the most novel element in Rost's leadership definition is that of ethical intentions, one of the concepts deeply studied by Kant. An ethical issue is how decisions are freely entered into, without coercion, manipulation, or edict, within contemporary organizational structures. More seriously, his analysis is considered to be an inadequate treatment of the dilemmas raised in considering what is ethical leadership. His advocacy of a collectivist approach leaves unanswered the issue of absolute standards, or directive principles. He avoids the deep issues of the nature of 'real' leaders and 'good management'. His espousal of the Kantian principle of ethical intent requires further consideration of principles of ethical imperatives, which he side-steps.

CONTEXTUAL MATERIALS

CM 11.1 deals with the social psychological approach to social identity, which has been recently examined for its relevance in reshaping our understanding of leadership and power relationships. The approach has become associated with the concept of prototypicality, which offers an explanation of otherwise puzzling aspects of leader–member relationships. These include how followers identify strongly with their leaders, and yet regard their leaders as different and special. CM 11.2 looks at the concept of emotional intelligence (EI), and its claim that high EI leaders are more effective than low EI leaders. CM 11.3 proposes a positive approach to leading in turbulent environments rather than by ineffective attempts to reduce turbulence and avoid necessary innovation and change. CM 11.4 asks perhaps the most important question of all: has leadership a future?

CM 11.1: The Social Basis of Influence

POU 11.1 identified the dominance of simple models of leadership that ignored the possibilities of active rather than passive interactions between the leader and other group members. Yukl urges attention to be turned towards a collective focus. The broad thrust of Rost's map (POU 11.2) is towards leadership as an influence relationship that tries to deal with different social goals. Yukl and Rost both consider weaknesses in twentieth-century leadership studies and encourage efforts to develop new maps.

The direction of travel is towards approaches that examine the social basis of leadership. One such emerging map is that of social identity. The work can be traced to the ideas advanced in the 1970s by Henri Tajfel and colleagues.[17] Shared social views emerge through interactions and dialogue. Social identity theorists have suggested that group members have greater chances of acceptance as leaders if they are particularly well able to represent the social identity of group members, and tend to be perceived as more effective leaders. Politicians (and many organizational leaders) try to show that, despite other differences, they are really 'people like us'. This strategy implies that prototypical leaders are very ordinary, and is a kind of dilemma. Politicians and leaders are well aware that they are in some ways unusual and perhaps extraordinary – in respect of their position of power, for example. However, prototypicality does not have to infer equivalence of status, or of leadership capabilities. Group members are looking for leaders who are prototypical of their map of their idealized selves, 'someone like me' in many ways, 'someone I would like to become' in others.

One conclusion from a social identity perspective is that leaders have to be aware of the consequences of offering 'individualized consideration' to members of the group. A privilege granted for one member will be interpreted differently in high-consensus and low-consensus groups. Just to make the issue more complex, the leader accepted in a high-consensus group is less immediately vulnerable to charges of favouritism because actions will be interpreted more generously by other group members as being in the interests of the group.

Social identity theorizing offers new insights into charisma and trust. Groups with high consensus may be prone to construct or interpret leader behaviours on social identity grounds, which intimately connects the leader with the values and aspirations of the group. These processes will thus be linked to the charismatic processes we have encountered earlier. This explanation suggests that a leader's actions play a part in the maintenance of identity as an in-group member, and helps to differentiate them from members of out-groups. According to social identity theorists, stereotyping and derogating others are widely observed group processes. Leaders contribute to the creation of in-groups and out-groups.[18] This is one more explanation for the culturally widespread practices of workplace bullying and teasing rituals.

CM 11.2: Emotional Intelligence and Leadership

As the twentieth century drew to a close, there was a surge of popular interest in a concept known as emotional intelligence (EI) as a predictor of leadership effectiveness.

Intelligence has been one of the most thoroughly examined of human characteristics. The most established tests of intelligence have been recognized as only a sub-set of mental activities. For most of the twentieth century (1900–70), intelligence and emotions were largely separate fields of study. In the 1970s and 1980s, precursors of EI began to emerge. Work on social intelligence, a concept suggested by Thorndyke as early as the 1920s, has been deepened by contemporary workers to indicate the possibility of multiple intelligences, within a structure of intellect. In the 1990s, EI research developed, and formal studies were popularized.

A major review clarified the concept, suggesting that it involves the processing of emotional information, including the adaptive regulation of emotion (a means of personal development).

Popular interest in the EI concept is traced to a best-selling book entitled *Emotional Intelligence*. Its author, Daniel Goleman, assembled evidence that intelligence as measured by IQ tests was not a particularly strong indicator of leadership performance. In contrast, differences in leadership characteristics suggested that emotional ('affective') skills explained a significantly greater proportion of the differences in leader performance.

Goleman concluded that leadership skills were due to EI, and that EI was the 'something special' that differentiated leaders. In empirical studies, the differences that could be explained by IQ were estimated at less than 50 per cent of the differences unexplained and attributed to EI. After Goleman's book was published, several assertions gained common currency. It was assumed that EI was far more important than IQ for leadership effectiveness. It was also assumed that a leader could become far more effective by developing his or her EI skills.

This conclusion has been challenged by other researchers, who have pointed out that EI remains inadequately researched. The popular claim that EI is twice as important as IQ for leader success has limited scientific justification at present.[19]

It would be a mistake to dismiss the EI concept on the grounds that one popular treatment has been found methodologically suspect. EI work has drawn attention to non-cognitive leadership competences that were previously under-regarded. The work reminds us that emotions convey valued information, and that awareness of and reaction to the emotions of others and self may well provide indicators for leadership and leadership development.

CM 11.3: Positive Turbulence

Countless books have been written describing the increasingly uncertain business environment facing leaders, often referring to its turbulence. The term is borrowed from studies of physical systems (air and water turbulence) and is used to imply unpredictable and unstable organizational environments. Extreme turbulence has become a popular application for the new mathematical ideas of chaos theory.

One non-mathematical analysis offering practical advice for dealing with turbulence was written by Stan Gryskiewicz. He identified Eric Trist, a pioneer of the action research methods of the Tavistock Institute, as having popularized the term's metaphorical use for a dynamically uncertain business environment.

Drawing on extensive experiences as a vice-president for global initiatives at the Center for Creative Leadership, Gryskiewicz argues that turbulence is now widely accepted as the inevitable context of work life, and is often presented as a threat and undesirable. This results in a tendency for leaders to seek to manage and control the impact of uncertainties in the traditional manner for organizational problem-solving and risk management. He argues for an approach that faces turbulence head on and that actively seeks out ways of using turbulence constructively. To direct efforts towards control of turbulence is misplaced. Strategies of 'riding the waves' and working with the conditions are more appropriate. Positive turbulence seeks to seize opportunities through appropriate strategies.

The approach acts to overcome a natural tendency under turbulent conditions for an organization to seek the protection of preserving the status quo in its actions and strategies. This may be contrary to what will ensure corporate survival and renewal.

Gryskiewicz believes that innovation occurs at the periphery of knowledge boundaries. A general principle is to accept the potential benefits of encouraging contact with information that comes from outside the organization's dominant experiences and mapping (including people who are information carriers). By bringing together people who use different maps of their world, it becomes easier to challenge assumptions. Central to his approach is the belief that the chaotic conditions at the interfaces of two organizations can be constructively harnessed.

Gryskiewicz instances ways in which companies have successfully institutionalized procedures that support positive turbulence. Intel, since the 1980s, actively encouraged its employees to challenge ideas regardless of their source. Open communications were also encouraged that crossed the typical status barriers of experience and corporate rank. Honda had a similar corporate story of enthusiasm for accepting change. This is hardly surprising from a corporation whose CEO publicly stated the importance of intense efforts by all employees to face up to environmental turbulence.

Turbulence calls for team-based activities. The teams are likely to be highly diverse in terms of experiences and knowledge bases. The management of diversity requires a highly facilitative and supportive style from the team leader, encouraging improvisation and offering scope for testing innovative ideas. This captures the broad principles of a creative leadership style developed by the so-called founding fathers of creativity research, including one of Gryskiewicz's early mentors, Don MacKinnon. It also draws on ideas of improvisation.

Various strategies are proposed for harnessing diversity. Team members are encouraged to have good networks of experts in their specialized fields. In addition, specialists should be regularly introduced to the ideas of experts from outside the set of competences of the existing team, in search of the unexpected and fortuitous connections between the fields of knowledge. Under turbulent conditions teams benefit from high-intensity support systems–leaders. There is an absence of well-established guidelines in high-intensity environments. Support systems for change become as vital for organizational health as are control systems for production quality in traditional environments.

Implicit in the other three strategic perspectives is a leadership approach that is receptive of new ideas. This captures many of the procedures outlined as a form of creative or trust-based leadership in Chapter 6. (It may also be compared with the facets of transformational leadership described in Chapter 4.) The leader is creative at the level of the team and with a focus directed towards encouraging the creativity of each team member.

CM 11.4: The End of Leadership?

Keith Grint is a leading teacher and researcher of leadership after working in a wide variety of manual roles[20] and as a senior labour negotiator.[21] His studies have drawn attention to the characteristic shared by traditional models of leadership, namely a taken-for-granted belief in an essential and objective core of leaders, which he has termed *essentialism*.

He observes as a widely accepted view that leadership may be taken as a contrast with management, the latter being concerned with routines and the predictable, and the former with the novel and the unpredictable. However, he argues that any attempt to reduce leadership to essential objective components will fail, in that leadership beyond recognition of its very definition is highly contested. From this position, no consensus may be possible. The simple distinction between managers and leaders is inadequate to explain the uncertainties.[22]

Grint emphasizes the manner in which leaders and followers engage in a mutually defining process. That is to say, leaders and followers co-create understanding and beliefs of their roles and potentials. He describes how his experience and studies had 'undermined whatever faith I had previously had in traditional "objective forms of analysis" for understanding leadership'.[23] He concludes that a better treatment would be one that moves away from assumptions of essentialism and towards approaches that consider leadership to be a social construct. This 'constitutive' or non-essentialist approach 'questions the significance of the allegedly objective conditions that surround leaders and implies that "conditions" are as contested as any other element'.[24]

This position suggests that 'the identity (or situation or leader) . . . is a consequence of various accounts and interpretations, all of which vie for dominance . . . leadership is an invention . . . primarily rooted in, and a product of the imagination'.[25] Grint examines this idea thoroughly, beginning with the construction of identity. While money is frequently important in various ways, 'the success of leaders is dependent on the extent to which they can construct and articulate an identity that pushes followers further than money can pull them'.[26]

This suggests the importance of visions that often leave the personal and social aspects difficult to disentangle. He notes a dilemma in that leaders need to imagine utopias which attract followers and yet which may turn from dreams into nightmares. Success is likely to depend upon 'not just how inventive the leader is but how inventive the followers are'.[27] Elsewhere, Grint remarks on a further paradox in that a 'strong' heroic leader may contribute to followers being unable to challenge the leader who has failed to act effectively.

He identifies 'an elective affinity' for various categories of social theory.[28] He specifically mentions constructivism, which appears to be close to what other authors have referred to as management of meaning; complexity theory; and indeterminacy. The common thread he considers to connect these is that of 'a foundational skepticism about the determinate nature of reality'.[29]

Despite the 'close affinity', these maps differ at a deep level. Arguably, constructivism is the most radical challenge to the DRM of leadership. It might also be argued that complexity and indeterminacy are widely accepted concepts in maps closer to the DRM within such professional fields as the physical sciences, mathematics, engineering, even modern business. Grint treats indeterminacy at the level of reality testing. This is the basis of his claim that leadership is 'always contested as a concept between competing ideas and positions'.

Grint's challenge is to leadership as it is widely taught and accepted. He offers up 'the end of leadership?' as a question, not a conclusion, indicating that he seeks to enquire into rather than eliminate the concept. In *The Arts of Leadership* he notes: 'I do not imply by this that we can do without leadership, but we could probably do without leaders.'[30] His objection is against essentialism, and implicitly against the DRM and traditional maps of heroic leadership. He uses case-examples as evidence that inconsistency can be a leadership asset, if only because predictability can be a fatal weakness – literally, in the case of military leaders. It takes him to the more recent maps of distributed leadership within which followers step up to assert leadership responsibilities when the situation appears to require it.

Grint's rejection of essentialism is also shared by the maps of postmodernism and critical theory. Postmodernism has stronger objections to the legitimacy of truth-claims made on the basis of dominant authorities and the wider influence of the DRM. Critical theory engages with the same sort of debate, for example, in its struggles over whether sociological paradigms (maps) are able to be reconciled effectively.

GETTING PERSONAL

The intention of this book is to offer leaders – existing and prospective ones – a chance to take a fresh look at personal leadership goals and ways of addressing them so as to benefit from other people's ideas (maps).

The advice offered by the authors of the first edition remains relevant, and can be found in Box 11.1.

Box 11.1: The Authors' Voice

The concluding words of advice offered by the co-authors (Rickards and Clark) of the first edition of *Dilemmas of Leadership*:

> Here, it seems important to introduce a few personal remarks from the perspective of the two authors. The convention in books like this is to give a voice to the authorial 'we'. Whenever someone such as a leader speaks of 'our' vision, and how well 'we' are doing, the same verbal convention occurs, with its implication of the merging of individual views into a social identity. We have used that convention throughout, and will continue to do so, without further emphasis of its textual significance. That is not to say that we, the two authors of this text, hold identical value systems, or decision preferences. As we constructed the maps, sometimes individually, sometimes working together, there was enough diversity and management of diversity to enrich the process and (we hope) the outcome. The process seems consistent with an overall treatment of leadership as a personal journey, and one within which the traveller was always bumping into ambiguities and dilemmas in thought and actions.

> We learned and refined our views through interacting within our networks of students, colleagues and leaders. At the simple level, we found considerable variation among our contacts (and sometimes between ourselves) regarding the relative merits of the maps we were suggesting. This confirmed us in the view that each reader would be advised to put something personal into the process of his or her map-making. This is consistent with the declared intention of the textbook to encourage the reader to be the most important leader and who stands to benefit from making sense of it all, drawing on personal experiences, beliefs and assumptions.

SUMMARY

Around the year 2000 many books were written speculating on the leadership context of the twenty-first century. Futurology is notoriously difficult, so we may treat these maps with particular caution. There are some widely shared assumptions, and from them we can compile a set of elements of the future context in which organizational leaders will operate. We would expect newer leadership maps to pay more attention to these elements, although we also 'expect the unexpected' from innovative map-makers in the decades to come.

Our future understanding of leadership will be reflected in our future maps. As Yukl pointed out (POU 11.1), new ideas will not replace and wipe out all knowledge gained from earlier maps. More typically, new maps hold on to old ideas, sometimes reworking them in a new context. We have seen how this process occurred within the ancient ideas of charismatic leadership, which were subsequently reworked within maps of transformational leadership.

As we review the maps we have encountered throughout this book we have seen how older maps could be tested and remade into newer ones by critical examination, revealing their dilemmas. To take a significant example from Chapter 2, the long-lived dominance of trait-based maps never succeeded in resolving the dilemmas of definition. Additionally, there was the dilemma of trait variability among leaders – the failure of research to identify a universal set of traits identifying 'the right stuff' of the great leader.

These dilemmas helped map-makers to replace trait theories with behavioural ones. The context shifted towards leadership operating levels throughout organizations, and from what leaders were to what they did. As proposed by Yukl, such new mappings did not completely eliminate the influence of older maps. The new maps retained the assumption of the leader as the prime factor in achieving excellent performance. They also retained the importance placed on rationality (rational leaders, rational expectations of followers). Also, evaluation of leader success in terms of measurable performance remained largely unchanged.

The shift from trait to behavioural maps increased the complexity of maps in some ways (more variables), while retaining the fundamental simplicity of leadership as a prime causal factor that influenced follower behaviours to achieve organizational objectives. Yukl had been pointing out for some years that the maps failed to account for reciprocal or mutual influence processes. An example of such reciprocal processes would be leadership behaviours influencing followers whose behaviours influence leaders. The turbulence of the environment is likely to grow in importance within future mappings. The shift will support mappings which will focus more on knowledge and learning aspects of leadership.

The shift to new leadership maps helped to place more emphasis on perceptual processes – including the importance of the management of meaning. The new leadership maps retained much from the older maps, while leaving unanswered some of the earlier dilemmas. The matter of a satisfactory definition of leadership persisted. Once again, however, older ideas were modified by context rather than completely exorcised. Studies of the symbolic and mythic aspects of leadership may provide additional life to the mapping of meaning.

Charisma became 'tamed' as the measurable aspects of transformational leadership. The new leadership maps still revealed dilemmas. The heroic leader remained an important figure within transformational leadership mapping. Difficulties remained concerning the malevolent and tyrannical leader who achieved transformational changes (the Hitler effect).

The heroic leader is a concept that appears vulnerable to further challenges as the frequently observed 'dark side of leadership' is more widely recognized through the pioneering work of Kets de Vries and Barbara Kellerman. The symbolism of the mandrill leadership style examined in Chapter 5 serves as a warning of such behaviours. Here is some evidence that a more self-effacing and less self-serving style has considerable social and organizational benefits (the fifth-level leader of Jim Collins is a promising example).

Rost's critique for the twenty-first century attempted to deal with the dilemmas of the contemporary leadership maps. His proposal was for a definition that he believed to be implied in the multiple other definitions of leadership. He defined leadership as an influence relationship among leaders and followers who intend real changes that reflect their mutual purposes. He thus excludes leaders who do not operate according to principles of mutuality of purpose. He argues that such a mapping helps to escape from an Industrial Age definition and suggest new mappings of distributed leadership (as indicated in the work of Manz and Sims, for example). Such attempts to claim priority for one definition over all others risks the very dilemma it seeks to address, namely the right of one perspective to dominate over all others.

Emerging perspectives include a social identity mapping for leadership. This is suggested almost in passing by earlier map-makers (leader–member exchange would be an example). The mapping seems to address several of the dilemmas we have touched upon. It also gets us closer to a broad theory of influence processes. The mapping does not appear to be a revolutionary shift from the maps of new leadership. The currently favoured methodological approach of prototypicality seems to be within older traditions of essentialist mappings of leadership processes. However, it offers a promise of more grounded examination of influence processes, with rich empirical possibilities. The approach may also help to map concepts of knowledge management and thought-leadership.

Emotional intelligence has become another emerging theme of late twentieth-century leadership maps. We have indicated how a comparative analysis of prevailing maps reveals challenging dilemmas of diagnostic accuracy and distance of the empirical measures from real-world leadership competences. More careful work is needed to explore such dilemmas.

Leadership maps of the last century conceal dilemmas of power and control that are revealed only though careful and comparative reading. Rost's appeal for leadership only as directed towards mutually accepted purposes is one attempt to smooth out the potential conflict. Enthusiasm in new leadership maps for shared visions and missions is another. The concept of empowerment tends to conceal dilemmas of multiple constituencies in organizations with different values and goals. The power-based maps have not adequately dealt with the dilemmas of power, coercion, and conflict resolution.

A less-investigated mapping is the one we have identified in these pages as trust-based leadership. Power is redistributed within a values framework that places a high priority on mutuality of goal setting as a creative and social process.

Other dilemmas also reveal the pattern of older ideas reworked to meet new contexts. For example, charismatic leadership (see Chapter 4) was an ancient concept reworked to fit the new leadership ideas of transformational leadership. Further examination of the dilemmas of transformational leadership reveals that it retained the concept of a vision from the more ancient map of charismatic leadership.

Visionary ideas were to be retained in the new leadership studies of the 1980s onward, but with a rejection of earlier 'essentialism'.[31] The wider shift in social science maps, as in leadership maps, had been towards the management of meaning, symbolic leadership, and the various maps that the DRM would have described as subjectivist.

This final chapter takes the form of a review of the wider terrain across which the reader has been invited to travel. It may be seen as a debriefing of the personal journey. It also offers one final set of maps in preparation for future journeys.

Now that the journey is reaching its conclusion, it becomes possible for a reader/traveller to see connections between the various regions mapped chapter by chapter. If you have been working through this textbook systematically, you will have carried out the exercises at the beginning of chapters to note your points of departure (your existing leadership maps). You have also had opportunities to revisit these maps (map-testing) at the end of chapters.

Exercise 11.2 provides a similar opportunity for you to continue the process of reviewing and revising your leadership map into the future. You are capturing your personal beliefs, which remain work in progress, to be revised in the future as your leadership experiences and study develop.

Exercise 11.2: A Final Piece of Map-making (for individual study)

Chapter 11 reviews the earlier chapters and suggests ways in which leadership ideas are changing.

Exercise 11.2 Discussion Questions

1 What ideas from Chapter 11 do you find promising starting-points for personal map-testing and map-making?
2 Referring to your notes from Exercise 11.1, what are the most significant ways in which you think the study of *Dilemmas of Leadership* will help you in your leadership journeys ahead?

The time has come when the advice from guides reaches an end. If you stayed the course this long, you will have found value in the maps provided during your leadership journey. That is not to say that you will not need to study any leadership maps in the future. Rather, you will be better equipped to carry out future explorations through map-reading, testing, and making.

So it's over to you. Up to you to retrace your journeys by referring back to the maps you have already made, and perhaps by discovering afresh where your map-making is still changing. Up to you to engage in further map-making efforts to support your leadership plans. Up to you to reject as much as you like. That final piece of unsolicited advice is offered not because guides no longer care what you do, but from precisely the opposite motives.

NOTES

1 Yukl, G.A. (2011) 'Contingency theories of effective leadership', in Bryman, A., Collinson, D., Grint, K., Jackson, B., & Uhl-Bien, M. (eds), *The Sage handbook of leadership*, London: Sage, pp. 186–298, at p. 297.
2 Fleetham, C. (2005) 'Why teams don't work: The benefits of "unrational" vs. rational leadership', www.allbusiness.com/human-resources/employee-development-leadership/479725–1.html, downloaded 1 February 2011.
3 Grint, K. (2000) *The arts of leadership*, Oxford: OUP, p. 419.
4 The classic paper remains Eisenhardt, K.M. (1989) 'Making fast strategic decisions in high-velocity environments', *Academy of Management Journal*, 32, 3, 543–576, stable URL: www.jstor.org/stable/256434. For evidence of the view more recently expressed see Alan Greenspan's memoirs: Greenspan, A. (2007) *The age of turbulence: Adventures in a new world*, New York: Penguin.
5 Goldstein, J. (1999) 'Emergence as a construct: History and issues', *Emergence: Complexity and Organization*, 1, 1, 49–72.
6 For rich examinations of earliest philosophic systems of thought (maps) see Russell, B. (1961) *A history of western philosophy*, London: George Allen & Unwin; Koestler, A. (1959) *The sleepwalkers: A history of man's changing vision of the universe*, London: Penguin.
7 The actions of Bob Diamond were discussed in these terms during the banking crisis of 2009–10: http://business.timesonline.co.uk/tol/business/economics/article5549510.ece, downloaded 7 February 2011.
8 Bryman, A. (1996) 'Leadership in organizations', in Clegg, S.R., Hardy, C., & Nord, W.R., *Handbook of organization studies*, London: Sage, pp. 276–292.
9 Parry, K.W., & Bryman, A. (2006) 'Leadership in organizations', in Clegg, S.R., Hardy, C., Lawrence, T.B., & Nord, W.R., *Handbook of organization studies*, 2nd edn, London: Sage, pp. 447–468, at p. 453.
10 Editorial preface, Bryman, A., Collinson, D., Grint, K., Jackson, B., & Uhl-Bien, M. (eds) (2011) *The Sage handbook of leadership*, London: Sage, p. xi.
11 Compare this approach with those implying replacement of one map with a newer one involving a complete paradigm switch, e.g. Kuhn, T. (1967) *The structure of scientific revolutions*, Chicago: University of Chicago Press; or Gladwell, M. (2000) *The tipping point: How little things can make a big difference*, New York: Little, Brown.
12 Fleetham, C. (2005) 'Why teams don't work: The benefits of "unrational" vs. rational leadership', www.allbusiness.com/human-resources/employee-development-leadership/479725-1.html, downloaded 1 February 2011.

13 See Myora's essay for a contemporary analysis: www.adm.fukuoka-u.ac.jp/fu844/home2/Ronso/ Shogaku/C50–2+3/C5023_0143.pdf, downloaded 18 February 2011.

14 Yukl, G.A. (1999) 'An evaluative essay on current conceptions of effective leadership', *European Journal of Work and Organizational Psychology*, 8, 1, 33–48.

15 To this list could be added social and domestic obligations, and the dilemma of work/life balance.

16 Attempts to provide new interpretations of terms will always risk influences from earlier contexts. Since the Second World War, the term 'collaborator' has had negative connotations, as indeed has the Germanic term 'Führer' or leader.

17 Tajfel, H. (1981) *Human groups and social categories*, Cambridge, UK: Cambridge University Press.

18 Turner, J.C., Hogg, M.A., Oakes, P.J., Reicher, S.D., & Wetherell, M.S. (1989) 'Rediscovering the social group: A self-categorization theory', *American Journal of Sociology*, 94, 6, 1514–1516.

19 Brown, F.W., Bryant, S.E., & Reilly, M.D. (2006) 'Does emotional intelligence – as measured by the EQ1 – influence transformational leadership and/or desirable outcomes?' *Leadership and Organization Development Journal*, 27, 5, 330–351.

20 www.windsorleadershiptrust.org.uk/en/1/kgrint.html.

21 Grint, K. (2000) *The arts of leadership*, Oxford: OUP.

22 Grint, K. (2005) *Leadership: Limits and possibilities*, Palgrave Macmillan, www.home.no/ emarum/artikkel2.pdf, a synopsis for students of leadership.

23 Grint, K. (2000) *The arts of leadership*, Oxford: OUP, p. 2.

24 Ibid., p. 4.

25 Ibid., pp. 11, 13.

26 Ibid., p. 411.

27 Ibid., p. 417.

28 Grint, K. (1998) 'Determining the indeterminacies of change leadership', *Management Decision*, 36, 503–508.

29 Grint, K. (2000) *The arts of leadership*, Oxford: OUP, p. 1.

30 Ibid., p. 419.

31 Grint, K. (1997) *Leadership: Classic, contemporary and critical approaches*, Oxford: OUP; (2000) *The arts of leadership*, Oxford: OUP.

INDEX

Page numbers in **bold** refer to figures, page numbers in *italic* refer to tables.